PERSPECTIVES IN SOCIOLOGY

THE OLD LOVE

AND

THE NEW

Divorce & Readjustment

WILLARD WALLER

INTRODUCTION BY BERNARD FARBER
FOREWORD BY HERMAN R. LANTZ

Carbondale and Edwardsville

SOUTHERN ILLINOIS UNIVERSITY PRESS

FEFFER & SIMONS, INC.

London and Amsterdam

TO

Ellsworth Faris

HUMANIST

FOREWORD

By Herman R. Lantz

The Old Love and the New was a significant work when originally published. First, because Willard Waller focused on the social-psychological consequences of divorce with reference to those involved and the implications which these consequences might have. Second, because his treatment set *The Old Love and the New* apart from the traditional writing about the family that had been in vogue; writings that still possessed historical and evolutionary preoccupations. By shifting the inquiry from the broad macroscopic examination to the microscopic, Waller was ahead of his time and anticipated a major development in family sociology which is current today.

The text remains intact although some statistics in the chapter on economic adjustments, dealing with consumer prices and adjustment of women, are now dated. While there have been significant changes since the original publication of this work, it is important to understand the times in which Waller wrote in order to understand the work itself. Omitted from this edition is Waller's original introduction and glossary of terminology; each add little for the reader today however important they may have been earlier.

It is altogether fitting that the present work, the

first major contribution of Willard Waller, be republished by the Southern Illinois University Press. Willard Waller was born only a few miles from the University and spent his youth in this area; the Willard Waller Sociology Club at Southern Illinois University was named in his honor. At the dedication of the Club in 1953 the members were privileged to have as their guest speaker the author's father, Elbert Waller, who described with warmth and nostalgia the early days and surroundings in which Willard grew. Here we learned of a highly intelligent and sensitive boy who was never really satisfied to accept, but who searched for ever ascending horizons. Following the death of Elbert Waller, letters sent by the son to the father were deposited with the Southern Illinois University Library. I have examined the nine letters that cover a ten year span (1929 to 1939) from the University of Pennsylvania, Pennsylvania State University, and Barnard College. These reveal a person sensitive to his surroundings beset by a series of difficulties, including constant financial pressures. Yet, one who seemed always to be in touch with the larger purpose of life, the transcendence of self. Thus, the letters tell something of Waller's reactions to the urban environment and his view of the world around him—academic life, the medical profession, and the depression. (These letters are in the Rare Book Room of the Morris Library of Southern Illinois University.) In a rather moving passage Waller conveys to his father his belief that the really serious problems of our society stemmed less from the radical ideologies of professors and more from the misused wealth of the privileged.

In view of Waller's perceptions, it is altogether understandable that Waller had an affinity for the case study method; for he was introspective, reflecting on his own life and the lives of others. Herein lie some of the roots of Willard Waller's pessimism on which Professor Farber comments; herein one may find Waller's unique capacities to depict the social scene. By contemporary standards Waller's methodology would be open to serious objection. Yet the ultimate test of this man's ability to understand rests in how well Waller's original insights have been upheld by subsequent empirical studies.

Professor Bernard Farber of the University of Illinois deals with this issue. Farber is well known for his significant work in the sociology of the family, and especially for his research in family organization in crises. His introduction relates Waller's effect on subsequent research in the divorce field; and he makes insightful comments about Willard Waller both as a person and as a professional sociologist.

CONTENTS

INTRODUCTION

By Bernard Farber

PUBLISHED INITIALLY in 1930, Willard Waller's *The Old Love and the New* for a quarter of a century constituted the entire body of sociological research on personal adjustment after divorce. In 1956, William J. Goode wrote *After Divorce*, reporting his study of divorced women in Detroit.[1] Since then, scattered research has dealt with topics relevant to postdivorce adjustment, but usually not directly with problems of the divorcée. As a result, supplemented by the findings of these few investigations, *The Old Love and the New* remains a major work on postdivorce adjustment.

This book is a relatively untapped source of hypotheses pertaining to personal adjustment. Although Waller is concerned with the crisis of divorce, many of his insights are relevant for other kinds of family problems as well. Waller's perceptive discussion is still as valuable today for understanding problems of personal adjustment as it was a generation ago.

This introductory essay can be regarded by the reader as an appreciative critique of *The Old Love and the New*. It will first describe some of Waller's

---

[1] William J. Goode, *After Divorce*, New York: Free Press, 1956 (re-issued in 1965 in paperback as *Women in Divorce*).

views as a sociologist and reformer. The essay then will indicate how Waller's hypotheses in this book have fared in empirical investigation. Finally, it will suggest an affinity between Waller's treatment of divorce and the characteristics of tragic drama.

Waller as Sociologist and Reformer

Willard Waller was born in Murphysboro, Illinois, and attended high school at Albion, Illinois. He received an A.B. degree from the University of Illinois in 1920 and an A.M. from the University of Chicago in 1925. His first teaching post was at the Morgan Park Military Academy near Chicago. Later, he taught at the University of Pennsylvania while doing graduate work. After receiving his Ph.D. from Pennsylvania in 1929, Waller taught for a short time at the University of Nebraska (1929–31), then at Pennsylvania State University (1931–37), and finally at Barnard College, from 1937 until his death in 1945.

The Old Love and the New was Waller's first of a series of extended essays combining social criticism and theoretical insight. Each of his succeeding books discusses a different social problem. The *Sociology of Teaching* (1932) portrays what goes on in schools and in the classroom. *The Family* (1938) elaborates upon Ernest W. Burgess' definition of the family as a unity of interacting personalities. *War and the Family* (1940) and *The Veteran Comes Back* (1944) deal with Waller's theories on war and the experiences of soldiers.

In his critical essays, Waller uses interaction as the central concept of analysis. This emphasis on interaction reflects the impact of Georg Simmel on American sociology in the early twentieth century.

Waller writes, "The influences that men exert upon one another, their interactions with one another, are the commonest things of life and the least understood. It is the business of the sociologist to call attention to patterns of interaction, and to dissect them in order to lay bare their true nature." Waller's interpretations of interaction have contributed to the understanding of the workings of various institutions and of the elements of tragedy involved in them.

Significantly, Waller dedicates *The Old Love and the New* to Ellsworth Faris. This dedication is appropriate because the book follows the paradigm developed by Faris, regarding disorganization and reorganization. Faris sees change as occurring in the following way: An individual's habits persist until a blockage occurs. This blockage produces some form of disorganization. As this disorganization occurs, the individual makes many attempts to think through his problems and to arrive at a reorganization of his life.

Yet, Waller has gone beyond Faris by suggesting that habits developed by the individual prior to the divorce consist of more than daily routines and particular dislikes and likes; they also involve the basic drives which Freudian psychology emphasizes. Viewing divorce as an event in an individual's life history, Waller speculates upon unconscious motivations which produce conflict in the marriage and affect the adjustment of the divorcée.

In dealing with irrational interaction leading to divorce, Waller stresses circular reaction mechanisms in emotionally-charged behavior. In circular interaction, the responses of one person evoke more decided responses from the other, and once people are involved in this process, it keeps snowballing until it culminates in some sort of climax or break. According to Waller, "husbands and wives who have begun to quarrel find themselves unable to stop until it is too late." In alienation, distance grows between the marriage partners, their attitudes toward one another change, and the couple revises its orientation toward persons outside the marriage. "When people have begun to drift apart, the group enters as a wedge which forces them further and further away from each other. The maintenance of the privacy of the home demands that the polite fiction . . . be kept, that there be no public quarrels, trials of strength, or commands between the partners." Waller here suggests the kind of teamwork (described later by Goffman) needed for the management of personal impressions made upon others.[2] By acting as they think they *should act* in front of others, the married couple sharply defines the discrepancy between the actual marriage and the ideal. By presenting themselves as unified to others, the husband and wife dramatize the failures and uncertainties in their own relationship. This dramatization stimulates further emotionally-charged behavior. *The Old Love and the New* focuses on these irrational elements in interaction, both before and after divorce.

As a family sociologist, Waller was influenced profoundly by Ernest W. Burgess. Sociologists concerned with the family can be categorized by the extent of their emphasis upon either husband-wife relations or parent-child relations. Those who stress husband-wife relationships view the family as emerging from marriage. On the other hand, those who focus upon parent-child relationships regard the

---

[2] Erving Goffman, *Presentation of the Self in Everyday Life,* New York: Anchor Books, 1959.

family as an institution primarily for the propaga-
tion and socialization of children. In describing the
family in modern urban society, Burgess regards the
affectional relationship between husband and wife
as the primary bond in the family.

Burgess has developed two polar ideal types of
family life.[3] At one extreme is the companionship-
family, emerging as an adaptation to urban society.
This family is held together by affectional bonds of
the husband and wife. In the extreme case, there are
no external pressures to keep the family together,
relationships are equalitarian, there is minimal division of labor between husband and wife, and interaction depends upon the personal needs of the family
members rather than upon fixed traditional norms.
The husband and wife consider themselves mainly
as companions to one another and only secondarily
as occupants of statuses designated as "husband" or
"wife." Loss of companionship leads to divorce.

Burgess identifies the polar opposite of the companionship-family as the institutional-family. The
institutional-family emphasizes the place of the
family in society through focusing upon socialization
of children and upon economic relations. In 1848,
J. A. St. John may well be describing the institutional-family in his statement that, in families
where happiness of husband and wife is not paramount, the family becomes like a business concern.

The object of marriage must be admitted to be the happiness of those who enter into it, not their mere worldly pros-
perity, or the well ordering of their household and families,

---

[3] Although Burgess formalized this typology in later works, the
distinctions are apparent in his earlier writings. See, for example,
his "Foreword" to Ernest R. Mowrer, *Family Disorganization,* Chicago: University of Chicago Press, 1926, pp. vii–xi or his "Family
as a Unity of Interacting Personalities," *The Family,* 7 (March,
1926), pp. 3–9.

but, in a moral and intellectual sense, their own individual delight and tranquility of mind; where this is not aimed at, marriage degenerates into a mere social connection for mere economical purposes, and in which both husband and wife become subserviant to the property they bring together, or may happen to amass. The man becomes the steward of the estate, the wife degenerates into a housekeeper and both plod on more or less comfortably together, according to the accidents of their temper, and the values they set on their worldly acquisitions. This, however, is not really marriage, but a partnership in business, of which the husband and wife constitute the firm, the former attending to the external relations of the home, the latter to the internal. If they have children, these are by degrees taken into partnership, and the great work of money-making, or accumulation of property, proceeds *pari pasu* with the multiplication of the partners. In such industrial connections divorce is seldom needed, money being the great ruling divinity of all the parties concerned. Love has no opportunity to intrude itself, to introduce disorder, or to disturb their calculations.[4]

The institutional family can be regarded as functioning to sustain the social structure of society rather than the personal gratifications of its own members. Since divorce interferes with maintaining order in society, those groups which predicate their continued existence on the stability of the existing social structure discourage divorce.

The question of divorce is, therefore, a central issue in problems related to family organization in modern society. The companionship-family is associated with divorce permissiveness and change in social structure, and the institutional-family with prohibition of divorce and stability in social struc-

---

[4] J. A. St. John, Introduction to "Doctrine and Discipline of Divorce," *Collected Prose Works of John Milton,* Volume 3, 1848, pp. 169–70.

ture. In this issue, Waller has sided with Burgess.

The issue of the relative importance of husband-wife and parent-child relationships in family organization has had a long history. The views expressed by Burgess and by Waller have been described many times in different social contexts. For example, in the seventeenth century, John Milton wrote of the primacy of the husband-wife relationship in the Bible. His tract was intended to persuade the English Parliament to liberalize divorce laws. Milton suggested that marriage was ordained for the "apt and cheerful conversation of man with woman to comfort and refresh him against the evil of solitary life." He considered the "purpose of generation" as only an afterthought and a secondary end.[5] J. A. St. John, the mid-nineteenth-century editor of Milton's prose works, indicates that "Milton's notions of married life are highly flattering to women, whom he evidently contemplates as the equal companions of men, fit to converse with them on all subjects. He insists perpetually on their intellectual qualities, and believes that the greatest and noblest men, after they have refined and enlarged their minds to the utmost extent by study, can still find fit companionship among women."[6]

Similarly, Francis Hutcheson, the Scottish moralist, in the eighteenth century, pointed out "the intention of nature that human offspring should be propagated only by parents first united in stable friendship." He also suggested that marriage should be "an equal friendly society."[7]

---

[5] John Milton, *op. cit.*, p. 181.
[6] *Ibid.*, p. 196.
[7] Cited in Gladys Bryson, *Man and Society*, Princeton, New Jersey: Princeton University Press, 1945, p. 179.

The perennial concern over the conflict between the importance of congenial marital bonds and the role of the family in sustaining the society emphasizes the gravity of the problems with which Waller dealt. Divorce has been justified by its proponents throughout history as being beneficial to the psychic state of society. However, Waller's study highlights the misery and suffering associated with divorce. If instead of releasing the unhappily married couples from their suffering, divorce provokes further misery, then it is not fulfilling its purpose. As detrimental to the general happiness, divorce either should be abolished or its aftereffects mitigated. The abolition of divorce would be inconsistent with values in American society regarding personal freedom and emphasis on status achievement rather than status ascription. The only feasible alternative therefore is to mitigate the misery associated with divorce.

Although Waller does not state his reason for selecting problems of postdivorce adjustment as a subject for analysis, his treatment of the topic is consistent with the viewpoint just described. Waller perceives divorce as analogous to surgery. Although the individual who has had an operation would have been better off if he had not needed one, he has no choice but to recuperate. In accordance with this view, Waller is concerned with the means of adjustment rather than with the social conditions relating to divorce and remarriage. He writes about utilizing the experience of divorce effectively, and he discusses minimizing the personal and social costs of divorce.

In this work as in others, Waller displays a commitment to reform. Throughout his career, he viewed sociology as more than either a discipline which applies objective methodology to human society or a humanistic study of human relations merely to produce understanding. Rather, Waller was concerned with sociology as providing solutions to major problems in society.

Waller believed that solutions to some problems can be introduced without greatly inhibiting ordinary "habit patterns." These ordinary habit patterns (as suggested by John Dewey) constitute the customs of the society. If these habits were inhibited and crisis emerged, there would be much disorganization and drastic solutions would be required. Seeking a change in power relations in society might achieve rapid reforms but would risk a major crisis. On the other hand, reforming habit patterns through changes in the socialization of individuals is slower, but less likely to create such a crisis. Waller saw society as competent to overcome some difficulties successfully without the necessity for consciously introducing a major crisis or catastrophe. Thus, he focused upon problems of socialization rather than upon iniquitous power relations in the society.

The emphasis by Waller upon adjustment within the existing framework of norms and values does not imply that he regarded these as superior to others. Instead, he insisted that reform must begin with the existing situation. In order to understand what is wrong with the existing norms and values, the reformer, according to Waller, must begin by studying social process. "Reforms must ultimately be processed through thousands of concrete situations as defined by the mores." [8] Waller believed that describing the crisis of divorce and its aftermath constitutes a critique of the existing norms and values

---

[8] Willard Waller, *The Family, A Dynamic Interpretation,* New York: Dryden Press, 1939, p. 604.

regarding divorce. Therefore, he considered the problem of adjustment to divorce not only as an individual social-psychological one but also as a reflection upon the particular organization of norms and values in the society at that time.

Waller's Contribution to the Study of Postdivorce Adjustment

The first major study of divorce in the United States was undertaken by James P. Lichtenberger.[9] In this investigation, Lichtenberger pointed out that between 1867 and 1886, there were 329,000 divorces granted in the United States, whereas in the next twenty-year period from 1887 to 1906, a total of 946,000 divorces occurred. His study then treated divorce in terms of the growth of a social problem. Lichtenberger traced the origin of divorce in primitive society and indicated its modification in recent history. He regarded as especially important the transformation of society through "our unprecedented economic development, our unparalleled achievements in social progress, and our remarkable transition in ethical and religious views."[10] Inasmuch as Lichtenberger and other sociologists who followed him concentrated on divorce as a social problem, they paid little attention to the aftermath of divorce.

Waller's contribution in *The Old Love and the New* was in part a shift in focus from divorce as a social problem to divorce as an event in an individual's life history. Waller was then able to ask how the status of the divorcé was defined and what this

---

[9] *Divorce, A Study of Social Causation,* Privately published, New York: 1909, Ph.D. dissertation, Columbia University.
[10] *Ibid.,* p. 19.

status involved. For Waller, divorce implied change —and change, in turn, implied crisis, disorganization, and reorganization. Waller emphasized the persistence of the habits of married life, and the modifications required of the divorcé in a new "social world."

For twenty-six years after *The Old Love and the New* appeared, no other research on postdivorce adjustment was reported. Following World War II, however, the divorce rate rose sharply, and experiences with personal problems following divorce became more common. William J. Goode undertook a study of the adjustment of divorced women in Detroit. Goode reported that he "assigned two budding librarians to summarize all the research literature on post divorce adjustment. . . . No such body of work existed, other than Willard Waller's *The Old Love and the New.*" [11] In many respects, Goode's research was based on Waller's. Since the Goode investigation in 1956, there has been a slow growth in the research literature on the aftermath of divorce. However, Goode's work remains as the successor to the Waller study.

The paragraphs below indicate the extent to which later investigations confirm hypotheses and conclusions by Waller with regard to postdivorce adjustment. Waller's analysis deals with a variety of problems in postdivorce relationships: Difficulties in (a) reorganization of the divorced person's sex life, (b) recovery from loss of pride accompanying failure in marriage, (c) readjustment of the many habits and daily routines developed during the marriage, (d) rearrangements of relationships with friends and relatives, (e) economic adaptations, and (f) resolution

---

[11] Goode, *Women in Divorce,* p. iii.

of personality conflicts resulting from the general upheaval of the divorcé's world. The intrusion of irrational considerations in the handling of these problems is a central concern of the book. *The Old Love
and the New* presents numerous propositions about
diverse postdivorce problems pertaining to friends,
sex adjustment, economic adjustment, and social role
of the divorcé. Other propositions pertain to success
of remarriage. Waller's major conclusions about
postdivorce adjustment and remarriage will be evaluated with reference to findings of later studies.

FRIENDS

Waller paid much attention to the role of friends
in postdivorce adjustment. He suggested that usually
"the divorcé is surrounded by persons who know
him well and sympathize with him, all of whose references to his marital troubles are of such a nature
as to bolster him and disparage the other person,
all of whose remarks may set up as suggestions that
he should indeed hate this person who has injured
him." Prior to the divorce, these friends assist in
redefining the marital situation as an intolerable
one. In this manner, they contribute to the final decision to end the marriage. After divorce, friends
help relieve ambivalence over the marital dissolution. Waller thus implied that when a marriage
breaks up, the inherent weaknesses and conflicts are
not sufficient to explain the decision to divorce. The
decision is affected also by the friends and relatives
involved.

In his later study of divorce, William J. Goode found
that in general the husband's friends were indifferent in their
attitudes toward the divorce, while the wife's friends generally approved. The basis for this difference may lie in the

general view of divorce as resulting from an errant husband,
with the wife deserted emotionally or actually. Hence, the
Waller statement was supported by the data on women but
not on men.

According to Waller's analysis, the divorcé frequently breaks completely with the friendship group
to which he belonged during his marriage. Waller
mentioned two reasons for this break. First, the
divorced individual is an oddity in a circle of married
couples. Second, the divorcé must reorganize his sex
life and he seeks the company of those who are in a
comparable marital condition. This breaking with
old friendship groups fosters feelings of alienation
and isolation, and thereby multiplies problems in
personal adjustment.

Goode's investigation provided only partial support for
Waller's propositions on changes in friendships. He found
that regardless of religion, race, or age at divorce, about half
of the divorced women retained their former friends. There
was a somewhat greater tendency for those divorcées in higher
socioeconomic levels to maintain their same circle of friends.
However, irrespective of social background, when the divorcée was in love with another man prior to the divorce,
she tended to drop her old friends. Goode interpreted change
in friends as associated with the extent to which the divorcée
seeks to establish a "new life."

Although there was no overwhelming tendency in Goode's
study for divorced women to break old friendship ties, his
data indicate that new friendships are in fact formed. Of
those women in his study who had not yet remarried, about
one in six mentioned that she now had greater freedom of
choice over friendship. Goode reported such statements as
"Now I can go out and meet people," "I meet a better class
of people," "I can meet and make friends with the people I
want to." [12] Almost one-third of the women reported that

---

[12] *Ibid.*, p. 340.

they could now make friends or see old friends more easily. The Goode study thus indicates a tendency for the divorcée to expand rather than to change circles of friends.

SEX ADJUSTMENT

Waller proposed that in divorce the "sex impulse [is] reduced to its crudest form, stripped to its essentials, robbed of all glamour and romance, and perhaps purposefully cheapened and degraded." One obvious way to cheapen sex is to become promiscuous. Sexual promiscuity "serves to keep any one person from becoming overly important in another's scheme of life."

Subsequent studies have not tested Waller's proposition about sex adjustment directly, but they have provided some relevant data. Although Goode did not query his respondents specifically about the handling of sex problems, he asked, "Have you ever been in a social situation in which you felt someone thought less of you when he or she found out that you were divorced?" Seventy per cent of all the women in his sample reported that no such incident had arisen. Yet those under twenty-four years of age reported a greater frequency of discrimination. Goode interpreted this difference as indicating a greater risk by the younger women of being regarded as "loose," though they actually were not. Jessie Bernard reported that in her study "a high proportion of remarried previously-divorced men and women had sexual relations with their future spouses" before their second marriage.[13] Professor Bernard suggested that after the first marriage, sex can more easily be integrated into male-female interaction than is possible prior to the first marriage—sex loses its mystery and aura of taboo. In summary, both Goode and Bernard presented evidence of a realistic attitude toward sex by the divorcée, not of a degrading view of sex relations.

---

[13] Jessie Bernard, *Remarriage,* New York: Dryden Press, 1956, p. 180.

ECONOMIC ADJUSTMENT

In dealing with economic adjustments, Waller concentrated on money problems and the difficulties faced by the divorcée in making a living. He contended that the divorced woman faces greater hardships than the man. He considered the woman as needing money immediately without the time or resources to invest in a long-term career, as being out of touch with "the workaday world," and as "worried about her marital break, and worried about how she is going to live."

By the time that Goode undertook his investigation, a large proportion of childless married women were in the labor force. As a result, Goode found that only those women who were unable to work fulltime were facing major financial difficulties. However, about half of the women who had not yet remarried at the time of his study were living at reduced income levels. The divorced women received outside financial assistance, mainly from their own families. Remarried women, however, were considerably better off financially than they had been in the previous marriage. Consistent with Waller's views, the Goode study suggests that for women, although divorce represents downward mobility, this trend can be reversed by remarriage.

ROLE OF DIVORCÉE

Waller examined the role of the divorcée from several perspectives. Much of his discussion dealt with divorced women. One viewpoint was that of seeing the divorcée as a castaway. Waller proposed that the divorcée who has been cast away by her spouse first of all regards herself as a failure, and secondly tries to reassert control over her former mate.

Tendencies toward the castaway role appeared in Goode's study of divorced women. Goode found that the trauma of divorce was greatest among those women whose husbands took the initiative in divorce. Especially these women reported sleepless nights, physical symptoms, and personal problems. Moreover, until the husband's remarriage, the castaway women kept hoping that their husbands would return, and they expressed disappointment and hostility when the husband remarried.

Another perspective utilized by Waller pertained to the complexity of the social relationships of divorced persons. Waller regarded these complexities as beginning with the ambiguities about the status of persons who are separated or alienated but not yet divorced. Since separation is a transitional status, interaction at this point is highly complicated. The individual does not know when he is to act as a married person and when as a single individual. He does not know how much to tell others about his marital affairs or how much to engage in courtship and dating. After divorce, other kinds of complications develop. Whereas the divorced individual requires a simple situation for his readjustment, the disintegrated marriage produces many highly diverse, ill-defined troubles. With all of these problems, the divorced person is highly motivated toward developing defense mechanisms and compensations in behavior. Waller suggested that, because of increased complexities in living, the divorcée becomes sophisticated, circuitous, and indirect in interacting with others. However, Waller's hypotheses on the complexities of the divorcée status have not been tested.

Waller regarded the divorcée status as lower socially and economically than the status of married persons, and he suggested that the individual reacts against this downward mobility in domestic relations by establishing certain defenses and compensations. These defenses sometimes consist of belittling the former mate, blaming the other partner, compensating by adopting behavior patterns opposite to those which had been present in marriage, immersing oneself in work, or doing penance. This compensatory behavior may involve consolation in religion, the embracing of a new philosophy, or increased indulgence in sex, food, clothes, or self pity. In any case, Waller suggested that the divorce crisis may produce a complete disjuncture with the past in the life organization of the individual. To Waller, then, divorce was not merely the dropping of a mate; it was a crisis, evoking profound changes in life organization.

Later studies indicate less prolonged crisis and suffering in divorce than Waller's analysis suggests. Only about one-fourth of the Goode sample reported difficulty in sleeping, deterioration of health, or increased loneliness at the final separation. The greatest tendencies to exhibit such indices of trauma were found (aside from the castaways) among women over thirty, women who had been married 10 years or over, and those who felt ambivalent about the divorce. The brevity of this trauma is indicated by the findings that about three-fourths of Goode's respondents who had obtained their decrees twenty-six months prior to the interview were either remarried or were going steady. Results of other investigations are similar. For one, Glick reported that in the United States in the 1950's "about one-half of the divorced women remarry within five years after they have obtained a divorce and . . . about two-thirds of the women who obtain a divorce will eventually remarry. The fact that remarriage rates for men are higher than those for women suggests, furthermore, that close to three-fourths of the men who obtain a divorce eventually remarry." Data from England and Wales lead to comparable conclusions in that "about two-thirds to three-quarters of persons obtaining a divorce will ultimately remarry." [14] Moreover, Jacobson has suggested that the rates of remarriage are likely to be under-reported. Divorced in-

[14] Paul C. Glick, *American Families*, New York: Wiley, 1957, p. 139.

dividuals frequently do not indicate previous marriages in their applications for subsequent marriage licenses.[15] Hence, the divorce trauma may even be less pronounced generally than existing studies indicate.

REMARRIAGES

Waller raised the issue of whether or not remarriages are happier than first marriages. He thought that there were many a priori grounds against the happiness of the second marriage. He conceded that where first marriages represented a rebellion against a parent or where the first marriage was "so bad that any comparison must inevitably favor the second," a second marriage may present fewer problems than a first one. However, "an unhappy marriage which ends in divorce may have disastrous effects upon personality, which may prevent successful adjustment in a second marriage." He believed that feelings toward the first mate and fear of losing the second mate would create problems in adjustment. On the other hand, he thought that the experience of the first marriage could produce insight, tolerance, and "progressive liberation from . . . infantile love objects." In these instances, Waller believed that the second marriage could succeed in that "people love better for having had a little practice." Waller's remarks on the salutory effect of an unhappy marriage echo John Milton's statement that "they who have lived most loosely, by reason of their bold accustoming, have been as so many divorces to teach them experience." [16] In this passage, Milton implied that experiencing a series of steady relationships (whether or

[15] Paul H. Jacobson, *American Marriage and Divorce,* New York: Rinehart, 1959.
[16] Milton, *op. cit.,* p. 190.

not they are legitimated as marriages) can increase competence for marriage.

Since *The Old Love and the New*, several investigations have been undertaken to determine the stability of remarriages. Monahan reported that in Iowa stability of first marriages was much greater than of those in which either husband or wife had been previously divorced.[17] Jessie Bernard also pointed out that marriages between two divorced persons tend to have a lower chance of success than other marriages. A minority of divorcées in her investigation reported their remarriage as successful.[18] Locke found, however, that "divorced women are as likely to be adjusted in a subsequent marriage as women who have been married only once."[19] On the other hand, Locke found that divorced men were indeed poorer marital risks than single men. Yet, in the Goode investigation about nine-tenths of the remarried women regarded their current marriage as much better than the first marriage. As a whole, subsequent studies on success in remarriage provide some support to Waller's proposition that, although remarriages may be more successful than first marriages ending in divorce, they still present more problems than happy first marriages.

CONCLUSIONS CONCERNING WALLER'S
CONTRIBUTION

This section of the Introduction has attempted to determine the extent to which Waller's propositions regarding postdivorce adjustment have been verified by later investigations. Only major propositions were selected for analysis; the total list could not be discussed in this essay.

Waller had reasoned that friends would be instru-

---

[17] Thomas P. Monahan, "The Changing Nature and Instability of Remarriages," *Eugenics Quarterly,* 5 (1958), pp. 73–85.
[18] Bernard, *op. cit.*, p. 362.
[19] Harvey J. Locke, *Predicting Adjustment in Marriage,* New York: Holt, 1951, p. 301.

mental in arriving at a decision to obtain a divorce but would be dropped soon thereafter for new friends. Later investigations (mainly Goode) indicate that the wife's friends, but not the husband's, tend to influence the divorce decision and that Waller had overestimated the extent to which old friendships are dropped. Instead, divorcées seem to expand their circles of friendship.

With his emphasis upon Freudian mechanisms, Waller proposed that the divorced person would act in maladaptive ways because of a need for sexual readjustment after divorce. Later investigation indicates that young divorced women face some problems apparently because men assume that they are promiscuous, but that in general sex tends to be more integrated into male-female relationships than is true in courtship prior to the first marriage.

As Waller contended, divorce represents a lower economic status especially for women. Remarriage, however, generally means regaining financial standing.

Waller's propositions concerning the role of the divorcée were partially supported. The trauma of divorce is greatest among women in the role of castaways. Older women and women who had been married a long time also experience difficulty in adjusting to the lower status accompanying divorce. For most women, however, divorce does not provide the prolonged suffering suggested by Waller.

Findings on remarriage were mixed with respect to the relative happiness of the first and second marriages. The general tendency, however, is that divorced persons tend to be poor marital risks in remarriages and that relationships in remarriages are more complex than those in first marriages.

In summary, although subsequent studies on adjustment to divorce have supported many of Waller's propositions, they generally report less crisis and trauma in divorce than *The Old Love and the New* indicates. Several factors may be responsible for this difference.

First, Waller stressed the existence of certain problems in adjustment whereas William Goode, Jessie Bernard, and others were trying to determine conditions for adjustment in divorce and remarriage. Thus Waller could be expected to select extreme problem cases while Goode and Bernard were interested in the variation in adjustment.

Second, the Waller study was made prior to the Second World War, whereas Goode and Bernard undertook their studies in the 1950's. In the meantime, the divorce rate had increased and the cumulative number of divorced persons in the population had mounted. Attitudes toward divorce had changed. From the time that the Waller study was made to the later period when Goode and Bernard made their investigations, conceptions of the American family had been modified. In the 1920's the American family was seen as declining. The emphasis was upon a loss of functions and an increase in family disorganization with urbanization and industrialization. By the 1950's there was wide diffusion of the conceptions of the emerging companionship-family and of the independent nuclear-family as structural types. People did not consider divorce as indicating the demise of the American family but merely as a problem inherent in the kind of family life that was developing. Hence, the difficulties faced by divorced individuals themselves may have been decreasing.

The third possible basis for the differences between

the Waller investigation and the Goode and Bernard studies is their focus upon a different kind of population. Goode and Bernard attempted to study samples which were representative of a larger divorced population. Waller's sample consisted of intellectuals and friends who had to a considerable degree emancipated themselves from their traditional kinship and friendship groups. Isolated from kith and kin, they faced vastly different problems from those of persons studied by Goode and Bernard.[20]

Divorce and Tragedy:
A NOTE CONCERNING WALLER'S METHODOLOGY

For the most part, the discrepancies between Waller's propositions on postdivorce adjustment and the findings of later research may be attributed to a tendency by Waller to be overly pessimistic. However, his pessimism seems to reflect a sense for selecting elements of tragedy in social processes. The focus by Waller upon alienation, downfall, and despair in divorce reflects this sense of tragedy. Elsewhere in his writings, discussions of sexual exploitation, dating based on social-status ratings rather than on self-fulfillment, and reaching of a "dead level of interaction" in marriage also mirror this sensitivity.

According to Aristotle, a tragedy concerns an action which is serious and which arouses pity and fear in the audience. In the course of the drama, there is a catharsis of these emotions. Tragic drama involves certain characteristics of plot and persons. The persons are of high station initially, often in royal families. The action is such that the persons in

---

[20] See Goode, *Women in Divorce, op. cit.,* p. 340.

the drama move from happiness to misery. This change from one state of things to another, which Aristotle calls *peripety,* is a probable or necessary sequence of events and occurs through some kind of discovery by persons in the drama. This discovery by the *dramatis personae* is expressed as shift from ignorance to knowledge. This knowledge modifies sentiments and impels the persons in the drama to perform acts which change their fortune. Eventually, the discovery produces suffering in the persons involved. Thus, the peripety, taking place through discovery, arouses the pity or fear in the observer.

The Old Love and the New contains major elements of tragic drama. The persons have passed from a state of happiness to misery. The progressive alienation between husband and wife has resulted in the dissolution of the marriage. Since persons do not enter marriage with the intention of divorcing their spouses, they view the divorce as a fated and tragic occurrence. Waller deals with the reactions of divorcés to this event. He discusses the various kinds of suffering endured by divorcés—self-recrimination, self-degradation, loneliness, anxiety, and uncertainty. This suffering is generally accompanied by a change in social groups—consorting with prostitutes, becoming sexually promiscuous, joining "fast" crowds or "Bohemian" groups. Here, Waller emphasizes the loss of self-respect accompanying divorce. In the end, the divorcé turns to seeking personal salvation in a new life organization and remarriage.

Waller's handling of financial problems of the divorcé shows a concern with a fall from grace in economic and social aspects of community life. The reader can almost visualize the horrified reactions of a Greek chorus as Waller describes the physician who lost his practice or the painter whose life was spent in bondage to his ex-wife. At the same time, paradoxically, this decline in economic and social position provides the fallen protagonist with a sense of redemption. Stripped of his community position, the protagonist has only his honor.

Waller's methodology is consistent with his emphasis on tragedy in social process. His Methodological Note describes his views. Waller divides social scientists into two groups—"those who want what they say to be true and as demonstrable as possible, whether it is significant or not, and those who do not so much care whether what they say is exactly true as whether it is significant if it is true, or if it has some truth in it." Waller identifies himself as belonging to the latter group. The technique used in *The Old Love and the New* is the case study method. Waller believes that the method "is based upon the notion that what happens in one case will happen in another, and that understanding can be had from a study of the ideal typical, which may represent nothing which ever happened but something which always tends to happen." This statement is similar to Aristotle's conception of poetry (which includes tragedy) as opposed to history.

The poet's function is to describe, not the thing that has happened, but the kind of thing that might happen, i.e., what is possible as being probable or necessary. . . . The one [history] describes the thing that has been, and the other [poetry] a kind of thing that might be. Hence, poetry is something more philosophic and of graver import than history, since its statements are of the nature . . . of universals, whereas those of history are singulars.[21]

---

[21] Aristotle, *Poetics.*

The researcher as an observer of tragedy is not impartial. Instead, he may be horrified, terrorized, or moved in pity by what he sees. Furthermore, if the ultimate aim of social science is to reduce misery, then the researcher should focus his observations precisely on kinds of events which evoke fear, pity, or at least moral indignation in him. Given this view of social science, *The Old Love and the New* has an additional validity which grows out of Waller's sensitivity to tragedy. Waller was a poet among social scientists.

THE OLD LOVE AND THE NEW
Divorce and Readjustment

CHAPTER ONE

Problems of the Divorcé

THE world that loves a lover does not love a divorcé, although it may like to read about him in the newspapers. Preference for the tender emotion is not difficult to understand. Love is simple, direct, and beautiful. The lover knows what he wants and goes after it. Frustration, usually the lot of the divorcé, is complicated, circuitous, and ugly. The divorcé does not know what he wants and is not sure that he wants it anyhow. He has got what he wanted and found it was not good for him. The divorcé, further, has rendered himself vaguely indecent by violating a marriage taboo which, although consciously repudiated by the half-enlightened multitudes, yet remains a powerful element in determining their behavior. The very word divorcé, to say nothing of its more vulgar synonyms, smacks of sexual irregularity.

In the explanation of popular prejudice against divorced persons, there is another factor, of the most subtle, to be considered. People do not like divorced people because they have personal problems. A woman may lie, steal, murder, even lose her virtue, and there will still be those who say that there is some hope for her. But let her admit some difficulty in controlling her thoughts and arranging her life and she is forever damned. She has problems, personality problems! Away with her! A man may carry tales, libel, seduce, betray, he may yet rise to a position of power and trust, but if he ever admits any subjective difficulties he is branded as an impossible person. It is not a crime to have problems; if it were, the attitude could be faced and evaluated. It is simply impolite, and no gentleman would do it! And then, in these post-Freudian days, there cluster about the person who is not quite at one with himself splotches of masturbation and stains of incest.

The problems that the divorcé must face are of a sort well calculated to make him preoccupied and subjective, and therefore perhaps a bit harder to understand than he would otherwise be. They are of such a compelling nature that his energies are likely to run long in internal channels, so that all his acts are enfeebled with thought. It is not possible to imagine more thorough-going reorganization than is in extreme cases necessary after a divorce. One must reorganize his love life, he must salve over his wounded pride, he must rechannelize his habits, he must reëstablish himself in his social group, and he must settle the conflict with himself, always present, sufficiently well that he can go on living effectively. The divorced woman must in most cases face also the problem of economic rehabilitation; she must learn to pay her own way. The most casual consideration of these necessities of reorganization will suffice to suggest the explanation of the fact that real reorganization is rare.

This process by which one marriage partner is split from the other and learns to live apart is one process. It neither begins nor ends with divorce.

Marriage relations are carried over into the post-divorce period, indicating that there is much vitality in a relationship after the legal break has occurred. In other cases, the relationship is dead long before any mention is made of a legal step. It is the process with which we should be concerned, regardless of its location in time and space. And, though it be swift or gradual, this process must always take place whenever a marriage breaks up, and it must include, at one time or at separate times, reorganization along all the lines mentioned.

There are cases, it is true, when the divorce seems to represent only welcome relief from inhibitions. In these cases the marriage perhaps never had a strong psychic and social foundation, or it was broken by a gradual process of which the mates were unaware before the final severance. We must mention also some few very disorganized persons who do not mind the additional complicating factor of divorce. They were not integrated before marriage and do not expect to be afterwards; divorce means nothing to them. Their very unadjustment to society, by keeping marriage from being meaningful, has protected them against its dangers. Being weak, they seem strong; they have the strength of ten, because their hearts are inaccessible. But there are many other people who insist that their divorce has caused them no particular conflict and has given rise to no problems. Their very insistence upon this is usually diagnostic of some urgent conflict which would be revealed by further study, if indeed the problem does not obtrude itself while the person is in the very act of denying its existence.

It is worth while to consider at length the necessities of reorganization with which the divorcé is confronted. (1) Probably the most pressing necessity is that of reorganizing his love life. Habits of sex expression formed in the marriage are at some stage in the process of breaking up rudely interrupted, and either new outlets must be sought, or an arrangement must be made so that one can dispense with an outlet. If the former alternative is more frequently chosen, the latter is not unusual, at least for a while. Effects of blocking the sex impulse will be observed from time to time in the course of this study, and will not be expanded upon here.

Certain alternative courses which present themselves to the divorced person who does not wish to give over sex entirely, aside from the very common practice of continuing sex relations with the mate after the divorce, are as follows: (a) An attempt to cheapen sex, to satisfy one's self with merely physical love objects, doing away with all idealization. This is in general regressive,[1] a rebellion against the demands of the highly complicated ego and a reversion to the elemental. In its extreme form it may be accompanied by a revival of masturbation or by definitely explosive expressions of the sex impulse. This sort of adjustment may be consciously worked out, or unconsciously adopted. It verges over into

(b) Bohemianism, or promiscuity on a high level. In the previous form of adjustment, only the sex act is contemplated, perhaps without reference to the person or the circumstances, perhaps even with these purposely made degrading in their nature. In promiscuity on a high level one considers the act, the person, the circumstances, and the subjective con-

---

[1] See glossary for definition of terms, p. 339.

comitants of these, but is not ready to answer with his whole personality for the consequences of the affair, nor to give any assurance of its continuance. In its very highest form it approximates a marriage terminable at will; in its lowest it represents hectic enjoyment of sex affairs and drinking bouts with persons not of the very lowest levels of society. The point will be made again and again in this book, and may well be stated for the first time here, that both these first two adjustments, however satisfactory they may seem to the casual observer, usually indicate a considerable degree of inner unhappiness. They indicate at best an expression of only one side of an ambivalence, and a flight from the other.

(c) The third alternative is to find a real substitute and really to transfer one's affections completely to the second love object, giving to the second mate full emotional equivalence with the first. This is more easily said than done, of course, and many things conspire to make it dangerous. There is the danger of those rebound phenomena which the novels talk about, there is the danger that the second affair, produced by some inner compulsion and subjective need, will burn out its feverish life more rapidly than the first. There is the danger that no real transference will ever be made, for it is hard to put aside the love of one's youth. There is the danger that in choosing a second mate one will make a neurotic choice allowing him to perpetuate his madness. There is the danger that one may marry a second time without being as willing to make adjustments as he was on the occasion of his first marriage. There is the danger that security-seeking mechanisms set into operation by the dissolution of his first marriage will make him unable to hold the affections of a second mate. All this and much more stands in the way of finding an acceptable substitute, but this is not to say that the thing is impossible.

The divorcé who attempts to dispense with sex expression altogether may be successful for a short period of time, during an interim when it seems that the impulse has died down under the impact of other compelling emotions. Alcoholism, gambling, card-playing, social diversions, work, athletics, religion, and art may constitute in some cases substitute outlets.

(2) A second necessity no less compelling than the first is that one repair the wound to his pride which has been inflicted by the fact of divorce. For however completely rationalized it may have been, divorce is always a blow to pride. On this point we should not be deceived. If one justifies the divorce by repudiating the mate, then he has a lingering sense of shame that he should have failed so badly in his choice of a marriage partner, humiliation that he has placed his heart so ill. If one takes the blame himself, then he cannot avoid a sense of failure. If one simply says that the twain could not get along, and agreed to disagree, there is still a modicum of injury to one's ego feelings because better insight was not used in the process of living together. But people rarely agree to disagree; nearly always there is one or the other of them who takes the lead in bringing about the divorce, and one's reorganization afterwards is conditioned by whether he played the active or the passive rôle in this process. The real extent to which conscience and the current moral code have a hold upon the most disorganized persons is not commonly realized—indeed this is one of the prime factors in causing such disorganization—

and the wound caused by the violation of the mono-gamic code by divorce is deeper than it seems.

If one escapes the deep trauma of the experience of divorce itself, he is not yet free, but must en-counter innumerable opportunities to have his tender sensibilities lacerated by being treated as people think that a divorcé should be treated. If not the divorce, then perhaps his status as a divorced person wounds him. Thus a woman who experiences no un-ease in living away from her husband still stands to have her feelings hurt by frequent and casual solicitations to intercourse.

These injuries to one's pride must be dealt with in some fashion, and in dealing with them one fre-quently reorganizes himself quite completely. De-fense reactions,[2] whose function is to guard against the infliction of further trauma, and to avoid the further exacerbation of wounds already suffered, and compensatory drives,[2] intended to offset and neutralize, in one's own mind at least, the effects of the trauma, are the answers which one makes to ignominy's poisoned darts. In this matter as well as in the love-life reorganization is rarely complete.

(3) One's habits are usually disturbed by a mari-tal break. Let us here overlook the fact that love is something of a habit and that one's sexual life is regulated by habit, especially in marriage, and the fact that one usually has a habitual basis for the satisfaction of his ego drives. Habits of all sorts accumulate rapidly in marriage, and upon them and their smooth operation the institution depends much for its stability. When the marriage goes, these myr-iad little habits go with it, and their struggles to find expression again account for part of the vague

---

[2] See glossary, p. 339.

unease and restlessness which obsess the person whose break has been recent. This adjustment is of course easier where the marriage has been of short duration or where the break has taken place gradually over a long period of time.

There is a certain division of labor in matrimony which breaks down when the couple separate. Tasks in which one formerly had a certain erotic pleasure, since they were performed for the love object, are no longer necessary. One thinks at times with regret of even the unwelcome tasks of marriage, and would be glad if they could be performed again. It is not easy, when one's life has included another person, to reorganize on the basis of life which is to be lived to and for one's self. One may miss the material comforts to which marriage accustomed him, a car with a husband who acted as chauffeur, a home with a wife who acted as cook. The very compromises of marriage, compromises which in their accumulation made the marriage acceptable to both parties but satisfactory to neither, crystallized in habit, carry over after one is free to do just as he pleases. A man who once quarreled with his wife because she set the alarm clock for a time a quarter of an hour in advance of that at which the couple had to arise, so that she might prepare herself slowly and luxuriously for the ordeal of getting up to dress, ended by contracting the habit himself and carrying it through some years of life as a divorcé. Sex habits tend to establish themselves as a result of compromises between the marriage partners, and there is a special impulsion to carry these over.

(4) Because of necessities both internal and external to himself, the divorcé must reorganize his social relationships. He has lost the one person who

was more meaningful to him than any other, and he has not the solace of the bereaved person of allowing that one person to go on being meaningful. The divorcé must rearrange his whole system of relationships in such a way that other people who were not previously important may become so, and that the one person who was more important than any other may be held at a distance.

Because of things external to himself, because he no longer knows whether he belongs to certain groups or not, because the attitude of his friends is likely to be changed by the fact of his divorce, the divorcé has to work out a new status in his circle of friends. We have no clear definition of the situation with regard to divorce, and one who has just broken up his marriage does not know what his friends will think of him. Sometimes the group of friends centering around the married pair is split, part of them siding with one of the mates and the rest taking the part of the other. One does not always know who is who, or where anybody else is standing. The influence of other, and more subtle, factors is also traceable. Perhaps one's friends want to sympathize, and force their benevolent sentiments upon one who is too proud to take sympathy. Or perhaps one's friends have become somehow involved in the unfortunate circumstances of the break. Many divorcés do not attempt to salvage the remains of their circle of friends, but break completely with the people they have known or remove to another locality—a heroic remedy, but one which people often feel that they must use.

There is throughout the danger that the divorcé, because of his preoccupation with his own conflicts, will actually give some of his friends cause for offense, or that he will, through the familiar mechanism of projection,[3] put thoughts in their heads that are really only in his own, thereby disrupting his system of social relationships. There is the further fact, mentioned at the beginning of this chapter, that the divorced person is shunned because he has personal problems, which debar their possessors from respectable salons as thoroughly as lice.

Not the least unfortunate effect of divorce is that it exposes anyone who occupies a position of trust or dignity to criticism from his enemies and rivals. Malignant tongues may make of divorce itself an indictment of an entire life and all its achievements, and the revelations as to the details of one's private life which a divorce suit may bring forth may furnish material for endless scandal and ridicule.

(5) Often with women, and sometimes with men, there appear certain problems of earning one's living. By women this is sometimes regarded as the most difficult problem. It has some intrinsic difficulty, and is made in addition to represent the objectification of many inner conflicts. It is not, as they think, the whole of their unhappiness, but it is a symbol of it. Women are still not accustomed in our culture to self-support, and are often timorous when they assume that burden for the first time. Furthermore, there is involved in many cases a reduction of the standard of living in the readjustment after divorce, and in such cases one always wonders just how he is going to get along.

Compensating for this and other worries, women frequently plunge into any work that offers itself with great singleness of purpose, and over-react by an excessive devotion to their tasks for

---

[3] See glossary, p. 339.

a considerable period of time. They are sincerely worried about whether they are going to make both ends meet [4] and the work in addition furnishes an outlet for their energies. Men in certain professions, such as the ministry, or to a lesser extent teaching, find their professional careers interrupted by divorce. Both doctors and lawyers are hurt a bit by a divorce; Soames Forsythe did not fail to consider the economic consequences of the step that he was taking.

(6) Most important, most intangible, and most subtle of the necessities of the divorced person's new life is that of settling the rebellion within himself, of defending the central government against the various minor insurrections and the one or two great ones in process. In a sense all this volume is concerned with this single problem, which is not separable from any of the others, but which looms up as such an important single aspect of reorganization that it will be given extended treatment. It may be briefly indicated that the conflicts of the divorced person, although having multitudinous variety, concern mainly the lines of readjustment which have been previously indicated.

The task of settling one's conflicts is at first one of learning to live with one's self and with one's wounds, and only later does positive reconstruction become possible. What divorced people usually do is to work out a technique of living with their problems, sometimes it seems that they want these problems to endure. As real reorganization after divorce is rare, the problem of the description and analysis

---

[4] This is a form of speech not infrequently employed. A Freudian interpretation suggests itself.

of the mental conflicts of the divorcé becomes exceedingly complex.

We may turn now from this brief consideration of the primary problems of the divorced person to a discussion of certain things which may give clues as to the types of readjustment which will be effected. For as the marriage and the divorce are expressions of entire personalities and are best understood in the light of the entire life-pattern of the person, so is the person's conduct during the period of readjustment governed by the major trends of the personality as brought out by the social situation of which it is a function. Anything, then, that will tell us what sort of people we are dealing with, or that will bring out the essential characteristics of their life-situations, will serve as a key to the readjustment effected after divorce.

One such key is furnished by the reason for the delay, or for wanting to delay, in getting the divorce. It rarely happens that people wake up one morning, find that they want to get divorced, and proceed to consult a lawyer the same day. Such a decision is usually reached after long deliberation, if not debate, in which one or the other of the mates takes the aggressive rôle. Or if there is no discussion, then both know long before the actual break which way things are heading. Usually, however cogent may be the considerations which ultimately carry the decision, there are other reasons which for a time are equally valid and which are opposed. In listening to the narratives of divorced people one is moved to marvel at the powers of the human spirit to take abuse, to suffer punishment in intolerable situations. Making allowance for the fact that they give highly rationalized [5] accounts in which what they have suffered is not minimized, one still must believe enough to wonder why the people did not separate long before they did.

Why was the divorce so long delayed? In the answer to this question lies often the key to the readjustment which the couple effect after the divorce. What was uppermost in their minds while they were yet married will be dominant in their thoughts while they are reorganizing their lives separately. Other things which were unforeseen may come to affect the situation, or those foreseen may not be in fact important, but in general the motives operative in the life-situation before divorce continue to be so in that existing afterward.

If people have hesitated to split their ménage because of a reluctance to let their friends, or enemies, know that all is not well in their lives, then covering up before their friends will be of great importance in their readjustment. In such cases there is often a complete break with all the people who have known them. This desire to avoid having one's friends know the unfortunate truth may arise from fear of a loss of professional or social standing, in which case the attempt will be much more seriously made to hide the real state of affairs from the public. Such pretense is usually transparent, and is at worst considered dishonest and at best pathetic.

If a couple delay to seek their happiness separately because of religion or moral scruples, then religion and conflicts over it will predominate in the period of readjustment. If the reason for the delay is a desire for security on the part of one or both

---

[5] See glossary, p. 339.

of the mates, then we may expect to find in the period of readjustment a buttressing and intrenching of one's self which is intended to assure security in the possession of such personal assets as the divorce has left untouched. If people postpone making a break with each other because of real affection—and contrary to the general opinion there is a great deal of what is called love which is lost between persons who nevertheless decline to sleep beneath the same blanket—then the marriage partners may expect prolonged agony and anguish and turmoil of spirit on account of mental conflicts which they can never quite solve. All these factors operate to cause people to procrastinate, to postpone, to delay, hoping that after all it may not be necessary, for though people marry in haste they must perforce divorce in a leisurely fashion, and all these factors have an influence on the type of readjustment which people effect after the break.

The nature of the marriage relation has a great effect upon the process of readjustment after the marriage has broken. There are some marriages which are so very bad that the divorce furnishes an almost unmixed feeling of relief; these are probably not frequent—not nearly so frequent as divorced persons would have the rest of the world believe, but they do exist. In these cases any change produced by divorce is an improvement, and its price is gladly paid. Elsewhere we shall analyze the effects of breaking up marriages in which there is a well-established dominance-subordination relationship; we shall pay special attention to the case in which relationship of the container and the contained exists. The analysis of the different readjustments of the persons who take the lead in pushing the divorce through, and of those who are passive in the process, will also be developed more fully in another connection.

It has been suggested that for many people also the reason for the divorce determines in part the channels of readjustment. Some offenses are thought of as so heinous that forgiveness is unmanly and going on living together impossible. According to the common code, adultery is final, and the matter of the relation to the former mate at least is settled once and for all by the divorce, whereas if a couple suffer from one of the subtler forms of incompatibility the affair is not so definitely over, and we see misguided persons, whose hearts no doubt are sounder than their heads, going back again and again to the same impossible marriages. Now by all the canons of common sense incompatibility is much more conclusive as a cause for divorce than is adultery, for incompatibility, by contrast with adultery, is much more damaging and less easily eradicable. That, of course, is not in this discussion either here or there, for we are not here correcting popular notions but merely stating them. We must also not overlook the fact that adultery, as the most flagrant of all possible violations of the marriage contract, is often a dreadful blow to the pride of the other partner. Adultery is sensed by the mate as a great affront and a great injustice; these feelings give a characteristic tone to the period of readjustment. Anatole France, the story is, never forgave the taunt about horns.

A clue to the nature of one's problems and his possible solutions may be furnished by the question whether any pathological fixations, i.e., undue attachments to members of one's own family, entered into the causation of his marital unhappiness. The family slave will usually return to his family, if that is possible, or arrange in some other way to escape the responsibilities of adulthood. There are cases in which a real revolt was ushered in by the realization that it was really not the marriage partner, but one's own family, which was most to blame for one's domestic catastrophe.

Not capable of being separated from the above is the question of one's margin of heterosexuality. To modify again the famous bon mot of another generation, it is divorce which is the touchstone of heterosexuality. One who is but weak in his preference for the other sex, on account of undue attachments for someone in his own family which partially preclude a love object of the opposite sex but do not preclude one of his own sex, is likely to be easily discouraged, and to find a single joust in the lists of heterosexual love all that he is interested in attempting. Such a person may be clinched in the homosexual rôle by an unhappy marital experience. Others whose homosexual drives are latent will yet experience pronounced personality problems; it is submitted that such cases are much more numerous among divorced persons than is commonly said.

If we think of the extrovert as a person who finds significance in things outside himself, and the introvert as one who is chiefly concerned with subjective reality, with inner meaningfulness, we may say that the adaptations which these sorts of persons work out to changed conditions of life are characteristically different. But since these are ideal rather than actual personality types, and since the dominance of one or the other type of adjustment is often conditioned by a flight from the other, the application of these concepts becomes difficult. It seems that, barring a breakdown of the personal mode of life which necessitates a resort to the opposite attitude toward the objective world, or enables one to gain balance, the net effect is finally to accentuate ·the degree of introversion or extroversion. Temporarily, indeed, the introvert may turn from poetry and music and communion with the everlasting mysteries to counting nuts and bolts and reorganizing systems of bookkeeping, but since he has suffered by allowing a person and a thing to become meaningful, he is likely in the end to retire again to his inner fastnesses, and to make them more impregnable than ever. Similarly the extrovert may take away the meaning of persons and things by making them take their places among a vaster army of things and persons. The disappointed introvert loves no person, but an ideal inside himself, whereas the extrovert loves many, but none very much. Similarly, the readjustment of the person whose chief concern is with status will differ from that of the person who is chiefly occupied with problems of affection.

There is unquestionably a sex difference in the readjustment which is effected after divorce, although generalization must here be so hedged about with provisos and reservations that it becomes almost meaningless. On the basis of the cases studied in the preparation of this work, it could be said that men are more positive and dynamic in their attitude toward reorganization, whereas women are more inclined to face their difficulties frankly. More channels of activity are open to men, and this alone may account for the fact that they tend to neutralize their tensions by extraneous activity rather than by facing them and subjectively resolving them, but there may be involved other factors which strike deeper into the masculinity-femininity dichotomy of character types in our culture. For instance, with women the sex mores [6] are more subjectively real, and therefore more important, than they are with men, and it ensues that women have more difficulty than men in avoiding overt conflict concerning moral issues.

Objective factors of the greatest importance obtrude themselves here also. The problem of self-support is likely to be a severe one with the woman, but this is partially balanced by the fact that the man on the higher professional levels has more to lose as a result of scandal than his wife. Children in general affect readjustment, and their presence may cause the readjustment of the man and the woman to be strikingly different. As the custody of minor children is usually given to the mother, the father stands to lose his parental as well as his conjugal privileges by divorce, and this has occasionally been cited as a partial explanation of the fact that most divorces are sought by women. If the mother takes the children, the father is less tied to the past than she, but he is also more obstructed in the natural expression of his affections. But the advantage is not all in favor of the parent who has primary responsibility for the care of the child, for the other parent is usually allowed to see the child at stated intervals; these occasions by their very rarity are festive days for the little orphan of the courts, and he may by his childish enthusiasm wound the parent to whom he is chiefly indebted for care and support.

Alimony also enters as affecting the different problems of adjustment of men and women. Where

---

[6] See glossary, p. 339.

there are children, the payment for their support is usually made cheerfully, though perhaps not without some twinges of regret that one is shut out from further coöperation in their rearing. But where there are no children, the man who pays alimony is likely to feel that he is paying interminable installments upon a dead horse. The records show, of course, that these payments are not usually continued very long. The reason for alimony exactions, as well as for the alleged mercenary attitude of women in general toward matrimony, is that marriage is for women a matter of both affection and support; a woman choosing a husband is choosing a mate and a breadwinner; a woman divorcing her husband therefore wishes to keep him as a meal-ticket while putting him away as a mate.

That there is an age factor is of course a commonplace that hardly needs restating. For all the turbulence of young emotion, its poignancy, its pathos, the advantage is nevertheless all with the young. Women who have passed a certain age must realize at last that love is not for them, for time, and marriage, and divorce have done damage to fair faces that no beautician can repair. Men, too, have lost, but their straits are less dire, because they have not, in breaking their marriage, discontinued also a career, and because the male is less rigidly judged by current standards of pulchritude than is the female.

We may arrive at a better understanding of the divorcé's problems of adjustment if we compare them with the problems of people whose situation is similar in some respects but different in others. Such cases, to take only those within the ken of all, are cases where one has been bereaved, losing a mate by death, cases of broken love affairs which did not go to marriage, and the cases of those interesting married people who should have got divorces but did not.

Like the bereaved one, the divorcé has lost a mate, but in most other respects the psychic and social situation is different. Yet there are some essential similarities too. Both are brought out in the following statement prepared by Howard P. Becker, who has made an extensive study of the phenomena of bereavement in general.

In the academic year 1925–26 the writer carried on an investigation which he called "A Social-Psychological Study of Bereavement." [7] Among the research techniques used were a series of case studies of individuals who had recently been bereaved, as well as a rather comprehensive survey of pre-literate and historical material on the subject. Certain elements seem to be significant in relation to Dr. Waller's study. Some of these are summarized below:

1. There is a striking similarity between the taboos built up about sex and the taboos associated with mourning and bereavement behavior.

2. In practically every culture examined there is some sort of outlet, in ritual or other sanctioned behavior, for the emotions attendant upon bereavement and personality readjustment after bereavement. The culture, in other words, makes some provision for the inevitable trauma of death—perhaps because it is inevitable and common to all.

3. In spite of the similarity between sex taboos and death taboos, there are marked differences in the

---

[7] Howard P. Becker, unpublished M. A. thesis, "A Social-Psychological Study of Bereavement," Northwestern University, 1926.

rigidity with which they are enforced. In some cultures the death taboos are more rigid, in others the sex taboos. Our own culture is an example of the latter. We provide, in some measure, socially sanctioned means of working out a personality adjustment when a mate has died; we have practically no socially sanctioned means for the painful task of readjusting after a marriage or engagement has "died." Here there are no "consolations of religion." When the widower remarries after a "decent" period of waiting, he has at least the partial approval of his community and his religious group; if the divorced person remarries there is usually the unexpressed but none the less potent feeling among "respectable" members of the community that here is someone who is evading the just punishment for his or her sin, indiscretion or incompetence. To be sure, the sex taboos are in the process of becoming less rigid, but there is as yet no recognized social pattern by which the personality thrust out of its normal course may be redirected back into the main channel. One hundred years ago, and in some quarters even to-day, a widow was sought after rather than shunned, and the man who married her had on the whole performed a meritorious act. Certainly the same cannot be said of the divorced woman—she may not be shunned in the larger cities, or even in small towns and urban communities, but she is still regarded as an undesirable marriage partner, and still more certain it is that no positive approbation attends the man who marries her. One reason for the difference is not far to seek. Death is an "act of God" to which no moral blame attaches; divorce is the result of free will, which might have chosen otherwise. Divorce is a willful violation of the sex taboos in the unconscious moral judgment of most persons dominated by the traditional code, and herein lies its peculiar culpability.[8]

---

[8] Mrs. Ada Davis is now carrying on a social psychological investigation of the phenomena of widowhood.

Though divorced persons and those who have lost their lovers sometimes take advantage of their common misery to console each other, their problems are really of a quite different sort. They are alike in that both suffer, or may suffer, from the pangs of love which if not unrequited is at least thwarted. The advantage is of course with the person who has lost his sweetheart, for although there may be more idealization in extra-marital than in marital love, there are more guards and more barriers between the persons, so that the relationship is less close. Both may suffer from injured pride; the divorcé, having been injured the more publicly, suffers more. Both suffer from mental conflicts which may in the case of either become very severe, but the advantage is again with the person whose affair stopped short of marriage.

There are certain respects in which the situations of these two sorts of persons suffering from interruptions of their love life are altogether different. One suffers no loss of social standing from the breaking up of an affair which did not proceed to marriage. One's friends often do not even offer to sympathize with one over such a break, there is an element of humor in the quarrels of lovers. The disappointed lover has a great advantage over the thwarted husband or wife in that there is present for him a clear and unequivocal definition of the situation.[9] The break having been made, he should reconstruct, nor does anyone consider it indelicate if he begins that process at once. Further, as the habits of courtship are of but little account by comparison with those of marriage, the penalty for

---

[9] See glossary, p. 339.

breaking them is less. An additional factor is that since the affair is lighter in its nature, one is more likely to tell just how the break occurred, and is therefore more likely to talk it out, getting what is known as a "catharsis." [10] It seems, however, that it is even more important in these cases who breaks the affair, possibly because, the affair being of a less serious nature, the inner qualms of the one who breaks it are more easily hidden. The one case in which the situation of the divorcé is better than that of the lover who has suffered a disappointment is that of the woman who has lost her virginity to the man whom she is giving up. If she attaches an uncommon value to that physical attribute, she may well grieve over having lost it illegitimately. That, too, is passing, for this fragile thing, virginity, has in these skeptical days a waning value.

We have yet to consider how the situation of the divorcé differs from that of those pathetic persons who ought to get divorces but for some reason will not.[11] The life of persons who live together in marriage, when the rapport upon which the relationship rests is gone, is if anything more effectually thwarted than is that of the divorced person. Divorce is a lump sum, it is said, that one pays for freedom to work out his own life adjustments; since one is never really free, it is a lump sum with continued partial payments. But those who live together when the

[10] See glossary, p. 339.
[11] We are not discussing here those married people who separate but refrain from getting divorces. These separations are tantamount to divorces except for the fact that reconstruction by starting another home is impossible,—a fact not without important consequences, it is true, but one which we may perhaps be permitted to overlook for the time.

marriage has become hollow pay and pay and pay, and never stop until they die.[12]

It is amazing how completely a marriage may in fact have ceased to be a marriage and yet remain one in form. The alienation of the marriage partners from each other may be complete, so that there is apparent no vestige of an emotional bond between them. Their estrangement may even be public and admitted. One may satisfy his own desires for status by a public derogation of the other, which represents the opposite extreme to emotional identification with the love object. It may happen that the life of the married ones is completely split, the husband having his friends, his life, his work, his ambitions, dreams, and ideals, from all of which the wife is excluded, she being similarly independent. Under such circumstances it is likely that each will be completely objective about the other. Or, unable quite to break away, and yet unable to solve their elusive incompatibility, they may meet and quarrel, giving vent to their pent-up hate in violent, cathartic quarrels whose periodicity and satisfactoriness to the partners indicate perhaps that in some bizarre way their sex life has been shunted off into that unfortunate channel.. There are endless possibilities which it is not necessary to elaborate because every reader will be able to supply further examples from his own experience.

The penalties that one pays for such marital unadjustment vary but have an underlying similarity.

---

[12] Since this was written a case has been called to our attention in which this was literally true. A man who had hated his wife for many years, but who had not been able to divorce her, lay in his last illness. Whenever his wife passed near his bed he kicked at her. His last agonies were precipitated by one final attempt to express his hate in this fashion.

One can only live with such a situation at a cost of repressing some of the major impulses, as one can likewise only remain unaware of the real state of affairs by repressing knowledge of them.[13] That these persons do repress is indicated by their apparent unconsciousness of the real seriousness of their situation. It is also indicated by the frequency with which, in their cases, projection mechanisms are employed.[14] These projection mechanisms express themselves by a general attitude of inquiry into the marital life of others, the tacit assumption always being that what one will find there will not be nice, by unfair accusations of others, and by a general lowered threshold for anything sexy. Repressions are also indicated by an uncompromisingly hostile attitude toward divorce, and prejudice against people who have taken that way out. These manifestations can only indicate that one has had to build up impressive defenses against divorce, or that one entertains a subconscious envy of those who, having made a bad bargain, had the courage to admit it and go their separated ways.

One can only live in a marriage that has failed at the expense of considerable personality distortion. There is, of course, nothing to be said against the distortion of personality, for that, described in other terms, is always the mechanism whereby we adjust ourselves to the conditions of our lives, but here the distortion is, as has been shown, very expensive, and what one gets from it must be slight. It should be remembered that it is not only divorce which makes people neurotic, but living in an unsatisfactory mar-

---

[13] See glossary, p. 339.
[14] See glossary, p. 339.

riage; divorce and neurosis [15] (or other forms of personality maladjustment) represent parallel modes of escape from intolerable situations. There is the further disadvantage for this type of persistence in marriage that reconstruction, involving the formation of new and perhaps more satisfactory family relationships, is impossible.

He who explains divorce—and no one has, with all due respect to the present so numerous learned tomes—should also be able to explain why people go on living together, and he who first satisfactorily explains either the one or the other will have explained much. Fear may lead people to prefer the familiar misery of living together to the unknown sufferings of divorce. The fears of these people—which may in many cases be simple anxiety neuroses produced by lack of sex satisfaction—have many forms, fear of the loss of professional standing, fear of the future, fear of economic reverses, fear of social degradation, fear of names, fear of crises, fear of God, fear of hell. Then there are sometimes children whom people think that they cannot properly bring up unless they continue to live together. Apparently it was more customary to patch things up "for the sake of the children" in the times to which Victoria gave her name than it is in this postbellum period. There is the desire to stay and fight it out, and in the end to gain the victory. Associated with this is the intricately contrary connection of sex with marital quarrels, and the more gross connection of one's drive for status, since it is very easy for quarrels to turn out in such fashion that each person thinks that he has really carried away the

---

[15] See glossary, p. 339.

palm. There is desire for martyrdom, the will to unpleasure, of course not primary, but perhaps existent prior to marriage. Perversions, such as masochism,[16] or sadism [16] may bind, and even impotence [16] may chain one to an unsatisfactory marriage partner. Fixations,[16] preventing one from giving to the incestuous love object a real rival but allowing an unsatisfactory one, may also be involved. And religion and moral ideas may serve to keep people together, on the principle that these two by a cruel jest made twain should be sacrificed for the benefit of the many. This is of course a travesty on what the modernists call "true religion." All very intricate, and the writer makes no pretense to having unraveled it.

Divorce is expensive. The divorcé has his problems and this one book written around them is not sufficient for their complete treatment. Yet it is not the possibility of divorce which should deter young candidates for matrimony, not the chance that those who now look at each other with the silly little look of love may some time face each other from opposite sides of the courtroom which should make them hesitate, but the eventuality that if their marriage should degenerate into a hollow shell they will not have the courage to break it. The divorcé has his troubles, but when he contemplates these others, after all so much more unfortunate than he, he may, and, in fact, must forgive destiny, for he is spared much who is his own master and his lot is not so lachrymose who lives alone. With this cheerful reflection let us turn to the chapters in which particular problems of the divorcé are considered in more

---

[16] See glossary, p. 339.

detail. We shall have need of all our optimism before we have finished, but we may yet be able to conduct our people, or a few of them at least, through the mazes of conflict till we see them at last safely on the other side of hell.

CHAPTER TWO

Transition Pains

ONLY the newly wed can answer the question, "How does it feel to be married?" because the conjugal state soon becomes so much a part of himself that it cannot be examined and assessed, and he can no more tell how it feels to be married than he can tell how it feels to be alive. Likewise, only the person whose divorce is recent has clear-cut impressions as to how it feels to be a divorcé. No happy uproar accompanies it, no joyous song or ribald jest, no clatter of pans or showers of rice, no congratulations, but divorce ushers in a change of all the important details of life as truly as does marriage. The newly divorced still has his tongue where the tooth has been, and if we ask him quickly, he can tell us how it feels. In this chapter we shall discuss those first impressions, first conflicts, first struggles to take hold, the subjective experiences of those first days when one is trying to realize what has happened.

After any crisis which produces a really fundamental change in the conditions of life, the problem of re-integration becomes acute. The old self will not do; it has committed suicide by producing a change in the environment of which it was a function, the milieu in adaptation to which it was forged.

The chrysalis has destroyed its cocoon; now it must become a butterfly. The first mental conflicts of the divorcé represent the struggle of the self that was to go on functioning in the new conditions of life. That it cannot do, or cannot do without making fundamental changes within itself, hence conflict arises. Before the conflict is ended a new self must be evolved, or a new ego put in control of the personality.

Habits cannot continue to function after the stimuli that set them off and the objects to which they were attached have passed out of existence. Yet they cannot wholly die either, and must be utilized in any readaptation that is worked out. Techniques of adjustment to social situations cannot always be carried over from one situation to another; yet one has at his command when he is facing any new situation only the techniques which have previously been employed. Love cannot conveniently go on after the person to whom it was attached has been shut out of one's life, yet we know that it dies ever a lingering death.

What happens is that when one is faced with a new situation he tries to adjust to it at first by retaining the old system of personal organization, and only later faces the possibility of realigning himself in order to deal more successfully with the environment. First attempts at realignment may be in the nature of a resurrection of a previous form of personal organization; more than one person has temporarily met a crisis by pulling one of his former selves from the grave in which it had many years before been interred, dusting it off and making it do duty in the new life. But this is never satisfactory, since any really successful reorganization must utilize all the years of one's experience. And as no new situation is ever experienced like any preceding one, only a considerably different form of personal organization can ever be entirely satisfactory.

When habits are suddenly interrupted, a very special sort of unease is produced. These habits are like wires which, though broken, still carry a current; they discharge their vain sparks into the indifferent earth. One seeks for something which will satisfy his habitual craving; not finding it, he goes on seeking, urged by a great restlessness. Finally the habits are absorbed in the new personal orientation; they are, to renew the simile of the wires, given a different hook-up. In the following case record we have the story of the interruption of habits by divorce. This is complicated by an unsatisfied longing for response which leads the man to give emotional importance to strangers and even to fictitious persons.

"Since I was moving to a new city, the paper which I had read in my former home was not available. It was not the paper that mattered so much as the comic strips, so I bought all the papers published in the new city in order to piece out as many of the comics to which I was accustomed as I could. There was the further fact that not one of the papers in the new city really appeared to satisfy my craving to have the news. I would buy a paper, and hastily scan it. I would perceive that there was nothing in it, read the comics, and throw it away. On some days I bought all the morning papers and all the evening papers published in town, and some papers from nearby towns. I had a craving for news and soon became interested in following the adventures of the people in the comic strips as well.

"The problem was to stay out of my room as much as possible. I preferred to stay at the office in the evenings and would not spend an evening in my room unless I had to work there. You see, I felt very much the change from a home of my own to a furnished room in somebody else's home, and looking about the room when I was alone in it, used to feel great throbs of sorrow for myself.

"I had the most trouble with the week-ends, Saturday afternoon and evening, and Sunday all day, were likely to be very black for me. I had for years been spending the week-ends with my wife, and, as I suppose is the usual case with married persons, not a little of the time was spent in love and sexual indulgence. I had come to think of Sunday as the day which was most fitted of all days for that sort of thing and it was very difficult for me to face Sunday when away from my wife. Traveling men have often told me that Sunday was their hardest day. I can well believe them.

"Saturday afternoon I would usually walk around, by myself if necessary, but only if I could not possibly persuade anyone else to go along. I felt somewhat better if I could have someone along to talk to. Not that I always talked about my troubles. I do not believe that I did, but I needed people in the most naïve way at this time. I was alone and needed company. Saturday night it was not usually possible to get any of the men I knew to spend the evening with me, I am not sure that I ever asked them, I believe that I simply took it for granted that they were otherwise occupied. So I bought a number of papers, if possible the Sunday papers also, and went into my room. I read these very thoroughly, and took a special interest in all stories about divorces, about divorced people, above all about divorced people who had remarried, and in stories about dogs. (It should be noted that I missed my dog also, for he had been my constant companion on all my walks for years. I used to imagine him running along in front of me when I was outside, I would see him running up to other dogs and wonder whether there was going to be a fight or not, and occasionally the image of his instant response to any advance that I made to him would become so strong that I would call out his name. In this connection, by the way, I do not know that I have ever felt more hurt than I did when a few months later I saw

my dog and he did not recognize me.) Later in the evening
I usually wrote a long letter to my wife, pouring out my
soul in it. Saturday night was perhaps the low point of the
whole week, for I was then more likely to be lonely than
at any other time, and I faced a lonely Sunday. The sense
that all this was unreal, that I was a disembodied ghost
living in a shadowy world, living a futile useless life in a cold
and lonely world, this feeling became very strong on Saturday evenings, but it was usually dispelled by the sunshine
of Sunday morning.

"Sunday morning I went for breakfast to some place where
the people were friendly and willing to talk. I would usually
stand around and talk to the manager as long as I felt that
I could without becoming noticeable. At this time I became
very ready to enter into any casual discussion that might
be in progress. No matter how inane the conversation might
be, I was very grateful for the relief that it afforded me
from loneliness. I believe that I understand these tedious,
rambling arguments of the cigar-store and barber-shop
better now than I did before going through this experience.

"But I could never prolong my time-killing discussions
long enough to avoid the necessity of returning to my room
before going out again for dinner. Shortly before noon I
started on a walk of between two and three miles to meet a
friend with whom I usually took Sunday dinner at a certain
place. We usually prolonged the dinner and then went over
to his room where we talked or read until he had to leave
to keep an appointment with his fiancée. I would walk with
him to the home of his fiancée, and would then reluctantly
start for my room. I meditated on the way in which cruel
fate had given to every other person in the world a person
to love but had denied one to me.

"I fell into the habit of allowing the people with whom
I lived to furnish my light Sunday evening supper. I felt
that I was under a deep obligation to them for their kindness
in this as in other matters. On the evenings when I was
forced to remain in my room I found a certain solace in
eating some sort of indestructible candy or in munching

crackers. With regard to the candy, I remember that for a long time I had very considerable twinges when I purchased the small quantity that I would eat, and that I thought with pain and regret of the times before when I had bought candy for myself and my wife, which was by a tacit agreement between us always regarded as a gift from me to her, even though my motives in buying it were altogether selfish. I used to wonder whether I ought not to send a box to her, and sometimes did so.

"Sunday evening was not so bad as Saturday, because I was looking forward to Monday, and Monday was my day of days. The sound of my alarm clock on Monday morning was no unwelcome clangor that summoned me to assume reluctantly the duties of the day, but a sweet tinkle that invited me back to a welcome routine."

Frustration may be felt in a long or short period when the old self is endeavoring to express itself in the new orientation. But when a decision is reached after the deliberations there arises a certain willingness to abide by it. This may be accompanied by a greater or less degree of repression of discordant impulses. The repression, while giving a temporary semblance of integration, and enabling one to mobilize his personal resources sufficiently well to be able at least to act, in the long run hinders the completion of the process of adaptation.

The search for an attitude in a situation which is not clearly defined may be prolonged and painful. The old self, trying to adjust to the demands of the changed situation, may do so by a series of antithetical and opposed responses, none of which is completely satisfactory. Or the antithetical responses may both come to expression in the same instrument, as in a letter which declares love but sets impossible conditions for its expression. It is not until a radically different organization has been attained that we are at one, not until then that the vacillation between opposed extremes is stopped and stability is attained.

But lest this too generalized expression leave the reader uncertain as to the actual nature of the conflicts of the divorcé, let us state them more explicitly. They arise, it is true, because it is not possible for the personality to change as rapidly as the conditions of life, for personality is ever an adaptation. Certain general lines of reconstruction have been analyzed before—certain general conflicts concerning these stand out. There is the sex need, complicated more often than people realize by a very real love for the lost mate. There is sadly wounded pride, necessitating readjustment, demanding constructive experiences. There are habits, there are worries concerning economic security, there is concern over status in one's group. In every one of these one must face reorganization, and reorganization brings conflict.

By some peculiar mechanism the perceptual faculties sometimes seem to increase in acuity at a time of great internal turmoil. Perhaps this is due to the conflict which, forcing one to face a changed situation, renders him keen in perceiving all of its details. It seems more likely that it represents the common turning of attention from things inside to things outside, when inside is something which one cannot face; if we carry this explanation over into the less trying moments of the conflict it may account for the not uncommon phenomenon of increase of extroversion [1] after divorce. (Admitted that this extro-

---

[1] See glossary, p. 339.

version is forced, admitted that it is merely the obverse side of real preoccupation with one's conflicts, it is nevertheless real, qualitatively and historically as real as that of the first tough-minded pragmatist.) Lest we be carried too far afield in following out the implications of a rather tenuous hypothesis, let us document this observation that at a time of crisis one's senses are sharpened and one's memory of details outside one's self is made more keen, by a passage from one of our cases:

"All the incidents of the last few days we spent together and of the first few days we spent apart are etched on my mind like so many steel engravings. . . .

"My train came and I kissed my wife good-by and took my bags and went into the smoking-car and sat down. I suppose the reason for the excessive circumstantiality of my account is that every one of those actions was an achievement. I sat, hunched over, with my traveling bags scattered about, and the future seemed very desolate and blank. I suddenly realized that I was alone, that I was afraid, and that something within me was very sick. But I had a sense also of being an actor in a drama of high tragedy. Life could not go on, I knew that. I was very tired and very sick and the end was drawing near. The thought came to me that I had already died and that my soul had gone away, leaving my body to act as a mere automaton. I wondered if death were like that. As the train went on, I grew very dirty, but I did not care. I bought some candy and ate it, then bought some more and ate that and was still too numb to know what it was that had happened.

"A roughly dressed workingman came in and stopped by my seat. 'Have you got a match?' he asked. Something told me that he was anxious to talk. 'Yes. Won't you sit down?' I said. I am sure that I smiled. He was in a very difficult situation and he wanted advice. He had married a former

telephone operator a few months before. He loved her so
much that to save her from death he would willingly go right
out and lie down in front of this train. I thought that there
were worse things than death. I wondered if he loved his
wife more than I loved mine, whether I loved my wife
enough to do that. He was being bothered by a woman who
claimed to be his common law wife. He had lived at her
boarding-house for some time, intermittently, and had allowed her to introduce him as her husband, had even allowed her to use his name. When he had left her before, she
had looked him up and had induced him to come back to
her. This time he had nearly escaped her by going to a different state, and had thought that she would never find him
again. But she had found out somehow where he was and had
written to the pastor of his church and claimed that she
was his wife and that his formal marriage was not legal.
His wife had sent him over to see this woman and dis-
entangle himself. He had sworn a fearful oath that he would
not have sexual relations with her. He described her. She
was a hail-fellow well-met sort of woman, who had once
been known about all the saloons. He had on previous occasions denied her sexual satisfaction when she had begged
him on her bended knee to accommodate her. He would
refuse her this time, because he had sworn it on a Bible and
if he did he would get in trouble with God. Besides, he
thought a lot of his God. I was amused to hear someone
speak of God, for I knew that there was no God but only
an implacable destiny. I asked him some questions. How
formally had he acknowledged this woman as his wife? She
had introduced him as her husband to some people in a store,
but he had never introduced her as his wife. He did not know
whether she could find these people or not; she had no money
with which to put up a legal battle. It did not seem that she
could make such a clear case after all. He had not lived with
her very long, and not very openly. Only once, in a store,
had she introduced him as her husband. I asked if he had
ever taken her across a state line for immoral purposes. 'Oh,
yes!' he said, 'She's going to get after me for that if I say

she's not my common law wife.' I asked when and where and whether she had any way of proving it or not. It seemed that she had not. He made his own contribution, not a very strong argument. 'Well, I didn't take her across the state boundary anyhow. The train took her.' I told him to deny that she was his wife, that he had ever acknowledged her as such, that he had ever taken her across a state boundary, and to tell her that he had seen a lawyer who would take proceedings against her for interfering with the peace and quiet of a married pair. I was very emphatic. 'Admit nothing. Under any and all circumstances, admit nothing. Don't admit anything to anybody. They can't prove anything. She can't prove you ever allowed her to pass herself off as your wife. Tell her to go to hell! If she says she'll prosecute you under the Mann Act, tell her she can't prove anything, that she'll only succeed in ruining her own reputation.' I thought that I wouldn't mind having his mistress for myself. I told him many more things like that. He was still a little dubious, and if he went to the penitentiary he wanted me to get him out. I thought that I would just as soon go there myself. Life was worth nothing to me now. Freight trains kept going by on the other track and my friend always stopped talking while they passed. I thought that this showed a certain amount of good manners. My companion left, considerably heartened by what I had told him. I thought that it was tragic that I could solve other people's problems when I could not solve my own."

The same man then continues for several pages to describe his conversations with people on the train. This account was written more than two years after the event, so that it becomes remarkable as an exhibit of the tricks of attention and memory at such a time. The opposite reaction is possibly more common, many persons can remember nothing of what happened outside themselves at such times.

Grace Hegger Lewis, former wife of Sinclair

Lewis, has described a distortion of perception which may be very common. Upon alighting at the Reno [2] station, one finds, she says, that:

"As in a nightmare all things are out of focus, even the Reno porter and the bus-driver.... Weeks later, when your life has become pleasantly adjusted, you pay a visit to the railway station. A nice station, a cheerful station, certainly not the one at which you alighted that sinister first night." [3]

The same writer has described certain phenomena of this period which are a bit clearer as examples of the projection mechanism. (The accusations of her own conscience are put into the mouths of other persons.)

"No matter what the cause which has resulted in the cleavage, the psychology of the women, Reno bound, is significantly alike. Even if, as often happens, your husband-to-be sees you aboard the train with books and flowers and sustaining promises of a new happy future, once the train has started you retire to your seat with tears in your eyes and a feeling of being a marked woman from that moment. When the conductor asks you for your ticket you hand it to him

---

[2] Mrs. Lewis' article is one of a number of recent descriptions of the life of the divorce colony in Reno. The others are mainly attempts to exploit, for the magazine reading public, the picturesque features of the life of the persons who go to Reno for "the cure." This is the theme of *Reno,* by Cornelius Vanderbilt, Jr., an honest but amateurish book. The substance of most of the "Reno" articles is that the persons who go to Reno for divorces are in conflict about the matter, and that their superficial gayety is an attempt to escape from their inner uneasiness. Drunkenness, promiscuity, the cult of the jest, and gayety are thus merely compensatory behavior. *Reno,* while telling an insipid love story, also gives some interesting details concerning the folkways of the divorce colony.

[3] "Just What Is Reno Like," Grace Hegger Lewis, *Scribner's,* January, 1929, p. 36. From *Scribner's Magazine* by permission. Copyright, 1928, by Charles Scribner's Sons.

with a sense of shame, and though you may have bought a thrifty round-trip ticket to San Francisco, nevertheless the Pullman ticket is inscribed Reno, and should the conductor note the fact in a loud voice, you cower a little or look impersonally out of the window as if the ticket were no affair of yours. If you are all alone, without mother, children, friend, or maid, your aloneness increases with every day. A spirit of adventure may buoy you up for a while, but as Wyoming mountains succeed Nebraska plains you realize there will be no dear familiar faces at this journey's end— you are on your own, for better, for worse.

"The trains from the East and the trains from the West all arrive in and depart from Reno in the dark hours. You hope to descend unobserved, but a number of men passengers are walking up and down the platform for a breather, and when they see your luggage being piled up by the porter you at once become a person of great interest.

" 'There goes one of them,' you overhear. You begin to feel as if you had an infectious disease." [4]

Mrs. Lewis is an excellent witness. Before we allow her to leave the stand, let us interrogate her upon some other points.

"When you ask the permanent residents of Reno just what effect this daily contact with the divorce colony has upon their private lives, they will say, 'None.' It is true that the abnormal sustained can become the normal, but what a strange normal it is! It is normal for the benevolent hotel manager to see freshly arrived women on the verge of tears changing their minds and their apartments three times that first week. It is too hot, too cold, too high, too low, too small, too large, too quiet, too noisy. Patiently he will show another arrangement, for he knows the manifestations so well. The doctors are only too familiar with the effects of worry, loneliness, and altitude. They can divide your symptoms and

[4] *Ibid.,* p. 35.

recovery neatly into weeks. The beauty parlor attendants prescribe for the inevitable lifeless hair and dry skin, and throw in a kind word or two which looses a flood-gate of confidences. 'I know, I know,' they'll say, 'we've been through the mill ourselves.' No father confessor has listened to greater intimacies than do the masseuses. And before your three months are up you in turn will be the repository of the marital secrets of many of those who serve you. Bellboys and telephone operators and room service waiters, as well as the housemaids, may be only three-month-job-holders, and if you are sympathetic you will hear their stories, too." [5]

The discontent with room should probably be labelled as a displacement.[6] The uneasiness concerning her life-situation is there, but she refuses to admit its connection with her pending divorce; the emotion attaches itself to the otherwise indifferent subject of rooms. The illnesses of these women are possible neurotic symptoms induced by their acute mental conflict. (As another physiological effect of such conflicts, doctors sometimes mention chronic constipation.) The breakdown of social barriers is possibly due to the operation of the psychoanalytic mechanism of transference,[7] a mechanism by which we become emotionally attached to those persons to whom we tell our troubles, although it is explicable as due simply to an increased "consciousness of kind."

Most pathetic, perhaps, of all the things that people do who are not quite reconciled to divorce, are the desperate little attempts to reassert control over the loved one. Certain stimuli were known in the past to evoke the desired responses, now these stimuli are made to march before the indifferent one's eyes in a pathetic little parade. One may know

---

[5] *Ibid.*
[6] See glossary, p. 339.
[7] See glossary, p. 339.

that it is all perfectly useless, may realize that it would be a great misfortune if perchance the attempt succeeded, and have many misgivings as to what he will do if it does succeed—yet he cannot help trying to elicit the desired response, or offering the stimulus while pretending that the response will certainly follow, in order to have for one moment the delusive feeling that the old rapport is there. The following excerpt from a letter of a divorced woman illustrates this admirably. Notice the medley of motives involved, with the buying of the slippers emerging as an attempt, partly compensatory, to reassert control over the husband who is drifting away from her.

"You've changed a lot, haven't you? From the time when you liked to write me to the time when you can't find time to answer in less than a week.... I've written you nasty letters sometimes, that was when I thought you'd hold me in spite of myself, and I fought against it in the only way I knew, meanness. Now you've changed so I'll admit that each of the cross letters cost me days of misery. You wouldn't begin to realize the stark misery of this last year for me.... And think before you fall for someone because I want to stay away from marriage and the day you marry I'll be driven to someone else, too—in self-defense—I couldn't bear it unless I did something defiant. And so I'm asking you to hold steady, please, for both of us.

"I've done something perhaps I shouldn't have. I went to Walkover and bought an utterly frivolous pair of high-heeled pumps, and a rhinestone strap besides. I went in to get some much-needed hose, and was tempted to try on a darling pair of slippers, and I hadn't any money and I knew I simply shouldn't take them and so I did. And I charged them to you and the slippers were $10 and the straps $6. And I really needed a pair of low-heeled sensible ones and I've got no business with these, so I'm not wearing them, I'm just looking. And I wish you'd let me know if you care to pay the bill at once, because if not I must take them back as soon as possible.

"If you don't want to very well. I notice you still want immediate freedom.... I also notice you aren't much interested in writing me. I'll let you off from that, too. Just let me know about this bill and what arrangements you'll make with me. And I'd appreciate it if you managed to find time to answer in less than a week....

(Postscript).... "It must be great to be able to do nice things like that without asking first for permission and next for money. This business of being a woman—whew. The next time I get born I want to be a boy baby or else somebody's pet dog."

(Note the "masculine protest" in the last paragraph.)

Suicide threats are used for this same purpose. It is difficult to arrive at really sound conclusions as to the sincerity of these threats or the seriousness with which a person is considering that way out, because it is not possible to know that one has seriously intended to kill himself until he has done so, and then he cannot be interviewed. If he talks it over with some other person he gets a catharsis and the situation inside himself is changed, so that one cannot know how close he was to committing the act. At any rate, when people are caught within a situation, it is a powerful threat, and one which people do not ordinarily use unless they feel themselves desperately trapped. The various alternatives were rather clearly envisaged by the subject of the case study from which the following excerpt is quoted.

"The thought of suicide was never absent from my mind. I do not know how near I really was to taking that way out, one can never tell. I used to sit in my room and ponder upon the fact that my life had come to a place where I could never expect anything more than unhappiness as long as it might endure, except for the fact that the possibility of my wife and myself being together again was not absolutely excluded. (It looked very unlikely to me at this time that this would ever happen.) I would occasionally take my automatic, loaded, and point it at the spot in my temple where I thought that a bullet might enter most easily. I would put my finger on the trigger and say, 'Shall I?' but the decision was always in favor of thinking it over further and more completely exhausting the possibilities of reconciliation. I would sometimes hold a rehearsal with the gun unloaded, going through everything but the dying. I would think of the things that would happen after death, of my wife realizing too late that she really loved me, of her learning to her sorrow that this was really serious business with me. But what hurt was that this final dramatic stroke would gain me nothing that I could see or taste or feel, nothing of which I could ever become conscious except by anticipation. I used to take walks, and then I would think of suicide. I could face with equanimity the giving up of this existence, but I found it hard to think of my body, really young and strong and well taken care of, turned cold and filled full of embalming fluid. Sometimes on the walks, and increasingly as time went on, I had a feeling of strength and unconquerable spirit, and as I stepped along with my chest out I was sure that I did not want to die, however much I might at other times toy with the thought."

Proof is not, as has been said, available, but the first few months after separation or divorce seem to be fruitful in suicides. The causes in any individual instance are deep in the inner nature of the man, but there is something in the romantic definition of the situation, models of which are so often given to us in literature. Love having failed, the meaning of life is gone, and naught remains but to cast it away with one final desperate gesture. So they die who go to stay with Dido in the myrtle grove, who sit in the shadows of Sheol and mourn for themselves forever.

A temporary suicide is the numb withdrawal from the world so frequently found among the recently divorced. It is the opposite to the sharpening of the perceptive faculties and represents a conflict so terrific that nothing of the person is left for his relation with the world outside his head. The psycho-analysts would call this a regression, meaning that a person defeated in his search for adult satisfactions and in his attempt to live in the adult world reverts to the simple, probably auto-erotic and certainly quite sensual pleasure sources of childhood and attempts in the extreme case to reproduce the stagnant, passive, and comfortable conditions of life in the womb. Whatever the explanation, the cessation of all activity and a great decrease in the ability to make external adjustments is frequent among persons who have put aside their mates. Often this retirement from the world is followed by a period in which all the functions are hypertrophied and activity is feverish and incessant, representing, no doubt, a compensatory drive. Such a temporary suicide was once Napoleon. The story is told by Ludwig:

"Napoleon went alone to Trianon, which was at this time unoccupied. There he held a death watch such as no lover had ever held before over the love from whom he was to be eternally severed: he remained there for three days, absolutely inactive—this being as great an achievement as if a Buddhist holy man had for three days done Napoleon's work! He received no one, he dictated never a word, read nothing, noted down nothing; for three days the mighty wheel stood still, which for fifteen years had rotated by the strength of its own impetus. Soon afterward he visited his divorced lady at her house in Malmaison." [8]

---

[8] Ludwig, Emil, *Napoleon,* Horace Liveright, Inc., New York, 1926, p. 346.

A study of the psychology of the divorcé would perhaps convince Ludwig that this incident was not unique.

Resentment, which is thrown into relief by the re-focusing of attention induced by the incidents of separation and divorce, may serve to give morale or to render one indifferent to his injuries. If the personality is reorganized with the resentment in a dominant position, it may become a powerful motivation, enabling one to tap untold reservoirs of energy during the period of his readjustment. If the resentment is not conscious, or is later repressed, it may have the most far-reaching effects upon the personality, producing, in the typical case, aboulia, or a paralysis of the will.[9] Ordinarily, however, the first crest of resentment passes when one takes off the wedding ring, and the most obvious hatred is soon dissipated, so that one is left to struggle with his conflicts.

Another occurrence in the emotional life which may intervene to soften the shock of the first readjustment is the numbness which prevents full realization of the change which has been wrought in life. This numbness is apparently a partial dissociation;[10] one perceives the things which are happening, but does not entirely understand their relationship to himself. It is often followed in the later period of readjustment by the feeling that one has so greatly altered his personal set-up that the experiences in question were really those of a different person. But the effects of this anæsthetic, too, usually wear off,

---

[9] See glossary, p. 339.
[10] See glossary, p. 339.

and one comes to face his problems and his conflicts. Time assuages hatred and dissipates stupor, but the agony of a broken personality is left when they are gone.

Nowhere is the story of conflict better told than in the letters of estranged husbands and wives. The writer has been privileged to examine the correspondence of some such couples, reaching sometimes over a period of years. A book might be written concerning one such series of letters, and much knowledge concerning human nature would be contributed by such a book; unfortunately we will be able to give this topic here only sketchy treatment. Throughout every such series of letters, the crossed out words, the sentences that were deleted, the sentences that were deleted and the pages rewritten, the letters that were written and never sent, the letters that were sent and at once countermanded, the ambivalent [11] expressions of the letters, the opposed opinions that come to expression in different parts of them, the letters which when sent caused days of regret, the letters that one had difficulty in writing, the words whose cramped execution shows that they were unwillingly put down, the things that were written in as qualifications and as after-thoughts, the postscripts that were added to give a further general tone to the letter, letters which begin formally and deliberately but become tempestuously emotional, letters showing the undue systematization and formality of coldness not altogether meant, the letters that were never finished, reproachful praise, martyred love, the letters whose coldness gave the lie to their words, the letters which when received were at

---

[11] See glossary, p. 339.

once repressed,—all these things tell a vivid and a moving tale of conflict.

People in the throes of such conflict are given to writing long letters, long, pointless outpourings of their souls, in which affection and recriminations, vows and demands, pleading and argumentation, love, hate, fear, business matters, and commonplaces are all mingled together in an amazing conglomeration of the stuff of life. Sometimes these letters run very long, and great care is put into their preparation, what with the careful consideration of the phrasing of nice distinctions, the interlardings, the interlinings, the scratchings out and the substitutions, and the interminable post-scripts. They are so hodgepodge and so conglomerate that any description of them must have something of the same character. Sometimes it may take days to write these letters; the writer has examined one letter, written carefully in cramped long hand, which ran to thirty-six closely written pages; no doubt there are other more striking examples. The cathartic effect of such outpourings seems to be marked, for they are quite often not mailed; the emotion is fully expressed by being written down, and when the pendulum swings the other way, it seems best not to post the letter. (The above letter, by the way, was after all not sent. A letter only slightly less long was finally sent in its stead.) The writer has been privileged to examine, but not to print, a series of long letters which a man wrote to his wife who was divorcing him; in these is represented a perfect set of parallel expressions in letters which were sent and letters which were not sent. The letters which were written and not sent expressed bitterness and self-justification; those which were sent were more conciliatory in tone; the conciliatory tone was possible because the other side of the ambivalence had already come to expression. This was soon followed by compromise letters in which love was expressed, but distantly. The writer of these letters at this time formed a habit of holding his most important letters a day or so before mailing them in order to make sure that they expressed his sentiments exactly. Equally interesting as illustrations of the same point are letters which are written carefully and after which a letter is immediately sent canceling them. Telegrams are sometimes used for this latter purpose. In the ideal case these two sides of the ambivalence dispose of each other in the manner made famous by the gingham dog and the calico cat.

When these letters are continued it sometimes happens that the tone of the earlier letters, which was at that time a true expression of feeling, is continued in the later letters after the rôle that one plays in it has ceased to have such compelling reality. The rôle becomes empty long before one discards it; all the rest of one's life may then give the lie to the things that are said in a letter. A person who begins by protesting against a divorce continues to raise his virtuous voice against it, though it now represents his own desire. What strikes one most, perhaps, when he reads these long, pathetic letters, is the reluctance of the human mind to forsake a forlorn hope. How slow we are when we love to realize that it is to no avail! How slow to acknowledge the final frustration of affection! How loath to relinquish an accustomed pose!

These are the letters in the main of persons who are not satisfied with the decision. If the letters of one being divorced against his will are diffuse, over-diffuse and conflicting, those of the person who is pushing the thing through are scanty, severe, and all to the same point, except for slips, over-reactions, and other such give-aways. A person who has before been quite unhampered, almost inconsequential, is now most frugal of words and sentiments. Contrast the following two letters from the same woman:

(Before the divorce)

Dearest of my heart,

Lover I do love you so very much. Honey since you have been gone I have suffered something awful from that treatment. So mother is going up with me to-day to find out what the trouble is—I can hardly walk for my one leg has swollen badly— He has bruised me a little and that is what causes it, but I feel much better this morning.

I did the coaching of my play yesterday Honey I got through just fine.

I took about a mile and a half walk last night— Out to the end of Walnut and back on South Park—Fran went with me.

Darling, please don't work yourself sick, please dear heart take very good care of yourself.

Your check has not come yet and you have received no mail at all.

Honey dear I just love, love, love you more and more all the time. Bless your heart you are just too dear for words to utter.

Darling 'Daddy' I do love you more and more every second of the day. I'll sure kiss you to death sweetie when you do come.

Mr. White gave Anna $1 for those letters.

Guess this is about all the news for now.

Baby sends love.

With hugs and kisses,
Your loving wife,
JANE.

(After the divorce)

GEORGE :—

Your letter received and to the best of my ability I'll answer.

(1) Under no considerations at all will I withdraw the suit now—I cannot trust you that far again.

(2) Now that you have no obligations whatsoever I think you ought to go into the ministry if it is a real call.

(3) It is all right to send the baby money or anything you wish to her—(as you had me sign for), but, George, your letters to me are of no avail and cannot help matters along.

JANE.

This severe style by contrast with the diffuse expressions in the preceding letter shows the stimulus of a decision and quite likely indicates also the fact of repression, since she could hardly have become so thoroughly at one on the matter without the intervention of that mechanism. She has made her decision, and now she refuses to admit that there is any part of her that would not have it so.

The reactions of the one who receives these letters are not less illuminating. One man, in assembling the letters which he had received from his wife, found that all the really important ones were at his office. This was puzzling until he recalled the following facts: His mail that year came to his business address. When he got a letter that was a little kinder or softer than the rest he would put it in his pocket to read it again later. When he got a letter which was announcing some new development, i.e., some new hurt, or some further step, he would read it through hastily and would then put it at once in the drawer of his desk. This was a symbolic parallel in overt behavior of the internal behavior of repression.

The reactions of one subject on receiving his mail have been interestingly described as follows:

The letters which I got from my wife at this time were rather reserved. No salutation, no complimentary close, few or no words of endearment found their way into them. She was having her own troubles inside herself, and seemed to resent having to be worried with mine, although there was never any question that she was deeply concerned with what happened to me. Sometimes she wrote letters which were intended to sting in order to arouse my fighting spirit and prevent more complete disintegration. After receiving such a letter, and they were often blistering, I used to feel very much cheered and would write asking her to do it again soon.[12] Mostly, however, I dreaded reading her letters, not so much because of what was in them as because of what was not in them. After receiving one of her letters I would read it at once, then go outside to smoke, and I usually planned to take an hour or so to absorb the shock. How these shocks could continue to be so great when they were so often repeated I do not understand; I believe that in some way they were the major part of my sex life. I know that if the letters did not come I was even more on edge than was usually the case, and I looked for my mail at all times of the day, even when I knew that it was not possible that there could be any more for me.

Sometimes very peculiar circular reactions develop in which the letters of both parties are tied up in a recurrent definite stimulus response pattern. A marriage had been broken chiefly at the instance of the wife and the following pattern showed up in the letters for about a year, beginning after about three months. The husband, under the influ-

---

[12] Note the strong masochistic trend. A habit of submission during marriage was apparently metamorphosed, in this case, into a willingness to take abuse as a demonstration of affection, a desire to kiss the hand that held the lash.

ence of love for his wife, would write affectionate, and therefore disconsolate letters, for, the love for her being dominant, he was thrown into a very real depression by the fact that he could not have her with him. Then she would write one or two very sarcastic, aloof letters, taunting him with his lack of morale. He would become angry and from then on would write independent, and purposely cheerful letters, not admitting to his wife the reality of his involvement or confiding to her any of his troubles. Then the wife, moved to tenderness by his show of morale, and perhaps worrying for fear that he was drifting away from her, would write one or two tender letters. This would shortly place his love for her in the dominant position, and he would write affectionate and rather disconsolate letters. This pattern occurred again and again in the course of the year.

In our discussion of the letters of estranged husbands and wives, we have gone a bit beyond the first few weeks and months after the crisis of separation. We must now go back again and trace out the vagaries and maladjustments of the sexual life of the just-divorced.

CHAPTER THREE

Sex Life of the Divorcé

AN immediate effect of the decision to sleep no more in the marital bed is sexual starvation. This usually begins before the actual separation, because, the rapport having gone, the sex act becomes meaningless and undesirable to one or both persons, —a fact which gives ego gratification to those wise-acres who say, "Well, my idea is that when people break up there's something the matter with their sex life," and never question whether this is cause or effect.

In this chapter we shall follow out the divorcé's first attempts, necessarily rather crude, to reëstablish a satisfactory sex life, his attempts to make the most of his meager and unattractive opportunities for sex expression and his endeavors to reduce his demands to make them fit the quantity and quality of his available resources. We shall see the sex impulse reduced to its crudest form, stripped to its essentials, robbed of all glamour and romance, and perhaps purpose-fully cheapened and degraded. We shall see love made carnal and animalistic. We shall see vice triumphant over virtue, and we shall listen to the voices of those to whom virtue is a mockery and only vice worth while. Perhaps we shall experience some shame and disgust, but if we have a seeing eye and a heart attuned to the misery of mankind, we shall sense the elemental tragedy of it all and be moved to pity rather than horror. We must at this point remind the reader that these stories were told not by the dregs of society but by conscientious, educated, and essentially refined persons,—persons who were themselves not blind to the less pleasing aspects of their experiences. To prove to themselves that they were not going to starve they ate raw meat. Some, too, have eaten tainted meat, preferring sickness to hunger.

One who renounces conjugal privileges has a problem of control, perhaps a worse one than ever before experienced. Now become a cruel, driving necessity, sex expresses itself in physical acts often deprived of positive emotional significance. As control is once more established, the inner values of love may return, and the individual may run the gamut of all the types of sex expression which he has known, from auto-eroticism to the highest forms of heterosexual love. Perhaps most people do not sink to the lowest stage in the beginning, certainly most do not return to the highest at the end of the process.

Sexual starvation as a result of the cessation of marital relations and the frenzied quest for a new outlet may arise while one still sleeps in the marital bed. In such cases indulgence constitutes marital infidelity and is known by the ugly name of adultery. On this matter of adultery, be it said, the opinions of *hoi polloi* and those of the learned professors of one thing and the other are alike wrong. For adultery is thought of as the cause of poor marriage adjustment, and is recognized by the law as grounds for divorce, therefore it is much emphasized as a cause of divorce; yet it has seemed in all the cases which the present writer has studied to be important only as a symptom of an underlying maladjustment, as a symbol of alienation and a mark of estrangement.

There follows the story of a violation of the marriage contract by a woman who had known for two years that her marriage was going on those rocks of which the various unpaid experts on the navigation of the marital bark so often speak. She received almost no sexual gratification from her husband, not because of a holding off on her part but because he had become impotent with her. She had powerful sex drives. In addition, she was rather cruelly treated, and welcomed sympathy and respect. Her violations of the code during matrimony then set up as produced by sex needs, by the need for sympathy and respect; they may also have represented a protest. What kept her in this difficult situation was love for her husband and an unwillingness to admit to her relatives that her marriage had, as they had predicted, turned out badly, and this must be included in the analysis of the causes of her behavior.

"During the last two years I was married, at different intervals, I met a certain party in the park for purposes of intercourse. Shamefully, he was a married man with five children. Anyhow I never let him spend any money on me. I never took a cent from his wife and children. I saw him once a week for a few weeks, then no more for a couple of months, then I would see him again for a few weeks. I felt like a dirty dog about it all, but I couldn't help it. I had to have that outlet. The man was very likeable. He was kind, and sympathetic. He was an optimist. It was his sympathy that won me to him first, his sympathy when I had no one to talk to. There were women I could have talked to, I suppose, but I don't take my troubles to women. Possibly that is because I never took my troubles to my mother when I was a child. When I was a child I had to keep my troubles to myself."

A German woman who came to this country as a war bride decided to break up her marriage, which had been definitely a *mésalliance,* as she came from a much higher social class than her husband. Over a period of a year she engaged only in very limited intercourse with her husband, telling him that she felt there was something degrading about the act because the relationship had become hollow. The contrast between what had been and what was affected her profoundly, she did not wish to engage in mere animal love with a man who had once meant much to her, she would rather give herself, she told him, to the first stranger that she met on the street. She went home on a visit to her parents, and while there she received a letter from her husband, an eight-page letter from a man to whom writing did not come easily. He confessed that he had met a woman who was sympathetic toward him, had given in to the impulse of the moment and had been intimate with her. The woman was old enough, the wife said, to be his mother. He gave all the details. It was the details which hurt, and the wife went to bed for two days with a fever. She was surprised that she was hurt, because she had considered herself through with her husband forever. Then she met a man whom she had formerly known. He was married, but his wife was away. There was "the spark" between them. They spent a week together in Leipzig, a blissful, romantic, glamorous week. She returned to America, fully intending to break up her marriage at once. Her husband was waiting on the pier. She had a change of heart, and told him that she would go back with him. The sunshine of the next day brought a new decision, she told her husband that she was leaving him, and in five days was gone. Occasionally thereafter she would call her husband and ask that he come to see her. On these occasions there would be sexual relations.

Many things both inside and outside himself conspire to make the divorcé go through a more or less prolonged period in which his sex life is on a very low plane. He has just come through a period of sex starvation, for we have seen that the sex life in a marriage which is breaking up is likely to be unsatisfactory. Because his love is thwarted he may be bitter and may wish to conquer his love by degrading it. He may want to prove that he can get along without a particular person, and think that he can prove this by reducing his sex life to its lowest terms. To make things worse, the sex impulse is often the more ungovernable precisely when there is the least opportunity to satisfy it, not because, or not simply because of the accumulation of any such thing as the libido posited by the Freudians, but because of some deep-lying security mechanism within ourselves. As we know, too, sexual expression has a habitual basis; when this is destroyed, the sex demand comes to occupy a larger portion of consciousness; there was more than a jest in the ragtime words, "I hate to lose you, I'm so used to you now." There is also the fact that we sometimes compensate by sexual acts for thwarts in other departments of life, so that the person who thinks that he needs intercourse really requires some sort of salve for his ego feelings. Or a woman may think she wants a man physically when all she really wants is to be accepted by someone.

If a couple think of their difficulties as due to

some sexual incapacity, as they often do, to the obscuring in many cases of the real cause of friction, then each of the former mates and especially the one on whom most of the blame was laid will feel impelled afterward to prove that the imputation of coldness was unjustified. This may lead to frenzied indulgence. Such is the inner situation of the newly divorced person; let us see what are his opportunities for sex life on a high plane.

Precisely at the time when his internal needs are most pressing, the divorcé is least able to make contacts with persons with whom he might contract high level liaisons. He is still married and cannot therefore expect to find sexual outlets in his own social group. Indeed, it is often difficult enough to have any association at all with members of the opposite sex from one's own level of society. One whose marital status is undefined is just simply left out of things. The divorcé himself hesitates to enter into affairs which might prove to be entangling because he is rarely sure until some time has passed that the state of affairs ushered in by the separation is going to be permanent. Besides, a man or woman of moral delicacy hesitates to cause other people to be talked about. Perhaps, too, the newly divorced person is unwilling to make the effort and the expenditure of energy which would be necessary to carry on affairs with persons of any degree of status. At least for men, the financial stringency produced by the attempt to maintain two households may constitute a serious handicap in love. And though what one wants is an immediate outlet, even an amourette must move without haste among people who count. All this, where there are no detectives to be dreaded, and the separated couple do not live in fear of exposure in the courts. Such are the limitations upon the sex life; with some persons it must nevertheless go on. With men, recourse may be had to prostitution; with women, violent and explosive yieldings to passion. The divorcé sinks. It is sometimes long before he rises.

Divorced men, less frank than divorced women in nearly everything else, have been a bit more candid about this one. Several accounts from their narratives will be included.

"Well, sir, frankly, I was looking for houses of prostitution. The little cripple on the street car told me about a place close to where I worked but I walked miles and miles and never did find it. I finally found a house that answered to his description, but all I ever saw there was a respectable elderly family sitting on their front porch in the evening.

"Looking for that house took me into a pretty tough neighborhood, all right. I finally decided to ask some directions. I saw an old negro sweeping off the walk in front of a large warehouse. I walked up to him and held out a quarter. I said, 'Say, is there a sporting house around here?' He looked at that quarter superiorly, I guess you'd say, but I knew damned well he wanted it. He says, 'Yes, there's some houses around here, but I swear I couldn't tell you where none of them are. I wished I could tell you.' I put my quarter in my pocket and went on. I was embarrassed at having asked him and just about as well satisfied as if he had been able to tell me. When I got to the middle of the next block I heard somebody running after me. It was a half-grown negro boy. He yelled out, 'Say, are you the gentleman that was looking for a sporting house?' I was embarrassed to have him talk so loud. I said, 'Yes,' not very loud. 'Well, I know where one of them is at.' He gave me the directions as to how to find some place that was over a barber shop and what I was to say and everything. I asked him whether it was white or black. 'Black,' he says. I made a mental note of the place but

I never went near it. I just took a sort of pleasure in thinking how low I could sink if I tried.

"That turned out to be just an idea. The idea of going to a negro 'house' and mingling with the lowest people that there were appealed to me at the time. I was going to reduce my sex life to the lowest sort of an animal form, and be just as low and common as I could. I never went to that place, but I finally did patronize some prostitutes.

"I got enough frankness, or crust if you want to call it that, to be able to ask most anybody where there was a house of prostitution. One day I struck up a conversation with the bartender in a real good residential district. I started off. 'Say, there's one thing about this town that ain't so good. Where the hell's any amusement?' He answered in a pretty surprised way, 'Why, what do you want? There's plenty of shows, plenty of places to eat, plenty of dance halls and plenty of amusement parks and pool rooms. What do you want in a town?' 'Well,' I says, 'where the hell's the red light district?' He looked sort of disgusted, I guess he was disgusted all right. He said, 'Oh, well, I guess there's one of those, too. I never went near one of the places myself. I'm a married man with a family. If you look around you'll be sure to run into it.' Well, sir, I was embarrassed all right but I thought the best way was just to not let him see it. Anyhow he was just a bartender and I didn't see why he should be so high and mighty after all. I asked him, 'Well, do you think you could say about where it is? Is it a regular district or just a place where the girls hustle on the streets? You see, I don't know so very much about this place.' I did know all about the place, for I had lived in it nearly all my life, but had had no experience with prostitution. I just pretended, because I wanted him to think that I was tough. He told me to walk along certain streets in the evening. I walked there and tried to start a flirtation with every woman that looked at me sideways, but didn't have any luck.

"I had heard the fellows who went in for that sort of thing say that if you just know where you could go and buy something whenever you wanted to you would not mind so much going without it. That turned out to be so in my case all right. I also had less trouble because I got disgusted with the whole thing.

"When I finally did run into what I had been looking for I was surprised. I turned a corner and there I saw three girls and an older woman sitting on the steps in front of a large house. One of them singled me out for her special meat and yelled to me, 'Say, you, come here!' I got all excited and felt all faint inside. My heart went to beating about one hundred and sixty a minute. When I was near enough she asked, 'Say, how would you like to go in and have a nice time, stay a half an hour, and enjoy yourself?' I said, 'How's that?' I knew just what she was talking about, but I couldn't grasp it all at once. She said it again, and looked at me as if she thought I was awful dumb. I asked how much she would charge. She said, 'Three dollars for me, and two dollars for the room.' I went in with her and was very much disgusted with the appearance of the house, the room and the bed. I realized that I could not be squeamish, because I had come to buy something without any trimmings, so I decided not to be squeamish. As quickly as she could, she went out after another customer. I think I went back to her three or four times. I never liked her very much, but she was someone that I knew.

"Later on I shopped around a good deal. I found another prostitute that was not so hard-boiled. She would pretend that she really cared about it and was very much sweeter about the whole thing than the other girl had been. She lived by herself. I went back to her several times. Once I paid her ten dollars to let me stay with her an hour. Oh, yes, I must tell you about the pass word that she had. When I went there the first time I paid her five dollars. She had dragged me in from the street. She said then that the next time I came I was to give the pass word to the maid. The pass word was Clara. After I paid ten dollars she gave me a different pass word. She said that she had changed her pass word. Now I should say, 'Sally,' when I wanted to get in. She explained that she did not want anybody but her friends coming around to her place. I thought she was using the pass word to tell the five-dollar and ten-dollar ones from each other. I always felt bad even after I had been with her and thought that money had been wasted. I would curse myself for wasting the money. I couldn't help it. It was the first time I had ever felt anything like that in my life, because I had always thought that whatever I spent was all right. I knew I was pulling myself down, too. Well, that was what I wanted to do, so I had to be satisfied. But as time went on I didn't go quite so often.

"Then I got it in my bean that the way to really get tough would be to have relations with a large number of women. So I shopped around in the district and added three or four more women to my list that way. One of these when I first met her I thought was very nice. Oh, yes, my experience with her was a turning point in another way, too. I almost forgot to tell you about that. Maybe it was important, I don't know, though. If it isn't you can stop me. My God! If I don't ramble on! Before that time I had trouble in holding off long enough to get any real satisfaction out of the act. I sometimes had got around that by bargaining with the woman to let me stay with her so long a time. You know, a half hour or so. I would tell her, 'Now you see I don't get anything out of it the first time. Just give me so much time and I won't keep you any longer.' Usually they would agree. Sometimes I got around it by not letting them know when I had a climax, but sometimes this would hurt and I couldn't come back. It wasn't so nice anyhow. When I first had this woman, I was telling you about, you know, the woman who seemed more attractive than the rest of the women in the district, the trouble disappeared. I could control myself as well as ever. This difficulty disappeared as quickly as it had come. It didn't come back even when I found that the woman was not nearly so attractive as I had thought. I found that out the next time I saw her. But isn't that very strange and unusual?

"I got pretty disgusted with that. It served my purpose somehow; I kept telling myself I could afford to spend five or ten dollars a week but I didn't do it. I got more disgusted than ever by a feeble-minded girl. She didn't do anything in particular that I can mention as particularly disgusting. Something about her disgusted me. Just the way she whined, and begged me to spend more money and have a better time. She was disgusting all right. Then I had been disgusted before by the guys I met in such places. I would see some drunken bum coming out as I went in and I would know that he had perhaps had the same woman that I had had and that disgusted me. Very bad. Then I was afraid of catching something, too. The first time that I had been with any such woman I had asked her whether she was all right or not. She had said that she was, that they were examined every week and she had never had a bit of trouble. I asked whether I could be sure and she had said, 'Well, you can wait ten days and see what happens.' I took a prophylactic that time and usually every other time. They hurt and sometimes they would make me bleed. I must have left them on too long or something. Well, that ended my experience with the prosti- tute. Oh, yes, one other thing I should tell you. I was awfully afraid that somebody would see me who knew me, you see, I was very well known in musical circles in town. I was afraid somebody would see me that knew me and I always put on other clothes than those that I usually wore. I would put on an old army raincoat and rain hat and would go down there looking like a buck private that had just got his discharge. I also had a mortal fear of being caught in a raid and so when I went I would take just as much money as I thought I would spend and I would leave all the rest at home. I guess my experiences with prostitutes lasted six months."

The man who told the story above does not seem to have been severely in conflict about the matter of sexual indulgence, and we do not find in his story the strong upsurgings of disgust that we do in some others. It is significant that he is consciously at- tempting to degrade sex. Many men tell of experiences with prostitutes and other easy women after which they have a profound disgust for the woman, probably the projection mechanism. They were disgusted with the women that they might not be disgusted with themselves. Typical of such accounts is the following:

"The sexual urge was strong, and kept demanding gratification. During the summer of the year after my wife divorced me, I became restless very often, especially in the evenings. Once while I was out walking I was attracted by a female form with very pleasing legs and breasts. I followed her, and made her acquaintance. She turned out to be a street-walker, who was attractive, apparently, because still new at the game. We went to a hotel and had intercourse. Immediately after, I experienced a great rage and resentment and could barely restrain myself from striking her in the face with my fist. This experience was very hard for me to reconcile with my idea of myself at that time."

This experience represented the explosive indulgence of a man who in general idealized sex. The disgust is the reaction to its cheapening and is not wholly free of projection.

Masturbation and other regressive sexual behavior seem to occur in a good many cases. Masturbation was admitted by some women subjects, but it probably is more frequently resorted to by men. One man told of his experience with masturbation in these words:

"While I slept, I thought that my wife was in my arms, for she had always been there when we were together. This lasted for many months. Sometimes I would wake up with a start when I found that she was not there, and I wouldn't be able to go back to sleep. Often I would dream of a sexual seance with her, and then when I would wake up the whole thing would be that much worse. More than once, though, I had dreams that were so realistic that I carried over after them a real feeling of satisfaction. I was exhilarated as I would have been if I had really had intercourse with my wife. Then for a day or so I had something like happiness. I used to wish that these dreams would come more often, and slept in the positions where I would think that they might occur. A few times I had homosexual dreams. I suppose there were others which anybody who really knew anything about the subject would have recognized at once. Several times I woke to find myself masturbating, and I once or twice had reason to think that I had masturbated in my sleep. I used to dream that I was having a nocturnal pollution, and would wake to find that I was producing it with my hands. Once or twice while I was sitting and thinking about my wife and all the amorous hours we had spent together I masturbated. And once or twice it had happened before we broke up, I think I was taking a bath in a bathtub. At these times I would be very bitter with my wife, because I thought she was really to blame for it all. Then someone figured it out for me that the reason that I demanded to have intercourse immediately, and was not willing to wait, was that I was unconsciously afraid that I would go back to masturbation. Well, then, I just said, 'If I do, I do and that's all there will be to that.' Then the whole problem vanished. I had never worried about it very much anyhow."

These accounts tell of the first and crudest attempts to solve the sexual problem. In these attempts, sex is regarded as purely physical, and is degraded, whether intentionally or of necessity, and adjustment on this level probably indicates in the majority of cases that the spiritual side of love is still attached to the absent mate. There is more opportunity for unification of these in one object after that attachment wears away, in part at least. Some divorced persons, mostly men, remain in this stage of adjustment. But nearly everybody progresses at least as far as the next stage, and many never sink any lower than it.[1] It is hard to give a name to the adjustments of this level, although they may be identified by a very clearly defined philosophy of life which recurs again and again in the cases. Love is no longer merely a physical act, both the person and the circumstances matter, but no obligations are regarded as going with the indulgence of love. It is of course non-commercial, but with that exception it can be said to range from a level almost as low as that of prostitution to one almost as high as the highest type of marriage. Such relationships are regarded as highly transitory, and imply no very important sharing of the resources of personality between those involved. There may be idealization of sex, usually in the nature of a rationalization of one's sex practices. Elaborate philosophies of promiscuity may be developed. This too is a way station, but it is one at which divorcés often stop in the reorganization of their sexual life, and this may be said even of those who remarry.

An account of an affair which would come in the lower range of this category might be in order here. This affair was on a very low level, but was definitely above prostitution, and even above the highly casual affairs that are sometimes had with "charity girls."

"I met a servant girl with whom I had an affair that lasted a couple of months. Seducing her was ridiculously easy, although I did not have an opportunity to take advantage of my conquest till I had had several dates with her. Then I

---

[1] We are taking the liberty of presenting this material somewhat more schematically than the facts warrant.

took her to a rooming house for the evening. After that she used to come to my room once or twice or three times every week. She helped to restore my self-respect, because she bragged of my sexual powers, and my wife had made me think that perhaps I was not very potent. When she would come out I would kiss her and she would lie down on the bed. Then we would have a couple of drinks. I could not stand it except by doing a lot of drinking. I was careful never to introduce her to anybody."

An experience in which some tentative sexual attempts with "charity girls" were made was recounted by the same individual:

"Among the friends whom I came to know during this period were some drug clerks and younger business men. One of these fellows invited me one evening to go on a party with their group. There was to be drinking and there were to be some very charming and very obliging young women. These girls, whom I have since come to consider rather typical charity girls, were rather undesirable individuals, and there were only three of them to four men. One of them, a tall hard-looking creature, was a well-known figure and she was the center of the party. The whole party was carried on in one double room in which the young men lived and the music was furnished by a small victrola. When the girls came in they demanded cigarettes and gin, immediately after the introductions were made. The liquor was gin, and we used a large amount. I paid for most of it, I believe. Pretty soon the party began, and the girl whom I have mentioned before rendered her favorite selection, a very obscene ditty about a lady who lived on Beale Street and some of her physical characteristics. I drank a large amount of the gin, tried to have intercourse with each of the girls in turn, and had no success, so I got sick, threw up, and went to sleep. The girls stayed over night, but I do not think there was very much intercourse because everybody got too drunk. The girls did not seem to mind getting their clothes mussed up and bespattered with a little of everything, nor did any of them mention in the morning their need of changing their clothes. I am not well qualified to speak of just what did happen, because I was the first one to go to sleep. The last thing that I remember was that one of the young men was imploring one of the girls to tell him truly if she was 'virtuous.' In the middle of the night I awoke and tried to have intercourse with one of the girls but the effects of the gin were still with me and I could not. The next morning everybody insisted that the party had been a great success."

A philosophy of promiscuity has a self-protective function, in that it serves to keep any one person from becoming overly important in another's scheme of life. On this account promiscuity may be very important in the life of the individual who has been hurt once. It protects, but it hampers, too, and may, by not allowing love to be fully meaningful, produce certain distortions of personality in the. individual who is thus playing safe. In affairs which are intrinsically quite satisfactory, considerable conflict may be produced by the balancing of the desire to be safe and the desire to carry the affair through to its natural culmination in marriage. Conflicts are also precipitated in the other partner to these affairs. Some of these difficulties, apparently inherent in a free love situation in our culture, are brought out by one story told to the writer:

Harry thought that he had made it quite plain to June that this intimacy presupposed nothing at all. He was later to learn that she had not taken his words to heart. The first effect of the experience was to cause her to regard herself as a fallen woman and to give her a lowered threshold for any admonition from pulpit or press with regard to such degraded persons. Later she adopted his point of view.

From then on her conflict became one of a different nature, a conflict perhaps inherent in a free love situation in our culture. June was wholly in love, sure of herself, satisfied that he was her perfect mate. Harry was not so; he regarded his feeling for her as one of very real affection, but certainly not of love. The relationship developed satisfactorily from the sexual angle. For June, it was so beautiful and so near an approach to the perfect that the fact that it was not quite perfect, in that she was not exclusively and permanently chosen to continue it, made it painful. For she made the assumption that this free love association, being so wholly satisfactory, would go on to marriage. Herein is contained the reason for the compromising of her self-feelings. That is, when Harry, who was following out the mechanism that we are tracing, made it apparent that he was not going to marry her, it set up to her as due to her own lack. She did not quite measure up to her lover's requirements. She had been tried and found wanting. Actually, her ego demands were not particularly great, she would have been satisfied to be the servile, subordinated wife, the situation is not exactly the same as it would be if she were the sort of person who is ordinarily concerned about status. But Harry was her first lover, her first sex object. As such he was meaningful and completely satisfactory, while she was not quite good enough. This conflict would seem to be inherent in the free love situation in our culture, especially where the divorcé is concerned, for he is a bit more likely to be concerned with protecting himself than another lover would be.

Elaborate philosophical systems based upon the fundamental notion that what one does with his sex life is after all his own affair are built up by both men and women who wish to justify promiscuity in sexual relationships. They can "love as many people as their heart can hold," or promiscuity enables them to realize the human values of all sorts of people, or promiscuity is natural and therefore virtuous while all else is vice, etc. These carefully worked out systems of thought are intended to serve two very necessary purposes, one, that of convincing one's self, and possibly others, that one's actions are not morally reprehensible, the other, that of convincing one's self that one should be satisfied with such opportunities as are offered by such associations. A number of things conspire against the happy working out of any life plan based upon free love or promiscuity. One is the fact that the majority of the persons who give lip service to such ideas are in fact but partially liberated from conventional morality. Although they may have rebelled against such morality, it is still subjectively real to them, still a matter for concern, which is indicated in part by the fact that they seem over-anxious to justify themselves. But where this is not operative complications of the sort described in the excerpt just quoted may arise. In almost any case promiscuity as a permanent adjustment is a particularly bad philosophy for the divorced person, for it enables him to avoid a real solving of the problems of his personal life, and allows the former mate to stand out in his life as a person who has really never had a rival for his affections. It is therefore peculiarly unfortunate that so many divorced persons should attempt to make this sort of adjustment permanent. But where all these things are absent, there is one other more fundamental and more important than all the others put together, and that is the fact that the sex act has such intrinsic importance in the emotional life of human beings that we remain essentially thwarted by sexual indulgence in which we do not have full and ideal emotional participation. Therein is an argument for monogamy which is worth more than a thousand moralistic tracts.

Philosophies of life and arrangements of one's activities are resultants of many factors, and consciousness and destiny alike may represent compromises between habit and impulse, desire and duty, the ego and the unutterable, compromises which could not be matched for intricacy and smoothness of articulation by a roomful of diplomats. A woman of about thirty, divorced some five years, reported that she had had several love affairs, accompanied, in each case by sexual relations, since her marriage broke up, but that for some reason they had always been with men who were leaving town very soon. Upon analysis this was found to be a resultant of a combination of behavior trends. She had not intended, after separating from her husband, to "take the veil." This was against her own disposition and the tradition in which she was reared. But sexual relations without love were unthinkable to her, both because of moral scruples and because of a certain refinement. The men she was to love had to fulfill certain social and esthetic requirements. She did not, however, want to fall in love, for she had been very badly hurt once because of her susceptibility and she had a six-year-old daughter to think of. Therefore she fell in love with a naval lieutenant who was to leave the port in three months. Similar affairs involved her with other men. (A certain sexual periodicity and a lowering of guards by fatigue seemed to be brought out by the fact that every one of these men came into her life at a time when she was very tired of life and somewhat discouraged with the struggle to keep up.)

Among the philosophies by which people justify

following the whim of the moment in their sex life appears one derived from and given the scientific sanction of Freudianism. "You can't suppress your desires or you'll go crazy." "Sex activity is only human, and everybody has got to have just so much of it or he won't keep up in good trim." "Freud says you'll go crazy trying to do everything society wants you to do." The anonymous author of *Ex-Wife* dismissed Freudianism by calling it, "The Great Excuse." Freud, it seems, has demonstrated that failure to follow one's impulses is harmful, and suppression of sexual desires is positively dangerous. It is perhaps worth while to point out what a garbled and misrepresented version of psychoanalysis we have here. The theory is, indeed, that certain impulses if repressed, that is, if dissociated from the rest of the self, may produce certain disorders of personality. That is, they make a person want to do strange and incomprehensible things for reasons which he does not understand. But there is nowhere in the Freudian literature anything which an intelligent person would interpret as sanctioning the giving of overt expression to every whim of the moment. The implication is more nearly that if we know what it is that we want to do we may not want to do it. Freud found, for instance, that according to his interpretation many men wanted to kill their fathers and mate with their mothers. He does not give us the impression that he advised them to do literally this, in order to avert damage to their personalities, but rather that he taught them to live with such an impulse, admitting its existence but not giving it overt expression.

It has been seen that the divorcé in certain ideal typical cases gradually works out modes of sex expression which are at once more refined and more satisfactory to himself. It should be noted, that, still keeping separate the physical and spiritual aspects of love (which is in itself unfortunate), the divorced person may begin to seek to reëstablish himself in a legitimate and permanent love affair while his definitely sexual life is still on the basis of promiscuity.

We have taken certain liberties with the facts in presenting them thus schematically.[2] Now we must correct our error by emphasizing the fact that the sex adjustment must differ in every instance, since there is involved a total personality reacting to a total situation. In a case analyzed by a competent psychologist a man carried on an extra-marital affair until his divorce, seeming to find in it great emotional fulfillment. After the divorce he dropped it. Several interpretations are possible; the one preferred by the man who studied the case is that while this man was living with his wife his sex impulses were excited but not satisfied, so that he turned perforce to the other woman for gratification. Later, the wife was not present to arouse him and the need was not so keenly felt. There is much in this sort of interpretation, for sexual behavior is definitely a matter of stimulus and response as well as a response to internal motivation.

A different interpretation of this man's behavior, offered not as conclusive, long-range diagnosis, but as a mere suggestion based upon the other cases, would be that he desired to get rid of his wife for reasons which were perhaps not known to himself, or were at least unrecognized, and that he used his

---

[2] Since this scheme was devised, two excellent literary studies of the divorcé, *Dodsworth* and *Ex-Wife*, have appeared, which seem to fit very nicely into our categories.

sexual indulgence as a protest against his wife. This interpretation would make the case fit in well with some others which have been studied; in these sex is an instrument and infidelity an act of rebellion. (There is a notion in the case of the men who patronize prostitutes that in some vague way they are getting even with their wives. One type of thought here is: "My wife has forced me to this. How terrible she is!" Another: "All women are alike. As I have been with my wife, so I am with these degraded creatures. All women serve the same purpose to me, and my wife is like these others.") To return to our case, a third and less plausible interpretation is based on identification with the conventional moral code after a break with it has once brought disastrous consequences, and a delayed turning against the person who has caused so much trouble. This interpretation is not the preferred one in this case, but it represents a not uncommon mechanism.

It should also be noted at this point that there are many cases of divorced persons who do not go through these peculiarly disorganizing experiences, but who solve their problems at once either in a healthy manner or by the use of the mechanism of repression. Where there are sex repressions which are already established the resort to these is easier. There is always danger of course in the use of repression, and we find our divorcés who have repressed often developing neurotic symptoms or further problems of adjustment afterwards. Hysterical splits in the personality represent in part the after-effects of interruptions of the sex life and attempts to solve the problems created by those interruptions.

Often, perhaps more frequently than not, there

is an occasional recrudescence of conjugal passion after the marriage as a social unit and a habit of life has completely broken down. Of all the things that bind people together in marriage the carnal link is supposed to be the most ephemeral, but this same physical bond many times outlasts all the supposedly imperishable joys of comradeship, and animalistic love lives to make mock of the grave where spiritual affection lies buried. After a period of separation, during which their mutual animosity has had a chance to lose its edge and loneliness and mounting desire have made the absent mate seem blooming and fair, the divorced couple meet. They chat pleasantly, like two friends who meet after a long separation. But there is a difference; between these two reserve is not possible, and if the circumstances permit, the mating is consummated. Often reconciliation partakes of this character. Since, however, the fundamental causes of friction have not been remedied and grievances have not been redressed, but only glossed over, such reconciliation is likely to be short-lived. There may be produced, by the equilibration or alternation of attraction and repulsion, strange compromises between the divorced and the married state. People live, act, and think as if they were divorced, but periodically they meet for the satisfaction of their sex needs. Or, divorced, with wrongs still unredressed and hate still high, they live together in misery enforced by the need for the sexual union, but not mitigated by its consummation. Snarling, hating, divorced, they remain, during months, years, or decades the slaves of noisome passion.

However the sexual problem is solved, various substitute activities come to have significance. Sublimations may be developed, or substitute outlets found in work, drinking, or gambling. Music and art, athletics, phantasy, and dream may furnish catharsis. Undoubtedly after every sharp break in one's life, phantasy plays an important rôle for a time.

Sublimations may develop most easily where some line of thought or activity has a definite relation to the love object. A young woman who had been in love with her English teacher in High School, but who, on account of her marriage to another, was shut off from all hope of having him, wrote to him as follows:

"Dear, I am realizing at least one great benefit from our acquaintance. My lil' youngsters come to me and say, 'Miss Black, we like English better every day.' This is so unusual as English is such a detestable and meaningless subject to children in the grades. I get a glorious thrill out of the period and sometimes forget that I'm teaching anything else."

In the following account phantasy and the writing of letters furnished a considerable outlet:

"During all this period there was a great deal of phantasy activity. I used to sit by the hour and dream of the time when my wife, yielding at last to my persuasions, would come back again to me. Always the same theme, with variations only in the details. I was at the time pouring out my soul in letters. I remember remarking to her many times in these letters that after writing to her for a long time I felt for a little while as if I had just had a little chat with her. When I stopped to think of the time that would have to elapse before my words should reach her eyes the pleasure was gone from the thing. Sometimes they were love-letters that I wrote, but I have a notion that more often they were of a rather complaining tone. They sometimes threatened suicide, and the nearness of madness, which was sometimes explicitly stated, was no doubt many times hinted at by the form and content of the letters. I would usually start them in a rather restrained manner, the phrasing was commonplace and the writing small. As I warmed to my theme the language grew less restrained and the writing grew bolder and more irregular. These letters were almost manic in their directness and their intensity, highly theatrical in their phrasing, and must no doubt have served to make things much worse for the poor girl who was to receive them. I must confess that the whole thing was a little piece of self-dramatization, although I was myself deceived by it. I really was not going crazy, and so far as I know I never developed a single bona fide symptom, but I kept thinking that what I had on my mind was enough to drive anyone crazy and then would reflect that perhaps I was really losing my mind.

"Another phantasy with which I was much concerned in the early days of my separation should perhaps be recorded. My wife had told me just before we separated of the rather brutal attempt of a man who was associated with us to force her to have intercourse with him, and it seemed likely his advances had something to do with the ultimate breakdown of her personality. He was a man much larger than myself, and I would not have been able to contend with him unless I used weapons of some sort. I used to brood for hours upon the trouble that he had caused me, he who spoke so glibly about sportsmanship and fair play, and I used to plan his death, or his disgrace and the ruin of his career. I was going to kill him in some deserted spot at a summer camp which he usually attended, or was going to contrive to tell his wife, who was somewhat older than he and had a reputation as a virago. My plans for a dramatic vengeance led always to a dénouement that was convincing, terrible, and beyond appeal. Alexandre Dumas could not have done it better. This phantasy disappeared from my mind only very gradually, and has not even yet lost its power to rob me of my sleep.[3] Just what it represents psychologically I do not know."

---

[3] This is a displacement mechanism. The phantasy disappeared when this man at length spoke out his resentment against his wife.

Phantasy activity of a slightly different nature is illustrated in the following account:

"The complete inaccessibility of my wife and her complete indifference to my pleas is evident in the correspondence. I idealized her, over again, I pictured her a sweet, innocent, delicate creature whom I had heartlessly despoiled of all life had to offer...a beautiful chrysalis whose silvery wings I had smashed in trying to help them unfold with clumsy impatient hands."

The release of tension by plunging into one's work is a familiar mechanism which has been again and again illustrated in the cases studied. A further mechanism which is perhaps worth illustrating is that where tension is released and some ego-gratification obtained by drinking and gambling.

"I gambled a lot, but fortunately I won. I can't imagine what I might have done if I had lost. An added depression might have caused some strange things.

"I drank some, but not much. It's not so pleasant drinking by yourself when you're gloomy, and it was usually too hot for most other people to drink a lot. In addition to a half-hearted desire for drink, I also imbibed for this reason: I liked to think that this woman was driving me to the dogs, that she was turning me into a dissipated and dissolute bum. I tried to lay the blame on her for my descent to the depths, which seemed imminent. This seems very childish now, but it was a grave matter then."

CHAPTER FOUR

Why the Bohemian Adjustment
Is Unsatisfactory

IMAGINE a group of ten or twelve men and women crowded together in a small room. All the people are well-dressed, though some are disheveled, the men's coats and trousers a little out of press, the women's dresses and hair a tiny bit awry, or showing a few stains of one sort or another. Some six or seven of those present are crowded together on the chaise longue, somewhat mixed as to sex, and perhaps not equally divided, or definitely paired off. The rest are scattered about the room, sitting, standing, walking, running, dancing. There is the racket of the inevitable victrola or radio. If the radio, then it is tuned in on some dance orchestra which is broadcasting. If the victrola, it is playing over and over some record which is a favorite of the person who has delegated himself to furnish the music, perhaps because he has not this evening been able to find a complaisant person of the opposite sex. Perhaps the record is scratched, certainly the needle needs changing; nobody minds if only the noise does not cease. Sometimes there is a player piano which keeps grinding out something like *My Blue Heaven,* on and on into the night, loudly, mechanically, determinedly. But there are other noises. Somebody pulls a good

line, or thinks of one of the latest wise-cracks,—
he raises his voice loud enough for everybody to
hear it. Then a few minutes later he says it again,
or somebody else says it,—it is still funny and again
everybody laughs. There is conversation which includes everybody and conversation which includes
only one or two persons, mostly the latter, so that
the room tends to be infused with the low murmur of
voices. And through the clear murmurs of conversation are heard the throaty tones of passion, a man
in the corner is pleading and urging in the sight of
the assembled multitude, the woman is but faintly
protesting. Their low murmuring voices, their nasal
"Huhs," with the rising inflection, their reassuring
answers, their long eye-shut kisses, go unnoticed and
unremarked upon. Other couples not so far advanced
or not so brazen are paired off in more serious tête-
à-têtes, exchanging confidences, laughing together
at their little jokes just for two. As the music starts
afresh there is a sound of shuffling feet, the dancing
grows as animated as it can in such a small space.
One of the men does a Russian dance; another couple
gives an exhibition. Once in a while there is a shrill
scream as some woman decides to enter into the
spirit of the occasion. There is loud answering
laughter, a few yells from the men. No matter, the
neighbors hereabouts do not mind, for the management of this apartment pursues a laissez-faire policy.
Of course there are drinks: whisky, gin, wine, Ba-
cardi, mostly mixed with ice and ginger ale, but
served straight for those who want to feel the effects
at once. Someone enters and is supplied with several
drinks in a row so that he may have an opportunity
to catch up. The guests ply each other with drinks,
continual accusations arise that so-and-so is holding

back. The women sip their drinks slowly, setting them down by their sides until they become thirsty, or drinking them at last with great gulps just before another round of drinks is to be served. Once in a while one of the tall glasses gets knocked over and somebody's clothes are spoiled, or there is a fresh stain upon the rug, or some more varnish is taken from the table or the victrola. Nobody minds; those things will happen. After a while somebody passes out, and has to be carried into the bedroom and put to sleep, or taken home so that he may recover. Or someone gets sick, and has to be helped through his somewhat disgusting rites. Or someone offers to fight. None of these are serious breaches of etiquette, for here the adage, "A Southern gentleman must know how to carry his liquor," and the other one, "Gentleman drunk, gentleman sober," do not apply in their full force. The real crime here is to be sad, for this is an atmosphere of jollity and levity, and people are met here to make themselves happy. This is light love, here nobody "pulls up a ladder," and any man is free to poach upon the preserves of any other man, to show jealousy is nothing short of a crime. Everywhere is noise, everywhere is laughter and song, everywhere is feverish, hectic gayety,— determined gayety. Who says we are not happy? Who says that this is not the way of gladness? He lies! Out with him! Drink him down! We'll have another! For we are making merry to-night, and we shall prolong the sounds of revelry far into the not so stilly night, we shall gladden the night with our lightsome cries till the streaks of dawn are almost ready to show themselves in the East. To-night we must make Hey! Hey! while the moon shines. We are merry!

That mythical individual whom we are accustomed to designate as the casual observer would, when confronted with such a group, perhaps say, "These people are very happy. All they care about is drinking and dancing and love affairs of a light nature. This just suits them, and they are glad to be rid of their marriages so that they can do this sort of thing. They are the world's irresponsibles." The observer possessed of a bit more insight would say, "These people are merry because they are unhappy. They are merry because they make themselves so. There is something inside them from which they wish desperately to get away. Divorce represents to them welcome relief from inhibitions which have become intolerable, yes, but they are not so wholly at one on the matter as it seems. They are gathered together here to drink and dance and make love in a light fashion in order to forget something inside them which hurts. Happy? Perhaps, but the happiness is too determined to be real." If this observer were skilled in the concepts of modern psychiatry he would go on, "We are seeing one side of an ambivalence, the side which these people are most anxious to keep dominant, and the side which they are most desirous of showing to the public. The greater the determination to be happy, the greater the insistence upon that state, the more frantic the reaching out for the various sorts of indulgences which are supposed to give pleasure, the greater the flaunting of those values which are dear to other members of the community, the greater, on the other side, is the unspoken and perhaps unadmitted misery from which, as a compensation, this other activity springs."

This sort of activity which has been so minutely

described is what the writer thinks of as typical of the Bohemian adjustment. Bohemianism represents seeking solace for more or less unadmitted misery in frivolity. Very often this frivolity of a sub-group is a kind which is definitely laid under the ban in the larger group. It implies that one must separate himself from the larger group in which he has been accustomed to live, and organize his personality about this sub-group, choosing from among the activities of this sub-group the things which he is to do, and therefore what he is to be. But since such integration can never be complete, Bohemianism represents always a partial integration. One cannot escape the larger group, neither its manners, nor its laws, nor its morality. The Bohemian is likely to be a person who has at a previous time been much enslaved to a very much subjectivated code of mores, and his frantic attempt to escape represents only his continued enslavement to them. One cannot say that he is free of a thing as long as he is only in rebellion against it. The Bohemian—closely allied here to the neurotic proper—represents the incompletely liberated individual, the one who cannot quite escape his past and the larger group in which it was lived, and yet who cannot quite adjust by going back to that group, from which for one reason or another he has fled. Often the Bohemian is intellectually but not emotionally liberated. Now this is what makes the activities of Bohemian groups vice. Vice is something which is personally demoralizing, a segmental activity which cannot be integrated into the major personal organization. Drinking is not vice when it is part of the mores of the group; it then becomes a part of one's personal organization. Sexual indulgence may be vice for the unmarried girl, but when she gets married it is part of her, and her personality is organized very much about her sexual functions. Bohemians, forming a sub-group, tend to buttress each other by their mutual acceptance of a divergent moral code, but they never quite succeed; all they succeed in doing is strengthening by sub-group sanction tendencies which nevertheless remain in essence segmental, unintegrated, therefore demoralizing and vicious.

We have seen that the divorcé frequently thinks it desirable to break completely with the group to which he belonged during his marriage. At the time of the break, then, he is faced with the necessity of forming entirely anew his circle of friends, and this precisely at the time when he feels most the need for companionship. Added to this is the necessity of reorganizing the sex life, the desire to belong to a group where his divorced condition will not make of him an oddity, and those inner problems from which he wishes to escape. This is the explanation of the prevalence of the Bohemian mode of adjustment among divorcés, of their tendency to form themselves into little divergent sub-groups composed almost entirely of divorced persons. (Several of the persons studied by the writer have commented on the fact that a very large number of those who are now their best friends have been divorced, whereas before they knew hardly any divorcés.) Needing friendship and sympathy, needing sexual gratification, needing to be accepted, wanting company, as do all the miserable, the divorcé knocks at the portals of the confraternity of the damned. He is usually admitted, for the social standards of that broad and democratic society are not such as to exclude many who are willing to enter and willing to pay with themselves for their entertainment.

Promiscuity in sexual relationships has been seen to be a not unusual development in the divorcé. Where this is complicated by Bohemianism in general, it is even more highly rationalized, more frankly admitted, and therefore enters much less furtively into the life of the person. Bohemia has its code, and if one is hurt in these light affairs he must expect no sympathy. The affair was intended to be light from the start, to take it seriously was a breach of etiquette anyhow. So if one falls in love in Bohemia, he conceals it from his friends as best he can, pretending that it is not so. This may in turn give rise to other personality problems equally serious with those initiated by the divorce; nevertheless, he must hide his wounds, for the pose is the thing in Bohemia.

Often correlated with Bohemianism and promiscuity in sexual relationships is the presence of a latent homosexual component strong enough to rob heterosexual relationships of their essential meaning and to make acceptance of them upon the lower levels possible. The Don Juan and the Messalina, always seeking, seeking for the unrealizable ideal, are often enough found in these Bohemian groups where promiscuity is the accepted custom. With them, promiscuity is not a defense or a something to be accepted in the place of something better but not attainable (if one except the homosexual ideal), but an opportunity, an opportunity to go on seeking for this thing which is never found.

An incomplete study of a man who apparently answers to this description was made. He was terrifically on the defensive, and would only agree to answer questions provided that he also was allowed to take a sheet of paper and write down the answer to a question for every question which was asked him.

This man is a receiver of stolen goods, having drifted into that illegal way of life out of a desire for the large financial returns and easy work. He is about thirty-five years old, has been married twice, and has had a checkered sexual career. He is of medium height, but rather slender, and does not give the impression of much physical force. In appearance, he is elegant almost to the point of daintiness, always sleek, neat but not gaudy, rather dashing. Although he has had only a high school education, he gives the impression of having a broad cultural background, and has, in fact, a considerable acquaintance with the arts and a speaking knowledge of literature. He has the soul of a social climber and delights to tell of his contacts with the elite.

His parents were Irish and resided in a good section of the city in which he now lives. Apparently he developed powerful inferiority drives while he was young, perhaps because of his lack of physical force, perhaps for more subtle reasons which could not be definitely made out.

Going while a young man to Cleveland, he took a position as a designer of dresses with a well-known firm. He was apparently very successful at this, making enough money to establish himself as a heart-breaker. He met his first wife quite by chance, and the acquaintance developed rapidly under an impetus furnished by her. She was the only daughter of a very wealthy family. The two were married against the opposition of her parents.

The first wife was a pretty, feminine creature who did not too well understand this husband of hers. Her mother was a good sort, and did not interfere with her daughter's marriage. The father is described by the subject very unfavorably. He was large, two-fisted, harsh, overbearing, efficient. Probably, successful, driving, masculine individual that he was, he was not pleased that his daughter should continue to live with this slight, subtle wisecracker, this "city-slicker," who designed dresses. He is given the credit for forcing the break between the two.

When he saw the break coming, the subject left town and consoled himself by adopting a Bohemian way of life. The break did not hurt him, he said, because he was at the beach at the time the news came, surrounded by a bevy of beauties. This was his answer. He tried a number of jobs, drifting into bootlegging for a time, and then into more remunerative crime.

His second wife, large, plump, forbearing, and female, may nevertheless have represented a compensating choice. He lived with her for five years. A child, a boy, was born about a year after they were married. The subject apparently participated less in this marriage than he had in the other, was always unfaithful, away from home often, and more than once cruel in a physical way. On one occasion he knocked his wife through the sun-parlor, and she was often to be seen with a black eye. He was very much interested, however, in fixing up his home (which he refers to as the "wigwam"). After five years of this sort of thing his wife left home while he was away on a trip, selling thousands of dollars' worth of furniture for much less than it was worth, and confiscating for her own use a considerable amount of his trading capital. This happened at a time when he was already in trouble with the law, so that he was unable to do anything to defend himself.

During this period a very interesting projection mechanism was noted. His own cruelty to his wife has been described. When, however, a friend of his happened to use profanity in front of his wife, he grew fiercely angry at him, plotting all kinds of vengeance. As far as his wife was concerned, he said, the break was simple and definite, but this fellow had no business swearing in front of her.

The subject was very much aggrieved by his wife's desertion, but chiefly because of the wrong that she had done him. In contacts with him at this time a number of homosexual slips were noted. First was perhaps an overreaction to certain homosexual jokes, at which he laughed with more than his usual heartiness, and which he retold with considerable gusto. Then he came out in the midst of a psychological discussion with a request for information about the psychology of homosexuality, and when this was furnished it apparently touched off a complex, if one is to judge by the interest. He then expressed the sentiment which has been found in other cases to be indicative of a perhaps unrecognized homosexual trend, that he would like to try everything, that if he had money enough he would. Then one or two homosexual jokes about himself, in which he apparently got some phantasy gratification from thinking of himself in that sort of relationship. His resistance, too, must be put down as probably a part of the same picture, although it may have been connected also with his profession.

Added to this was his utter ruthlessness where women were concerned, and the apparent lack of any meaningfulness in his relations with them. He had pictures of several women, among whom was supposed to be included his first wife, in the nude, and he showed these while referring to them slightingly. Especially did he find unattractive the large buttocks of his first wife. At this time he began drinking rather more heavily than he ever had before, and apparently went into a lower state of integration. It has been noted in other cases that divorce probably brings out such latent homosexual components as are present, and this seemed to be so in his case. He was quite ruthless, apparently not caring to what hazards he exposed the women with whom he was intimate. And there was every indication that every cross-sex relationship in which he was involved was quite meaningless. All women were belittled, they were referred to as bags, pigs, cows, turkeys, etc. For particular ones he had special names, "Flop ears," "The girl with the whistling gizzard," etc. To show the utter meaningless of women to him, he would say, "Black and white, they're all sweethearts," or refer to the fact that intercourse was becoming a burden to him, so that he needed other sexual stimulation.

Now none of this would be sufficient by itself as evidence upon which to base a diagnosis of homosexuality, but when seen together, and contrasted with the fact that his relations with men were characterized by the highest loyalty and the greatest emotional participation, this evidence indicates a powerful, but perhaps unconscious trend. This early diagnosis was corroborated all along by a further piling up of evidence all pointing in the same direction. His complete promiscuity, and this is the point in this discussion, was correlated with an utter meaninglessness in the relation, so that sexual indulgence came rather as a result of demand from the other person or the situation than as a response to a driving inner urge.

His cruelty, which is almost unbelievable to those who have seen him only in his relationships with men, is explicable as a fighting down of the feminine within himself, as is also his continual belittling of women.

A similar interpretation was made of a great litterateur by the psychiatrist Kretschmer:

The marriages of Strindberg are a pathological prototype of the psychic disorder in the relationship of an inter-sexual husband with his wife—a man who over-compensates his partly feminine traits by a rugged emphasis upon the male part; for whom the conflict with the woman, and through her the woman-question in general, has become the perpetually renewed central problem of his life; who therefore has been driven into a prophetic rôle in the modern struggle for power of the sexes, because the "masculine" and the "feminine" fight constantly within himself, since the desire for domination and the voluptuousness of subjection are mingled in the most irreconcilable contrasts of his own inherited predisposition. In this way his own marriages are always destructive tragedies, sizzling fireworks between ice and flame, hot amorousness and cold hatred, attracting and repelling, brutal, never satisfied, kept constantly feverish by the sensual desire to torture and be tortured.[1]

---

[1] Kretschmer, Ernst, "Physical and Spiritual Harmony in Marriage," *The Book of Marriage,* Keyserling and Others, p. 324.

In another case, which was somewhat better worked out, there was no promiscuity, but apparently the existence of fixations prevented complete outgo in heterosexual love, and perhaps led the woman to find relationships with those of her own sex a bit more meaningful than would otherwise have been the case. This woman remained heterosexual in her orientation, those were the meaningful relationships, but she was not sufficiently at one in them to receive and give sexual gratification, and on this account the outgo to women was more important than it would otherwise have been.

This case seems particularly valuable as typifying the Bohemian adjustment, and as illustrative of what happens to this sort of person while the trauma of the divorce is yet recent. This subject was interviewed just after the divorce suit had been heard, and on the eve of her departure to New Mexico.

She came from a family of well-to-do, rather horsey Irish. Her father had had a number of occupations, including, the subject said, being superintendent of schools in a small city. This statement was somewhat supported by the fact that she claimed acquaintance with a number of persons whom her father would have met in the educational world, including a famous psychologist and the director of an institute for adult education.

There were several children in her family, and she was the youngest. This is significant in itself, but it is made to assume much more importance when it is added that there was a gap of ten years between her and the previous child. Most of the other children were strange to her when she was in her infancy. She says that she would be going out with her nurse, and would meet some other children in the hall, and would hear, "That's your sister," or "That's your brother, John," but that they did not become real to her in her early years.

Later on she entered into the family group, but in a way which did not make for the development of the very best mental hygiene. Her brothers and her father spoiled her, took her with them, and encouraged her to engage in their sports, while her sisters and her mother had an extreme dislike for her. She said that she had always been in the society of men. She told of many occasions during the summer vacations when she played golf all morning with her brothers and then all afternoon with her father. The emotional tie to the father is quite strong, and she used to stay in the city during the summers because she felt that she ought not to leave him. Naturally all this golf and the riding that she did caused her to develop a rather good set of muscles. She is a large and heavy woman anyhow and is quite proud of her strength, although she is not by any means a completely masculine picture. She related with some pride the fact that she had once played in a father and son tournament.

Her general personality picture during her girlhood must have been rather tomboyish. She told of calling upon a newspaper editor who was a friend of her father. He was sitting on the radiator, and since she was a familiar of the office, he did not rise, but asked her to hand him his cigarettes. This she did, and then he asked for his matches. She struck one of her own matches, and he, seeming to be angry, muttered some imprecation and started to get down from the radiator and get his own matches. She started after him and forced him to stay on the radiator, telling him the while what she thought of his manners. He said later, "Well, one thing about old man H——'s daughter, she's not going to let anybody run over her." She spoke of getting some privileges for the social settlements in her home town. Of this she said, "Well, I put that over. That's the sort of thing I used to do before I was married." She said also, in a different connection, "Oh, my basic manners are pretty good. You see I was raised by my father and brothers."

She was, as the other little Irish girls, put in a convent for her education. Here she received a very thorough training in Catholicism, and the foundations for her later state of revolt were no doubt laid at that time too. Here she learned outward conformity, but she insists that she always internally disbelieved. This is not so far as it seems from outer nonconformity and inner compromise or belief.

She married when she was eighteen. The man·was ten years older than herself and was already a successful man of affairs. Their married life was probably never any too well adjusted. The subject has two children, yet she says that she is still a "psychological virgin," by which she means that she is still untouched by the sex act as far as her own feelings are concerned.

There had been five separations, always, it seems, at the instance of the wife. Her reason for leaving so many times was that she felt that her husband was not faithful, yet she admittedly has had a crowd of men about her during most of her married life. Each separation previous to the last had been terminated by her husband's repentance and her own "getting soft-hearted." This separation bids fair to be the last, since it culminated in a divorce suit, and the subject has already left the city.

Her outer Bohemianism is attested by a number of character traits. In the course of an evening she delivered a number of "wise cracks" (some of them rather cheap) concerning her husband and concerning matrimony. She was interviewed at a somewhat Bohemian gathering, and she had been called up at about twelve o'clock in order that she might be invited to attend. She had said at the time that she was in bed and did not care to "go on a party." A half hour later she called and said that she was coming. When she entered, carrying a banjo-uke under her arm, and attempting to give the impression of not having a care in the world, she turned to some of those in the group who knew her and said, "I'll bet you never can guess who drove me down." They couldn't and she said, "God." One or two of them tittered, but when the rest did not she went on, "You know. The pope, the outgoing husband." All said with the greatest air of nonchalance, yet with perhaps a too obvious attempt to be casual. She then explained that this name had been given to her husband because it seemed to fit in with his own opinion of himself. On a previous occasion he had heard himself so referred to, and had said dryly, "I accept the nomination." She soon delivered herself of the customary jests about matrimony, saying, "I was fool enough to suffer seven years of it. I ought to know." Altogether the Bohemian picture.

She then seated herself on the floor and tuned her banjo-uke after a fashion. She strummed the instrument softly and without the least appearance of self-consciousness sang in a passably good voice, but one which had perhaps been affected a bit by alcohol, a number of popular song hits, and some of the older sentimental ballads. Kipling was a favorite, and the refrain, "And I learned about women from her," was chanted with the greatest glee. She occasionally interrupted her renditions to take a sip of her cocktail or to take another cigarette from the very chic musical cigarette box. She was at once on terms of easy familiarity with all the rest of the party. She spoke of her friend, a certain William P. She said then that she thought that women did not mean much to him except as copy, that he had perhaps copied that one about being "a wet smack from the toe line up," from her. Then she said that after the last separation, when she supposed that both she and her husband "had their fingers crossed," William had come to see her about four o'clock in the morning, bringing "some public utility." The next day her husband called her to ask who that dreadful person was who had come in at that unearthly hour. She asked, "Does it really matter? The person means nothing to me." Later she added, "If you want any information, pay for it," which was a reference to the fact that her husband was having her shadowed in the hope that he might be able to pick a corespondent out of her numerous male admirers.

The use of French phrases to interlard her conversation and frequent allusions to her travels bespoke an attempt to qualify as a cultivated Bohemian. She was also very much given to swearing, preferring new and unusual combinations of words which struck her as witty. She casually referred to her custom of getting drunk every night and rang several changes upon that theme. "Since it was after eleven-thirty I was drunk, of course," etc. She made much of some of her sprees, especially some recent ones in which her companion had been one Caroline. She and Caroline had recently kept her butler up all night serving cocktails, and amusing them with a trick of falling down. The butler "would work for nothing if you kept on clowning all the time." After such a hilarious party she and Caroline would wrap themselves up together and sleep on the davenport.

Suggestibility is a highly developed personality trait. As she sat upon the floor and sang she was frequently interrupted by one of the other girls leaning over to her and saying, "Anna, let's laugh." She would then laugh loudly and with every appearance of relishing the experience. Every one would join in, which was the reason for urging her to laugh. She told of several incidents when this trait had led her to unusual actions. The afternoon before she was married was spent in this pastime in the company of another girl. That was the time when she did "the dirtiest trick" that she had ever done anyone in her life. A young man living across the street from her had written a note to her saying, "Anna, just as you are getting married I am going to blow my brains out." She wrote back, "All right, I am to be married at six-thirty." Then she called up a florist and asked them to deliver a funeral wreath at his home some time in the afternoon. This was a huge joke. The young man did not commit suicide, and she laughed the afternoon away with no unpleasant results. Whether the need for this release of tension bespoke an uneasiness about the outcome of the marriage was not made plain.

The external picture of Bohemianism should now be fairly clear. The idea of the investigator that this always indicated acute conflict was here confirmed in striking fashion. The first complex to be touched off was the one concerning Catholicism. To her it was "all rot," although she had had to conform during most of her life. She never had believed in it, had always thought it all "a lot of hokum." Nevertheless, she was not a complete atheist, she believed in a God who was a "directing force." "Of course, you understand I don't believe in some Christ-bitten old Jew in a bath-robe." Her statement of her determination to go through with her divorce was very intense. "I've had to fight the whole damn family, but I don't care. They can all go to hell. I'm going through with this this time I don't care what."

She had, she said, maintained her chastity throughout all the series of separations from her husband, although she had always had a number of men about her. As she put it, "My husband has not yet had a successor." Then, singing, "I'm funny that way." She absolutely and unconditionally repudiated the suggestion that her early religious training might have anything to do with this fact, and grew extremely argumentative about it. The existence of a connection between her chastity and her emotional tie to her family and the family code was admitted.

After this came the most striking corroboration of the hunch which the investigator had had that her behavior was compensatory and intended to gloss over some very acute inner struggles, for she told of three attempts at suicide. She broke down and confessed that she was very much troubled, that she felt that she had nothing at all for which to live, that life seemed a hopeless, futile proposition after all. She had tried suicide three times, twice by gas and once by shooting, and had failed, but she was going to try once more and the next time she would succeed. She would not be dissuaded, and intended to go through with it. Happiness? That was Sunday School talk. Why be a damn fool? She cried a little and seemed to feel better. A psychoanalysis was suggested to her, and the idea was at first repudiated and later more or less taken up.

The existence of a father or a brother fixation is probably involved in this case. She classified herself as a "supreme egotist," which may indicate something of the nature of her conflicts. Another feature of her personality which should be noted is her motherhood complex. She sang with much interest little songs from the "Child's Garden of Verses," and put a great deal of expression into her rendering of "I faw down, Go boom." One of her friends, she said, called this "acute maternity." It is to be doubted that she is a very consistent or practical mother.

This subject shows some homosexual traits. One other girl was present with whom she seems in very close emotional rapport, and the only physical demonstrations of affection which were made during the evening were between the two. Both seemed to relish some jokes about a famous actress reputed to be Lesbian. A further evidence of homosexual traits is her indifference to men, for although she has had a number of them around her always, she has, she says, never yielded to any of them. She was very sure that even under the melting moon of New Mexico she would not be likely to get interested in the game on her own account. "That's the secret of my success, I never get soft." No doubt this is true. She told with some sympathy of one of her admirers, who said that he knew that all one could ever get hanging around her was a heart-break. She said that he needed to be disillusioned. For all the homosexual outgo, however, she remains essentially heterosexual and feminine in her general orientation.

The two cases which we have discussed at length deal with persons who have adhered to the Bohemian way of life for a considerable period of time, and who seem very likely to remain in it. It seems to be more common for people who are lonely and discouraged and in conflict about their divorces to make an excursion into Bohemia, subsequently finding their way out and taking up a different manner of life. Typical of these stories was the following:

"In the next six months I had just one date. That was with an old friend, a boy younger than I, and we went to the movies. I felt terribly guilty about it all, and did not see the boy any more after that. All I did during those months was work and stay at home. I used to get lonely sometimes, and wrote Lloyd once or twice. The sex urge didn't bother me. I did not think of it one way or another. I got dreadfully sensitive and reacted in a hurry to any slight. That is a thing that I have had to fight against ever since I have been divorced. I am too likely to think that people are looking down on me. I did not have that trait before I was divorced.

"In April I saw Lloyd again a few times. We thought we were going to get it all patched up again, but somehow we did not succeed. He still wasn't working. I had intercourse with him then.

"In September I heard that my husband was going out. What did I do then? I ran wild, just went absolutely on the loose. I was out on wild parties every night, and I drank a terrible lot. I met a really vulgar crowd. I went with them a great deal. Why, I don't know, but I kidded myself that I was having a good time, and there was always a party there and always some gin. They were really a terrible crowd, telling dirty jokes all the time, and always singing dirty songs. I knew that this girl's morals were minus but she was nice to me and I kept going there. I never had sex relations with any of those people, though.

"Then I went with another tough crowd which was not quite so vulgar. For about two years all told I was doing a lot of drinking and going on a lot of wild parties. It ended by my getting thoroughly disgusted. I had a party at my home, when the folks were away. It was terrible. One of the boys had intercourse with one of the girls, I feel certain. I felt terrible about such a thing happening in my father's house. And I got terribly drunk at a sorority dance, and resigned from the sorority. My former friends all dropped me because I got drunk and went on so many wild parties.

"After I had been going with these two tough crowds for about two years I met Jack, and I thought quite a lot of him for a while. We gradually quit going on wild parties then."

As the great humorists are ever the unhappy, the cult of the jest has its devotees of the most fanatical among those who live outside the conventions. Wise-cracks are more precious than virtue among those who would be merry. This addiction to jokes enables the divorcé to carry off his rôle, and also serves to release tension by tapping hidden springs of uneasiness. But there must be a sting in the tail of the joke at which Bohemians laugh. The joke must be on somebody or some thing, on matrimony, or love, or husbands, or wives. Technical humor belongs to people who are identified with the moral order.

Bohemianism, as it has been described here, is an adjustment by running from one's problems, by covering them over and pretending that they do not exist. It must be said that this is usually a courageous attempt, but that it nearly always works out badly. For if one runs away from his problems, they remain unsolved, the love for the former mate to whom one does not, following out a philosophy of promiscuity, give a real rival, the hurt pride which one wounds all the more by consorting with a group which is not accepted by the group in which his major interests lie. The Bohemian is a Philistine who has gone on an excursion into the land of the creative person, he cannot really live there,—his home is elsewhere. Always the person who flaunts the mores is insufficiently liberated; he is between, and unfortunate in that he is between; if he were less liberated he would not rebel against the mores, if he were more liberated he would not find it necessary to do so. What the

Bohemian does not realize is that it is only the good little boy who wants to be bad, and that only an essentially naïve person can take pride in his sophistication. Let the Bohemian go back to conformity, and face his problems with that orientation, or win through to the other side, and solve them from there, but let him not stay in the valley between or he will be drenched at length in the waters of the river, a river whose waters are composed of gin and ginger ale, with a goodly percentage of fusel oil, and on whose banks rest many thousands of dead soldiers.

CHAPTER FIVE

The Process of Alienation

A POET has remarked upon the hate of kindred that grows so deep that its roots take hold on hell. If he had been more of a psychologist who said this, and something less of a poet, he might have elaborated his point by showing that this is a very unfortunate peculiarity of human nature, for it has most lamentable results. There is no pathos in all the life and death of these talking apes equaling that of those who have been friends in youth, but who have come to "stand apart like riven oaks." No waste of good like that of love misunderstood or kindness repaid with ingratitude. The friendless monarch left to his misery cries, "Shame, shame, on a dying king," or bares his breast to the wintry wind; and the eye that can remain dry at so sorrowful a spectacle looks out from a soul that is dead indeed.

There is always an element of betrayal when we break with a friend, and our distress is made all the more poignant because we have betrayed not only the friend but the part of us that was in him; although we may, being all essentially auto-morphic, experience the thing with the reverse emphasis. People can hurt us in proportion to their meaningfulness to us, and the worst wounds are ever inflicted by those we love.

The pathos of a marital break attaches not alone to thwarted love and pride bowed down, but to the very essence of the process by which those who have been one flesh are made separate. Personalities that have been fused by participation in common enterprises and that are held together by their common memories can only be hewn apart at the expense of great psychic travail; a scar is left when the beast with a double back is cut apart. For marriage is stronger than people think, and there are reasons for its permanence which no one yet can understand.

The process by which those who have learned to live together learn to live apart is one process, and it is neither initiated nor ended by the legal step of divorce. In this work attention is centered upon the later stages of the process, but these cannot be understood unless one has the beginnings in mind as well. This process by which people who have been meaningful to each other become less so has many inner and outer complications, and is almost too intricate and evasive for the human mind to comprehend or words to describe. Attention in this chapter is focused upon one phase of this process, upon the elements of group influence which make themselves felt in it.[1]

Alienation is of course implicit in every relationship, as death is implicit in life, but it only becomes apparent when it has assumed more than usually formidable proportions. Perhaps that helps to explain the seeming inevitableness of alienation between marriage partners, when once that has shown itself. Alienation once begun, it moves on as ineluctably as if a thousand Titans were pushing it and the

---

[1] We discuss elsewhere the dissolution of the love-complex. See Chapter Six, Old Love and New.

actors were but puppets in a show. How impotent is Man's design! How powerless is he to unravel the skeins of Fate in which he is entangled! All who have ever been involved in such a situation will realize how utterly caught they were. There is a circular interaction in which the responses of one person evoke more decided responses from the other; once people are involved within such a process it is almost impossible for them to break it. (The concept of summation has been applied to explain these processes by certain sociologists. The distinguishing mark of processes to which this concept may be applied is that once one is involved in them he is carried along. An excellent example of a process in which this is involved is the mating process: the responses of one person release the responses of another which in turn evoke more decided responses which serve as stimuli in their turn; the culmination in the act of mating is almost inevitable.)

Husbands and wives who have begun to quarrel find themselves unable to stop until it is too late. Mayhap their disagreements bring heartache to both; they discuss them fully and frankly and agree to stop; no matter, the quarrels go on. (It is the idea of the writer that these quarrels which no one can stop and which neither party can understand are due to little things which the couple have insufficiently talked out, or to actual repressions on one side or the other, but this remains to be verified by more controlled observation.) When alienation starts it marches inevitably, love alone cannot stop it, soon the relationship is bankrupt and those involved do not wish any longer to become reconciled.

Elements of this process which we may separate

out by analysis are the growth of distance between the marriage partners, the change of attitudes toward each other, and the rearrangement of the psychic and social orientation of the mates toward persons outside the marriage. Each of these elements is of course implied in all the others, all are functions of each other. The entire process has its causes in the nature of the relationship and in the minds of those concerned in it; to analyze these causes would carry us a bit further back than we care to go. (For a treatment of this subject the reader is referred to Mowrer's *Family Disorganization*.[2] This is unquestionably the most scientific work on that general topic now available, but we cannot endorse it unqualifiedly, for the complicated system of tensions seems topheavy and the whole treatment lacks life, as if it were based upon the study of case records rather than upon an intimate knowledge of people. The present writer would find more useful a treatment more essentially dynamic in its nature, with family disorganization treated as a function of the interaction of recognizable and understandable personalities rather than as a process in itself, like the interaction of chemicals.)

Whether one thinks of alienation as a function of sexual dissatisfaction or explains it as a manifestation of the masculine protest (the drive toward mastery), he will have no difficulty in recognizing the active participation of the group outside at every stage in the process. For marriage has two elements of strength, one, that it is private, the other, that it is public, and from neither of these is the group out-

---

[2] Mowrer, Ernest R., *Family Disorganization,* The University of Chicago Press, Chicago, 1927.

side entirely excluded. It is a public privacy; privacy
is assured and its value enhanced by the public character of the arrangement. This public-private character of the arrangement is a source of both strength
and weakness in the institution, and of both happiness and unhappiness for the married. For when a
man loves his wife he is proud to have his friends
know that she is his; he does not see her faults as do
people who do not love her, and he does not realize
that most others, if they trouble at all to speak
of him as the husband of a particular woman, say,
"Well, I'm glad it's he." If he does not love her, he
sees her defects more clearly than anybody else, having more opportunity, and more motivation to do so,
but he imagines that others see her as he does;
thereby his unhappiness is increased. But as love is
made stronger when people at large know of it, so
its frustration is the more keen if it is glimpsed by
persons outside. And when people have begun to
drift apart, the group enters as a wedge which
forces them further and further away from each
other. The maintenance of the privacy of the
home demands that the polite fiction, if not the reality of mutual preferment be kept, that there be no
public quarrels, trials of strength, or commands between the partners.

Previous works have shown that the group can
keep people together in marriage, but the inference
has always been that when a marriage broke up it
did so only because of its own inherent weakness, or
as a result of conflicts arising mainly within itself.
This is like saying that a house can be preserved by
painting, but that if it is not so preserved it just falls
to pieces of itself, wind and weather being left out
of the demonstration. What we are here attempting

to show is that there is an element of group influence in such cases as well as a fundamental unadjustment in the marriage. We would not wish to say that the group never keeps people together, unquestionably it does so, but that is a different question, and we are here concerned only with marriages which from the nature of the case the group did not preserve intact, sometimes with marriages which would have rotted if they had been kept in heaven where they were supposedly made. We have certainly not explained the influence of the modern world upon the family when we have simply shown historically that society has relaxed its efforts to preserve the home; for we must supplement this negative explanation by a description of the way in which the group takes a hand in actively splitting a married pair apart. When a marriage is destined to break, the very efforts of relatives and friends to save it may only serve to make it all the more intolerable for the two persons most concerned. Any effort, too, to mediate between a husband and a wife serves at least partially to destroy one of the assets of the home, its privacy, although the same could not be said of those indirect buttressings and protective mechanisms which are part of the current moral code.

When the home is functioning in a healthy manner, whether this is accomplished in accordance with the doctrine of the inferiority drive, by avoiding status conflicts, or by maintaining a perfect sex adjustment which makes possible complete identification with the love object, as the more devout Freudians would believe, the home is impregnable to attack from the outside. Frank Harris has interestingly told what happens to the luckless member of

the group whose head is thrust into the home at the
wrong moment:

> While we were talking the door opened and Lady
> Randolph appeared. Naturally I got up as she called out
> "Randolph," but he sat still. In spite of his ominous silence
> she came across to him. "Randolph, I want to talk to you."
> "Don't you see," he retorted, "that I've come here to be
> undisturbed?" "But I want you," she repeated tactlessly.
> He sprang to his feet. "Can't I have a moment's peace from
> you anywhere?" he barked: "Get out and leave me alone!"
> At once she turned and walked out of the room.
>   "You ought not to have done that, for my sake," I said.
> "Why not," he cried, "what has it to do with you?"
>   "Your wife will always hate me," I replied, "for having
> been the witness of her humiliation; you, she may forgive;
> me, never." He laughed like a schoolboy. "Those are aston-
> ishing things in you," he said; "you have an uncanny flair for
> character and life; but never mind, I'll say you were angry
> with me for my rudeness and that will make it all right!"
> "Say nothing," I retorted, "let us hope that she may forget
> the incident, though that's not likely." Ever afterwards Lady
> Randolph missed no opportunity of showing me that she
> disliked me cordially. I remember some years later how
> she got into the Express train for the South in Paris and
> coolly annexed an old man's seat. I spent ten minutes in
> explaining who she was and pacifying the old Frenchman but
> she scarcely took the trouble to thank me. She showed her
> worst side to me almost always, and was either imperious
> or indifferent. (Frank Harris, *My Life,* Vol. II, p. 380.)

Thus the home as a functioning unity is a very
cohesive group, and one way in which it maintains
itself is by the transfer of hostility to convenient
intruders from the outside. Mr. Harris' psychology
is wrong only in overlooking the fact that Lady Ran-
dolph's hostility toward him might have been made

all the more keen if she had actually forgotten the incident. For even the best of marriages are likely to be founded in part upon repressions, and the animosity, originally aroused by the mate, based upon a thousand forgotten unpleasantnesses and un-recognized shortcomings, not being allowed to vent itself upon the person who aroused it may wait its chance and pounce with long contained fury upon some person who is conveniently near and not incon-veniently dear.

But the home does not always function so effec-tively and a gap may be opened that is large enough to admit a sizable wedge. Thus is initiated an in-teresting process which moves apparently in cyclic fashion to its dénouement. An alienation is begun,— for what causes some other writer must tell. The distance between the partners is sufficiently great that a wedge can enter, and their ability to dislodge it is decreased. They have lost the advantage of leverage. After the wedge has entered there is per-haps a quarrel, perhaps none, but from then on the couple live on a new level of alienation. As distance is greater, there is more possibility of misunder-standing, and thus new disagreements may arise. If so, these are added to the old and a further stage is reached. Thus we apparently have alienation occur-ring as a cyclic process resting on incidents each of which is followed by the establishment of a less sat-isfactory and more dangerous *modus vivendi*. Di-vorce takes its place in this process as a way station.

This is not to say that a couple might not become very thoroughly alienated from each other for rea-sons of their own quite unconnected with the life of the group. That is conceivable, but in the stories that have been told to the writer other persons have always entered somewhere although perhaps not till the melancholy business was well-nigh finished. Another possible variation of this mechanism for the preservation of the privacy of the home occurs where, a relationship having become hollow, people devote their efforts to covering up the defects of their marriage and find themselves at last bankrupt of love, like a business man who has wasted his capital in paying hush money.

A case in which the cyclic nature of the alienation, based upon recurrent crises after which adaptation was on a lower level, was noticed by the subject himself, is the following:

The subject, now a school-teacher in Chicago, was reared on a farm in the South. There is some evidence that he had a mother fixation; for one thing, the fact that he slept with his mother until the age of fourteen. He was also his mother's favorite.

Acquiring somewhere an urge for achievement, he gradually drifted away from home. He developed a personality that was adapted to a much more complicated environment than that of his home community. He went to live in a great northern city. All this happened by slow stages, so that the change was nearly imperceptible. He first went to High School, where he did well. Then he went to business college, then taught there, then went out as a business representative to solicit students. Still unsatisfied, he went on to college in the North, and finally took enough graduate work for his Doctor's degree. He was well established in his new environment.

The war came. The subject was two years in the service. For him it marked disillusion. He lost contact with the world that he had known, and reverted to the elemental. He had his first sex experiences, on a rather low level, but satisfactory enough to release his impulses from the inhibitions which had previously been placed upon them. He had a number of upsetting experiences, being in some of the most hard-fought engagements. He was shaken to the roots of his being.

All during the war he kept up a correspondence with a girl with whom he had renewed contact just before leaving home to go into the service. There had been no prior love affair, but they kept up a correspondence all this time. During the war his mother died. The girl was a friend of his mother.

After the war he returned home. He had idealized his home while he was overseas, he had waited for this moment, he was not disappointed. He fitted himself once more into the old ways of many years before, forgetting the interim. His mother was gone, yet here was the girl who had been her friend. The girl was evidently highly suitable in the group in which she lived. He was sorry for her, which was perhaps another fitting in with the mother image. They talked of marriage, and although there were certain obstacles presented by the fact that she could not leave her home, they were married.

Then the young man went back to the work which he had dropped before the war, back into the intellectual world in which he had been living when the war came. He took up his old friends and his old interests, all this implied that he left his wife behind, for she could not yet leave her home and parents. He came North after having spent just one night with her, although there were sex relations on other occasions, of course.

In their letters the couple looked forward to their meeting during his Christmas vacation. Not a very firmly established home, but no indication of alienation as yet. At Christmas time she came to see him. Then came their first shock. He introduced her to his friends, and saw that they were none too pleased with his choice. What he saw she saw as well, and they began to realize that they had made an unwise marriage. At that time she began to be quite unenthusiastic about sexual intimacies with him. Their coldness increased during the six months between Christmas and summer, when he returned home.

During the summer they lived together, at her home. Apparently they both tried to adjust, although of course not in either case as wholeheartedly as they might have. The subject said that there were at this time a number of recurrent crises, after each one of which the relationship was left weaker than it had been before. He did not care for her friends, and on some occasions said so. He had drifted away from the church, and there were one or two occasions when there were words over that. An incident that stands out in his mind as a particularly high point occurred when she wanted to go to a near-by dance and he did not. He told her to go ahead and go by herself. To his surprise she followed his advice. The husband's reaction was the more severe because he did not care for his wife's friends anyway. At this time occurred the first mention of divorce. It came from the wife, who had grown increasingly cold. Another crisis occurred when the husband decided to start back for school a month early so that he might work on his thesis. It was in reality in part an excuse to get away, but was taken by the wife as being wholly that.

During the second winter, the wife still stayed at home, although, her father having died, she might very well have come to live with her husband. The husband became better adjusted than ever to the complicated conditions of life in the city, and more and more at home in the sophisticated world. Letters now were less frequent than they had been before, and the topic of divorce was occasionally up for discussion in them.

A definite break occurred when he did not return home the next summer. The wife had expected him, it seems, and was much hurt that he did not return. Then the correspondence centered around the topic of divorce. The wife at first consented to a divorce, and later withdrew her consent.

At this point the subject met his second wife, and made, he says, a complete transference of his affection to her. Now his wife's refusal to let him have a divorce, on the basis of her standing in the home community, became a much more serious cause for resentment against her.

What clinched the matter for him, he says, was that he heard from home of some gossip about his wife. It was made to seem probable that she had other outlets for her affections, or at least for her sex impulses.

He started proceedings for divorce, suing in the city in which he lived. The wife came North to contest his suit. He was beaten, and the situation became somewhat nasty. Later she got the divorce herself at her home.

It seems pretty clear that this case rested on a number of incidents which were rendered dramatic by their meaning in the whole process. Each incident, more clear in its implications than any of those that had preceded it, marked a new high level of misunderstanding. Each one initiated a new stage in the process of alienation. At every dramatic point the group entered. The couple were prevented from establishing a home by the fact that the wife's parents needed her at home and by the demands of the group in which the husband lived in Chicago. The first realization of the unwisdom of their marriage came when she was not accepted by the husband's friends in the North; she had a high social standing in her home community. The couple lived at her home when they were living together. He did not go to church and the part of the wife which was attached to conventional religion was opposed to him. He did not like her friends; she resented his unwillingness to meet their demands and he resented the existence of those friends; the incident of the dance merely served to throw all this into relief. The demands of the husband's career took him away from the wife, or served him as an excuse to get away; the basis of the wife's resentment is obvious. During their separation each was buttressed in his or her stand by the group in which each lived. The struggle as to who should get the divorce had its roots in considerations of personal dignity and standing in their respective social groups. The finishing touches were given by the rumors and the nastiness of the divorce; the job was complete.

The same process is illustrated, somewhat differently, in the following excerpt from a record of the latter stages of a marriage. The parts played by both husband and wife are here a bit clearer.

This couple were living in an army post at the time of their break, and the closeness of contact with the other persons on the post made possible a clearer working out of group influences than is ordinarily the case. The man was an army officer of about thirty. The woman was several years younger. They had been married two years and had no children.

There was between these people a very real affection, although the germs of alienation were also present. Living in this marriage necessitated on the part of the husband some repression. He had very strong sex urges which he confessed were never quite gratified in his marriage. He was a dominant individual and yet in his home he was the submissive one. He seems to have had a considerable underlying motivation to better his condition in this respect but this remained long unrecognized. The wife had powerful status drives which were not quite satisfied; and she was never quite able to identify herself completely with her husband, to feel that she could not enhance her own prestige by subtly detracting from his. In addition, her internal necessity for domination led her to some unpleasantness with the other women on the post. Both the husband and wife were thwarted in some of their major wishes; the husband sexually and in his profession, for he did not consider that the army gave him an opportunity for a full utilization of all his abilities; the wife sexually thwarted by a self-blocking mechanism within herself, and thwarted in her attempts to gain the recognition she thought she deserved. Both to some extent lived by fictions, the husband by fictions of what he would do and become, the wife by fictions which exaggerated her present importance.

Life in an army post throws people into contact which is so close that it is likely to bring out any little defect in a personality or a relationship. It occurred so in this case. The first notable incident occurred when the wife became embroiled with some of the other women about the post. Their motivation was partly jealousy and partly a quite justifiable reaction to the tactless behavior into which the wife's status drive had betrayed her. The wife was accused of not caring for her home properly, of going away to too many parties and spending too much money for her clothes. She called upon her husband to defend her, which he did. However, he also attempted to get her to conform to the standards of their particular group, and although this was done privately she identified him with the opposition. He was also unfortunate enough in his arguments with her to appeal to her on the grounds of what people would say, which set off a hostility reaction which had originally been attached to her mother, who also had used that type of control with her. The wife thus felt a great resentment well up within her over the whole affair, she rebelled, and exposed herself to yet further gossip.

Now the gossip about her became more serious. The practice of going to shows and dinners with other men than her husband in her husband's absence or when he had to work was not clearly frowned upon by the group in which she lived. However, she began, as the other women thought, to take advantage of this privilege much too frequently, to the neglect of her home. She was again cautioned by her husband and by her friends to employ greater discretion, because of the openings which she gave to the people who did not like her, but her answer was further rebellion. The gossip increased, and there were vague rumors of definite sexual irregularity. Although the husband turned a deaf ear to these charges, and although they were quite unfounded, they had their effect upon the wife. And by this time the husband was rather clearly identified in her mind with the opposition.

Another incident marked a turning point. A man a few years older than either of the pair, himself unsatisfactorily married, hearing of the alleged sex irregularities of this young woman who was his neighbor, decided that he ought to be included as a partner. He then not only paid her public attentions, which caused his wife to become the bitter enemy of the younger woman, but privately tried by force to claim her sexually. There were one or two episodes which registered in the mind of the wife almost as traumatic incidents. On one occasion, at least, he was near rape, the woman escaping him, she said, with the greatest difficulty. He realized that she would not dare to call out or tell her husband, and he relied on that to give him security in his attempts. She was sufficiently alienated from her husband that she could not tell him of the latest development, but keeping it from him made her even more reserved with him.

These episodes marked the turning point as to several things in the relationship. They marked, for the wife, a definite turning against sex. It will be remembered that her sex expression was never very free, and after this it became much more inhibited, and something approaching real frigidity developed. It also marked a turning point in that she, who had previously confided very much in her husband, to the great betterment of the marriage, now turned away from him and kept her secrets to herself or shared them with outsiders.

The turning point as to sex was especially marked. Prior to this time she had perhaps been compensating in regard to sex, and had used it as a channel by which to neutralize strains in other respects. Now quite suddenly she turned against it. The husband, inclined perhaps to overvalue his sex life, made frantic efforts to get her to conform. Considerable hostility was developed on both sides and the affair became quite complicated. The wife was given further negative conditioning in regard to sex life, which, as the subject of so many arguments, became very definitely repugnant to her on that account as well as the others. But the sex act assumed to the husband a vast symbolic importance, for it represented to him as well as sex satisfaction triumph over the rivals for his wife's affections, and triumph over the situation itself. Further, the effects of the blocking of their sexual impulses became obvious in the increased emotional instability of both husband and wife. The wife developed a number of defenses against intercourse, all of which were evaluated by the husband as such, and all of which excited him to further resentment and to further frantic attempts to make his wife conform. The devices were such things as: pleading illness or distraction, postponement, indefinite promises, inviting visitors and keeping them in the house until the hour had become so late that sleep seemed imperative, etc. The group had now driven a wide wedge between husband and wife.

The wife then began to seek by various means to interpose distance between herself and her husband. Some of these were very ingenious, and were noted by the observer before the couple confided in him. The husband had in his group a name which he somewhat disliked; he was called Andy because of his receding chin. He never displayed his real dislike of the name to the persons in his group, thinking that poor sportsmanship, but he had often displayed it to his wife. The wife had always before called him by his given name both in conversation with him and in speaking of him to outside persons. Now she began to call him Andy, which he more than half understood and always resented. This led him to certain reprisals, such as quoting to her the things that had been said about her. This is a very clear example of the mechanisms of which we have been talking. The wife and the husband had always discussed at length their joint plans for their summer vacation, deriving much pleasure plans for this summer, and had definitely decided. The wife was asked a question as to where they were going and what from the phantasy activity involved. They had discussed their they were going to do. She parried, "I don't know, where are you going, Andy?" All of this implied her separation from him, and her lack of intimacy with him, in that she did not know where he was going to spend his vacation. Further, the wife began to speak of herself, probably at first without realizing it, as if she were a single woman, quite free to make her own plans and follow out her own career without any reference to her husband.

An event of both primary and symbolical importance was the wife's decision not to sleep with her husband. Primarily this was due to sex aversion, to a desire not to be exposed to the at times quite violent solicitations of her husband. It led to more complete sex frustration on the part of both husband and wife and finally deprived them of the outlet for other kinds of tensions and of the periodic rapprochement which the sex act had furnished. Symbolically, it meant to her the interposition of greater distance between herself and her husband, and gave her the chance to complete the unhealthy process of drawing within herself. The husband now assumed very definitely the rôle of the wronged husband and based his pleas to his wife on the lack of justification for the injuries she was doing him. There were several stages in this process. The couple possessed but one good bed, the other was quite unsuitable for frequent use. The wife decided one night to go to the small bed. The husband followed her; there was a long argument. After a while the husband returned to the other bed. After that there was an argument every night for a while, but the husband finally lost. The wife gained her point at length by promising to try to relax her attitude on sex matters. At this time her horror of sex was somewhat increased because she heard her husband and the man who had been most frequently mentioned as her possible paramour discussing the matter of sex. Finally the wife slept alone in the conjugal bed, and the husband in the smaller one, she promised that she would come in the morning to lie with her husband for a while, but she did not keep her promise. It was agreed between the couple that they were to keep this arrangement for sleeping separately a secret but the wife let it out in a Freudian slip before the man just mentioned. There was the further fact concerned in this part of the process that the husband's suspicions as to his wife's fidelity were aroused by the fact that she refused to sleep with him or have anything whatever to do with him sexually; he suspected that she might have an outlet elsewhere.

The breach was widened by persistent rumors about the post that that couple were going to separate. The wife on account of these rumors developed the feeling that everybody could tell from her face that something was wrong with her marriage, and that the frequent advances that had been made to her had been so motivated. This amounted at times to a belief that people could read her thoughts, and intensified her conflicts, already severe enough. She also developed profound guilt feelings at this point, and began to think seriously of divorce. The gossip had the effect upon the wife of crystallizing her opposition to marriage, and upon the husband of further motivating him to maintain the status quo.

Now developed certain arguments between the husband and the wife. In these, according to a principle of polarity, they tended to become more and more definitely committed to opposite policies. The wife demanded first living apart for a while, but this was opposed by the husband. Up to this point she had been reluctant to face a definite break, but she then developed a desire for a final and complete separation, which the husband opposed. He then offered the first alternative, but she had moved on from that demand. The whole situation was vastly complicated by the presence of other persons at these discussions. The wife usually arranged to have other people present whenever she and her husband would be together, in order to prevent quarrels and to ward off the now insistent solicitations to intercourse; nevertheless, the quarrels occurred and the presence of the witness merely exaggerated their bitterness and made their effect more lasting. The presence of other people also definitely committed the persons to their positions. This was perhaps the most trying period of all. Both persons involved were very conscientious, both were emotionally involved in each other, both were worried about the breakup of their marriage. They would agree after their quarrels to stop them, each would try to refrain. But the sex frustration, and the status involvement proved always too great, and soon they would break out with renewed intensity. Finally they agreed to a separation. At this point they consulted the present writer, but he was unable to do more than hear their stories and suggest a few compromises, not feeling that he had sufficient insight into the characters of these people to justify him in assuming responsibility for advice to continue or to break the relationship without a more complete study, which was not possible.

A psychological explanation would have to pay some attention to the fictions by which the wife and the husband lived. The wife was put in a situation where her fictions were rudely destroyed, and she was left disconsolate and helpless. She desired to retire within herself and rebuild them. A short vacation apart from her husband and a change of group might have saved the marriage at this point. Instead, the husband busied himself with tearing down these fictions yet further, taking advantage of the opportunity of proving that he had been right all along in his opposition to them. Thereby he caused the wife to identify him more definitely with the opposition and to interpose other persons between her and him.

Alienation with reverse English was also to be noted a little later in the case. The wife had developed her peculiar personality from living in a home which took its tone from a dominating mother. Her fictions, and the trouble can be thought of as arising from those fictions, had their origin there. Her rebellion had its roots in her ambivalent attitude toward her mother, and in rebelling against the authorities at the army post she had rebelled also against the loved and hated mother image. When she left her husband she went to live with her own people, coming again under the domination of her mother. Her mother strenuously opposed the daughter's separation from her husband and thereby gave the daughter one more reason for going through with her plans. This opposition of her mother clinched the young woman in her decision to get a divorce, which she accordingly did.

A question as to the possibility of arresting the process of alienation is suggested by this case. Although the desire to pick another person to pieces no doubt has its roots in some unspoken grievance, small or large, which attaches to the person or to some other for which he serves as surrogate, catharsis does not always destroy it. If the mutual interchange which should give catharsis becomes an out and out quarrel, with things spoken out in the desire that they may wound the other person, or if other people are witnesses of these domestic scenes, alienation is not stopped, but hastened, for the interchange has given not relief and increased understanding, but greater cause for grievance. There are of course innumerable cases in which the process of alienation has been arrested by a timely discussion, but this must occur very early in the game and while a marriage still has the asset of being unbroken before the public; a grievance must apparently be thrashed out before one has a chance of forming a habit of feeling aggrieved. On the other hand, too great a readiness to speak one's mind is not a trait which makes for happiness in marriage or anywhere else. A person who has it is likely to acquire a most unenviable reputation. But if the people who air their grievances frequently and well get into trouble, so do those who keep them altogether to themselves; slow accumulation of unrecognized and unspoken injuries sometimes accounts for our sudden hates. In any case the analysis of the group factor in marital alienation would suggest that it is never good practice for married persons to have disagreements in the presence of people. (This does not at all shut out the possible practice of having both parties talk to a trained individual who would allow them to get a proper catharsis and privately suggest modifications of conduct to both parties, maintaining the strictest confidence as to all disclosures.)

When we speak of the alienation of affections we usually mean the alienation of one mate from the other by a third person who intrudes. This third person is thought of as an individual of superior attractiveness who puts the mate to shame by comparison, or who wins by sympathy or sex lure or what not. The situation is never so simple as that, but is part of a highly complicated web of personal interaction, as may be illustrated by the following case.

This was the case of a doctor and his wife in a small town of the Middle West. They were both about thirty-five years of age, had been married about twelve years, and had no children.

The wife has a very strong urge to dominate; her clenched teeth and doubled up fists frequently make her the very picture of aggression. That the wife dominated during the years of marriage is certain. The husband, more suave and less aggressive, suffering from inferiority drives having a basis in his physical organism (he was barely five feet tall), outwardly submitted to his domineering mate and inwardly rebelled. From time to time in the marriage he had protested by having an affair with another woman. Usually they did not go to intercourse. The wife in the course of the interview recalled a long series of these, each of which in turn she had forgotten, but each of which had no doubt served to make her more domineering than ever before.

Another woman, not overly attractive, appeared. She had already a rather bad reputation, and had nothing to lose.

It appeared to her that to marry a doctor, or to be his accepted mistress, would be a distinction. She found the doctor ready to take an interest in her, since by so doing he felt that he would be striking his wife in a vital part. This woman saw the doctor frequently at his office, and arranged to have him as a guest at her own and her mother's home as frequently as possible. Apparently both she and her mother went to great pains to please the doctor, paying him many flattering attentions.

Soon there began to be gossip about the town. This was carried to the doctor and his wife. The doctor reacted by rebelling against it; his attitude was that people would just have to learn. The wife at first would not listen to it at all, but no doubt she took her revenge in other ways, probably by accentuating the domination against which the husband's affair was a protest. The wife's action, when one day a man delivering groceries started to tell her what he knew of her husband, is representative of her attitude in this period. She stopped the man at once and called her husband, who ordered the man off the place in great wrath. No doubt, without saying anything, she was nevertheless able to make the most of the situation.

A bit later, the gossip continuing, the wife's suspicions were aroused. She spied on her husband a bit, and her suspicions were confirmed. She confronted him with the evidence, and they quarreled. During these quarrels she made him feel his inferiority, emphasizing the low standing of the other woman and the doctor's probable loss of status by consorting with her. She had also certain church and social activities which she could use for compensatory outlets, and she began to take great interest in these; in some peculiar way things got twisted about so that these were made weapons in her struggle for prestige with her husband. The husband was thus driven in this struggle for status to take refuge in the other woman, and to make a more and more complete transference to her. (This is always the homewrecker's advantage, that his very presence interferes with the free flow of affection between the mates.)

Other people now entered more frankly into the argument. To some of them the husband said things which were carried to the wife, the things that he said not only committed him to a course of action, but when they reached his wife made his domestic situation worse, for she made reprisals. Others said things about the woman in the case, and these were carried to the wife. One day when this woman was going to the doctor's office some men noticed that she was wearing bronze evening slippers. The men passed some jesting remarks and these were carried to the wife. She said, "I never thought you'd fall for a pair of bronze slippers. If that's your level, go ahead and sink to it. I'm through."

By way of reprisal the wife began to humiliate the husband in front of other people, telling him publicly to stop this or that, or to shut up. The husband retaliated by telling other people that he was going to show her where the money came from.

Up to this point, although the woman had made definite sex advances, the doctor had not allowed himself to be drawn into intercourse. The wife found about the house a number of magazines and pamphlets relating to sex, and concluded that they had been given to the doctor by her rival. She also found in the doctor's clothing occasional evidence that he had been under intense sexual excitement. Therefore, when he said to her again, "I haven't fallen, I haven't fallen," she replied, "Yes? Well, I know why. You're just afraid you can't make good." That taunt must have struck a very sensitive point.

The situation became more complex when the husband and wife went on an automobile trip with another couple, and the other people saw the struggle which was taking place. There were few scenes but the wife was experiencing a terrific conflict, and the husband, seeing her distraught state, became more than a little afraid of her.

When they returned she went to the home of the other woman. She must have made something of a scene. When the doctor heard of this it furnished grounds for a definite break; the husband declared that his wife had done something quite unpardonable. From this point on there were no sex relations at all between the couple. They continued to live together for some months, although completely out of touch. The husband had vowed to treat his wife as badly as possible, and she made some reprisals, although she was at this time and later much more concerned with preserving the relationship than he. The social group had turned completely against the man, having passed a moral judgment upon him. He left the group and divorced his wife. Shortly thereafter the other woman divorced her husband. She is now living with the doctor, and the doctor is again making some headway.

The wife at first felt very much motivated to prove her innocence, and talked very freely about her husband and the wrongs which he had done her. This passed and she has now reached the stage where she is willing and even anxious to hear evil spoken of him by others, but where she nevertheless feels that she must defend him. She is quite pleased, also, by the fact that her rival has received no social recognition.

This telling of the story makes it quite obvious that the intruder, while an active element in the situation, did not operate by any means alone. It is submitted that alienation is very rarely so simple a matter as inducing a person to fall in love with one individual and out of love with another. These two processes are not, it is true, unrelated, for the individual who is at the center of such a situation is caught in two processes of a summatory nature (of such a nature that a person once involved in them has difficulty in extricating himself). He is quarreling with his wife, and he is falling in love; neither is an easily arrested process, and here they may set up in such a way as to reënforce each other. The more he falls in love with the other woman, the more he quarrels with his wife; the more he hates his wife the more he turns to her rival.

A man who attached great importance to a group of friends, mostly male, was hindered in this association by a jealous wife. He dropped his friends, except for occasional contacts, but he found that his wife begrudged him even those. The man resented his wife's attitude the more because of his actual fidelity to her. This led him to think of his wife as a jailer; they quarreled more and more bitterly, and were divorced.

There is the frequent situation in which a man becomes embroiled with his in-laws. The persons on both sides of the dispute are activated by the highest motives; on the one side, desire to see that the daughter is not ill-treated by her husband; on the other the blameless wish to be undisturbed in the enjoyment of domesticity, and the rights of the conjugal state. The in-laws say unkind things of him, to the great detriment of the marital rapport, and he may be led to reprisals which yet further alienate his wife from him. This cannot fail to affect his attitude toward his wife. Unless this circle is broken, all must sometime go before the judge with their stories of marital unhappiness. When divorce is in the air, those in-laws who "never did like so-and-so" have their chance at last. Before, their comments on their kinsman's wife have rebounded into their own faces, but now at length they get a hearing. Such conflicts strike deep always, and are further complicated by the presence of fixations or by living arrangements which interfere with the social independence of the new home.

Peacemakers deserve all the praise they have got, but it takes more than a good intention to be a son of God. When it is husband and wife who are at war, the peacemaker's is an unfortunate rôle, for he stands to lose whether he succeeds or fails. The great likelihood is that he will do more harm than good, for by entering into the situation as an arbiter he makes it more clear that one is needed. When a person would make peace between a married pair, he should remember that they may not know that a war exists. Many are they whose enmity is proverbial among their friends who privately congratulate themselves on their unfailing rapport. But even if love's blindness has not protected them from realizing the extent of their incompatibility, the entry of the conciliator may freeze them into their opposition, because they are ashamed that such a necessity should exist, and each, laying the blame upon the other, privately makes his conditions of peace more exacting. If the peacemaker succeeds, that is, if the twain become reconciled to each other in spite of his bungling efforts, they will hate him always for knowing that they have quarreled. It is better for a man to come between husband and wife than to go between them; the one may be construed as a compliment, but the other is always an insult.

There are innumerable variations. There was the case of the very elderly man married to a young woman. This woman was unfaithful to her husband, a younger man being the object of her passion. She wrote some letters to this man, and the man sold them to her husband, who used them as a basis for his divorce. Then there is the case of the man who lets a married woman tell him her troubles, gaining thereby a favorable transference and a considerable leverage for any advances which he may care to make, in addition to committing the woman by overt acts and the knowledge of the public concerning them. There is alienation or the clinching of the alienation by the sympathy of the parental image. Then there is the case of the mother-fixated child whose alienation from his wife receives its final touch from his knowledge of the fact that she is not good to his mother. The possibilities are in fact endless and we cannot hope to deal with them all. We must rather be satisfied to describe and explain a few typical forms of interaction, and show their relation to the personalities concerned.

The mechanism of alienation assumes an unmistakable form when disagreements culminate in actual separation. At this time the former friends of the couple frequently become wholly or in part attached to the one or the other of the former mates. These two groups then sympathize mainly with the persons about whom they are organized. (In other cases, both persons leave the former group and seek new connections, or one person leaves the group and seeks a new circle of friends. In these cases, too, the same sort of thing occurs.) The wife's friends see her in near perspective but see the husband only dimly—there are few of us who photograph well, few who can stand merely objective interpretation; they see the effects that the husband's actions have had on her; they see the extenuating circumstances for any acts of hers of which they do not approve, but they do not see the effects of her acts upon the absent husband; they must more or less depend on her for an account of the nature of the difficulties leading up to the break, and even though in telling the story she tries to tell the husband's side too she can never really tell more than her version of the husband's story; even the telling of a story which casts discredit on her really draws her friends closer to her, for they think that if she is so fair now she has always been that way—all these things work together to build up in the eyes of her friends the notion that she could not have been at fault in this matter, and the result is that sympathy for her runs quick and deep and enmity for the husband grows. Then there is the fact, which no sociologist would fail to point out, that this is an in-group, and that one sympathizes with those in the in-group and hates those in the out-group who injure any of those within. Often too, even those who are quite aware of the faults of the divorced person whom they know profess a sympathy that they do not feel—this may be from motives high or low—and give utterance to sentiments of hostility toward the absent person which they think will evoke favorable responses from the one present. (This mechanism must vary according to social and intellectual levels. With the more involved personalities, direct dispraise of the former mate will evoke often a very unfavorable response, indeed, discreet dispraise is one means of driving people back together. On the lower social levels, this sympathy with one partner and condemnation of the other can be direct; on the upper it must be only inferential—in the nature of a sympathetic understanding which assures the person that whatever he did surely could not have been so bad, that no doubt the other person did not have a real appreciation of his virtues. And in this latter phrasing, perhaps it is often true.)

Thus it usually happens that the divorcé is surrounded by persons who know him well and sympathize with him, all of whose references to his marital troubles are of such a nature as to bolster him and disparage the other person, all of whose remarks may set up as suggestions that he should indeed hate this person who has injured him. Thus we have often the anomaly of the divorcé hating his former wife much less than those about him hate her, for he is conscious of extenuating circumstances in her case, and sometimes of the extent of his derelictions. One's friends are more bitter over his injuries than he is himself. This whole situation powerfully influences the divorced person to build up within himself a feeling that the other person was wrong and he was right, a hatred for the absent mate. And it effectively deters reconciliation, for one has the feeling that if he goes back to his wife his friends will say, "The dog has gone back to his vomit." This is the mechanism of alienation. Under such pressure all the psychic and social arrangements which have made marriage possible must give way. Habits of life which made it possible for a certain woman to be dear must be given up at length, and habits of thought must be changed. The myriad repressions upon which marriage was founded must now at length vomit forth their memories, and emotions which have long been unexpressed may have their chance at last. Indeed, the wheel may be so turned that what was before unconscious is made conscious and the previously dominant system of ideas and emotions is relegated to the limits of the disremembered.

The mechanism of alienation is here made to explain much, and it is thought that it would be found to be important in all intimate relations which break up. A case may illustrate a bit further what happens when the process is more advanced.

"I was first conscious of the fact that I really did not want to go back to my wife, or that a part of me did not want to go back, about two months after our break. I analyzed this, and thought that it traced to the fact that I had introduced

myself into this new community on a single-man basis, and
people had sort of come to think of me as a separate individual, rather than as a married man. Then later I had
talked to several people and I wondered what they would
think if I went back to this woman who had caused me so
much trouble. They sympathized of course, and that made it
all the harder. Then, later, people insinuated to me that I
was such a fine fellow that it must have been my wife's
fault. In telling the story of our break I had always been
careful not to say anything against my wife, for two reasons,
one that she is really a very nice person and the other that she
might come to this new place and I didn't want people prejudiced against her when she did. But the very fact that I
tried to be fair with her and to take the blame myself made
my friends all the more certain that whatever had happened
had been her fault rather than mine."

Three levels of alienation are noticeable in the
above case: alienation due to the fact that the
subject had status as a single man, alienation due to
the sympathy of his friends, and alienation due to
the feeling of having committed himself on the matter. The point brought out by the entire discussion
is that one who is separated from his spouse gets
committed willy-nilly to a policy of complete break.
Little bits of self-defensive sarcasm are seized upon
and elaborated, little admissions that the other person may have violated the moral code in thought or
deed are made the most of; all is clinched by the
nastiness of the whole proceeding—a web of circumstance is woven from which the great Houdini
could not escape.

If a couple have escaped bitterness before, they
are likely to fall into it when the time comes to go
to court. And when the judge says the time has come
they talk of many things. Now it comes out, all the

essential nastiness of tearing the blanket in two; each person blames the other. The exposure of one's domestic arrangements cannot be made without pain, the mate must bear the blame for it. Often charges are unfair, and their falsity rankles. Now the world hears all about one's pathetic little deeds at violence, the attempt of the husband to kill his wife by throwing his coat at her, that of the wife to do her husband to death with a finger-nail file. The world sniggers because it is very funny to think that people should attempt to accomplish results so important by means so ill-chosen. But the divorcé hates.

When people speak who have not often spoken, their words have special force. A father who had kept silent for three years wrote as follows to his daughter, who he thought intended to go back to her husband:

"You know I speak with love to you and I do not want you to feel that I am guilty of an unwarranted interference with your affairs. While Henry was very sweet and gracious to me, I never felt that he was your equal or that he would contribute greatly to your up-building. He is responsible for a great—shall I call it misfortune or what? At least it is a period of extreme worry, certainly enough to bring gray hairs before their time. You can find a better one I am sure. I heard a lecture not long ago. The lecturer used the statement frequently, 'This, too, will pass away.' I wish I could tell you more about it. Your mind will eventually adjust itself to a view adapted to a new order of things if you simply allow it to do so. I do not want to lecture you but I wish we could have a visit of at least a day. I know it would be pleasant. If his life is saddened by association with you, his Dad's money will partly compensate, while nothing can repay you for the unwarranted interference with your well-ordered life. He left you to begin again as best you could with a handicap. I figure nothing can compensate for that and nothing can justify it. You owe him nothing. Forget him. I know you can. New visions and new possibilities will open up before you. Do not reënact old mistakes. Look forward. Press on to make new mistakes if must need be. 'Only a fool makes the same mistake twice.' "

In such unmistakable language the group speaks to the divorcé. Let him who can, avoid the influence of those about him. Perhaps he is wiser who does not try.

CHAPTER SIX

Old Love and New

THERE comes a time when inveterate love, grown stale, or seen to be a burden, is threatened by love of adventitious origin. Then ensue great deliberations, vast probings into the profound caverns of the soul, searchings and questionings of the self,—and this is true whether the new love has a self-justifying value which enables it to beggar any other or whether it is merely embraced as a substitute at best imperfect for that which, having once been, can never be again. Then surge forth, like bats fanning with breeze from leathery wings the face of the intruder in their forgotten caves, memories of times that were, and visions of faces that are gone. And only he is wise who reads the auspices well.

People remember longer than they know, and they do not so much forget as forget that they remember. For we know well that love remains when those we love have gone, and the aura of love is ever immanent in the place where it has been, and this, though love itself has died. And even those the pathway of whose love has led them to a fork in the road may go on loving yet while they travel in different directions. If that be not so, then it may be that the memory of a person is dear after the person is dear no more. Certain it is that often love lingers

long after people part;—for this, there are many
reasons.

The first and perhaps the most potent of the reasons for the persistence of love for the former mate
is the real strength of such attachments. Frequently
one marries the first person with whom he has a
serious love affair, and nearly always the affair that
culminated in marriage stands out as the affair in
which there was the most complete emotional as well
as legal involvement. It is likely at any rate that this
affair which was associated with marriage was the
one in which the bars were most completely down,
the one in which each person made himself most completely accessible to the other person and felt that
he enjoyed similar privileges with regard to the
mate. A man goes on loving his former wife because
she, being the first, was the one who had the opportunity to form his taste; he must have rare insight
who is able to liberate himself from the silken domination of a force so subjective. And this is not to
say that there may not be some deeper biological
something which binds people together who have
mated, something which holds a woman to her rav-
isher or brings a man back to the woman who has
often given him sex satisfaction. If a marriage has
been reasonably satisfactory, reasonably peaceful,
reasonably close, over a reasonably long time, the
wonder then is not that people should go on loving
after it has been broken, but that it could ever be
broken.

When the relatively very meaningful love of marriage is contrasted with such sex outlets as one gets
in even high grade promiscuity, it does not suffer.
It would be different if the memory, in running over
the preterite marriage, were always wont to dwell

upon the bad times of its close, but we well know that this is not so; it is courtship days and honeymoon nights that we remember best. We have seen that after divorce many persons adopt a philosophy of promiscuity which, brilliantly rationalized as it may be, almost necessarily connotes that love shall be less meaningful and less responsible than it has been in marriage. One who shapes his life in accordance with this philosophy finds that he enjoys many cheap and easy contacts, but since none of these is permitted to last beyond a certain time or to assume more than a certain set amount of emotional importance, the first love, the real love, the former mate, never has a rival. The barriers that are drawn as to time and emotional participation are not less clearly set up also with regard to the social class of the love object, and affect as well the opportunities for æsthetic enjoyment of the relationship. When we contrast affairs of weeks or months with one of years, affairs in which one is careful to define the amount of his responsibility exactly both to himself and the other person with an affair in which one writes a blank check to be filled in by the bearer, an arrangement in which each person is accessible at all times with one in which he is seen by appointment, and then for a short time only, involvement with a person of one's own class with affairs in which no limitation of class is imposed; when we compare love in a superheated atmosphere of alcohol and jazz with the quieter, friendlier love that goes with domesticity, surreptitious love with love that is proclaimed to the world,—it becomes much easier to understand why the one for-a-long-time-meaningful love object can hold its own through years of competition with promiscuity, and is perhaps able to reassert itself in the end stronger than all its competitors put together.

We have seen that when an impulse is dissociated it not only preserves all its original strength but may even seem to grow stronger. Herein lies much of the reason for the persistence of emotional involvement with the former mate. At the time of a break in the love life, one is confronted with a welter of conflicting impulses which it is very difficult to organize except by definitely banishing some of them to a convenient limbo, by making up one's mind one way or another and then refusing to hear any further arguments on the other side. Not only is this the sort of solution which one's own emotional needs are very apt to prompt him to make, it is the sort of thing which the prevalent philosophy of life of his group and the necessities of his social situation may dictate. The widespread notion that one must be bitter in order to assimilate a break with the former mate, that one has assimilated it if he has attained that happy state and has not if he has not yet reached it, is here in point. Popular ignorance as to the real nature of mental hygiene is appalling; a physician somewhat recherché for his wisdom and common sense declared to one of his patients, "You are still in love with your wife. You won't be free of her till you can say, 'What? That louse?' and mean it." What he is here advising is that his patient repress the love for his former wife, and develop a compensatory antagonism as a means of preserving the repression. But this solution, however common, however successful it may seem in individual cases, is always bad.

One who has been greatly hurt by the experiences of marriage and divorce may think that he needs a guard against another marriage; an admirable arrangement is to go on loving his former mate. This links up in some cases with the excellent arrangement of loving an unattainable person, a mechanism of morbid psychology which is by no means uncommon. This loving the one who has gone may in connection with just one or two other easily supplied elements furnish a highly efficient combination lock to insure the perpetuation of a neurosis. One should not, it is said, contract a new marriage while there is yet life in the remains of the old, and this is excellent reasoning not capable of being directly controverted, but only modified. Yet there will always be life in the memories and the remnants of the old marriage until the love that attached to the first love object is transferred to another; love is not an entity and not external to ourselves, but something within us which causes us to twine our tendrils first about this person and then about that. What makes it seem more certain in these cases that love is a defense reaction is that these persons themselves have a dim realization that their disease is incurable, and display a sort of beautiful indifference to that fact. The door is shut and the bolt is drawn and a lock is put upon it; reality may pound with vain hands upon the panels, but we shall dwell with our madness forever, secure in the enjoyment of our misery.

After people are divorced they have sometimes considerable difficulty in really wrenching their lives apart. If there are children, for instance, some arrangement is usually made whereby the parent who does not have custody of them may see them on occasion; this furnishes an opportunity, sometimes a necessity, for a continual renewal of the link. Common sorrow, or common anxieties concerning the children, may furnish a cement which not even the acids of hate can dissolve. The riven couple may see each other in the homes of mutual friends, or come into contact in the course of business enterprises in which both are concerned, or meet over the unclosed graves of their dear departed.

Often the psychic maladjustment of one or the other of the married pair which produces the divorce assumes the nature of a neurosis, or some milder form of personality disorder. This is frequently something produced by the intolerable conditions of married life, conditions intolerable for this particular person, not necessarily objectively so, and the divorce represents a mode of escaping from them. While these conditions and the reaction from them are in existence, the person does not realize or does not express the affection which he has for his mate, but when after the divorce there has been a partial recovery from the neurosis produced by the marriage the underlying love is again free to express itself. This may lead, perhaps in conjunction with the accumulation of sexual energy, if we may be privileged this once to speak of "energy," to advances made once more to the other person with a view to reëstablishing the marital relation. As a result of this sort of reaction on the part of one of the mates, decision may be long delayed for both, or there may actually be two or three marriages and two or three divorces with the same couple involved in all, or remarriage with another person, followed by a divorce and remarriage with the first mate.

If after divorce one does not adjust, or having adjusted runs into further difficulty, recrudescence of love for the former mate may arise as a regression. Thus it happens that the person who has loved many women since his divorce can still love his former wife after all the other affairs, during which he felt no affection for her, have run their course. Naturally an infantile channel might be chosen here also, but love for the mate is sometimes more compelling than any of those.

One's moral ideals are frequently injured by divorce. Ideals are tendencies to act out rôles of a certain sort. Intolerable circumstance may serve as an anæsthetic to these impulses, but when the strain has been temporarily eased off, the ideals reassert themselves. Or, one who has played the passive rôle in these schismatic events, who has always stood for the preservation of the relationship, may have maintained a consistent rôle in this respect too, and have steadfastly refused to stop loving the erring mate.

Sometimes one learns after divorce that it has been more expensive than he had thought that it would be, not in money, but in terms of status in his community. This may lead to a reconsideration of going back to the marriage, which may in turn involve a recrudescence of love. In this case, as in some others, we must think of love as produced to meet a necessity in the environment.

Pathological sex needs may well be such as to lead both to a breakdown of marriage and to the persistence of an emotional involvement afterwards. Sadism and masochism are quite obvious examples. There are others more difficult to diagnose. A certain woman because of a fixation on her father could only love a man who was very large, powerful, hard, and mean. But she also rebelled against such a man and found living with him impossible. This meant that she would be forced to break up her marriage with such a man, but would go on loving him nevertheless. There is the more involved case of the woman who dominates her husband, but cannot love a man who can be so handled. The husband leaves, fights the thing out, and conquers her. Then she loves him, but he is gone. The quotation from Jung in a different chapter has explained how the contained one is made more complicated, and therefore more able to fulfill the love requirements of the container, by a discontinuance of their association.

The kindly hand of time mellows our pictures of the past. The good times are ever the times that are gone. This mechanism of idealization, whereby the image of the one we love is softened, retouched, and painted over in the dark room of the mind, helps to account for the continuance of love. Aside from the fact that as time passes our unpleasant emotions are dissipated so that we may think more kindly of the one we loved, there is a real touching up of the picture by our failure to remember the small things that displeased us. Over the years a man forgets that his wife has a peasant laugh and only remembers when it roars once more unpleasantly in his ears.

These are the less complicated mechanisms. The list is already long, and we will not increase it unduly by the introduction of the more involved permutations and combinations. Perhaps we should mention the possibility, where the original fount of love was deeply tinged with ambivalence, so that the loved person of one's early days was devoutly loved and hated, that when a transference of this ambivalent love has been made from the former mate to a newer love a wholly unambivalent affection may be found to be yet attached to the former mate, so that love is won by its losing, and lost if one wins it back again.

All these things make it hard to forget the person whom one has loved and married. But no such discussion is complete which does not allow for the fact that one finds it hard to put his former love aside because he cannot and will not forget his own youth. This mechanism is powerful because unrecognized, and more or less unavoidable because it is impossible to evaluate it. Impossible to think of "that first fine careless rapture" without a sigh for what has been. Those first stirrings of the tender emotion were destined to be of permanent emotional value. Who can think of the youth that he was without pining for the times that were? And to think of the youth that one was, is not that to think of the woman to whom one was married? Unavoidable,— and pathetic. One did not marry in youth? Well, youth is always the time when one was younger. Now this is peculiar about us human beings, that as we go along we must leave part of ourselves behind, and only by so doing can we go on, and we love ever those who received our earliest emanations, and cannot recall the thrill we had in giving without experiencing a wish that we might have it again.

After so many possible reasons for the persistence of affection for the divorced husband or wife have been cited, it may well be questioned whether one is ever able to put it behind, but it is nevertheless true that one does, as is attested by the numerous cases of divorced persons who are living happily and affectionately with their second mates. It is possible in part because adult love is always a substitute for an infantile one, or may be so thought of. The attitudes that one has had toward his various love objects in childhood are combined and reorganized, somewhat altered by the adventitious elements of overt sex behavior; this is the love that one has for a husband or a wife. Fixations, pathological attachments so strong that the affects cannot be freed from the infantile images, greatly hinder this process, or thwart completely its consummation. When the adult sex object is denied, the affect may revert to the primal images—this would help to account for the increased attachment of various divorced persons to their parents—it may be diffused among many persons, or transferred to one who is made to serve as a real substitute for the first love, who may be in fact more meaningful than the first because of the practice that one has had in mobilizing himself for love. This process of coming to love somebody else has many ramifications, and is worth our attention, this chapter is centered around the problem of the old love and the new.

If love be thought of as a complex,[1] then the association chains that once touched it off may be broken by allowing their elements to be recombined in so many different ways that they can no longer be said to be organized about this one central object. This is one of the earliest tasks and the most difficult to accomplish. If it occurs smoothly, the whole complex will gradually lose its emotional importance. If, however, the complex is repressed, there will be no opportunity either for the dissipation of the affect or the breaking up of the complex by the recombination of its elements. One self-analytic individual has described the process as he thought it occurred in himself in the following words:

---

[1] See glossary for definition of terms, p. 339.

If the set of emotions connected with my wife could be called a complex, I was able to trace the gradual disappearance of that complex from the foreground of consciousness. I did not become aware of any progress in this direction until after about a year of separation. For a long time it was difficult to become used to sleeping without her. The time came when I could go to bed in a very matter of fact way without thinking at all of the fact that I used to have a companion. Naturally it is much harder to tell when a thought disappears from consciousness than it is to tell when one arises, although the latter is difficult too, but I believe that I could place the date at approximately ten months after separation. It would still happen once in a while that I would experience the feeling of loss when I went to go to sleep and found that she was no longer there, but I believe that this became increasingly rare from that time on. Other things, too, that had previously set off a very painful chain of emotions, now began to lose their affective power. At one time the sight of a woman wearing a fur coat of a certain sort, the sight of dainty underwear displayed in a shop window, shapely legs, a trim foot, a flashing smile, eyes with a certain sort of luster, any of these things would at once throw me into a terrific emotional storm. But I came later to evaluate all these apparently without reference to my wife. When I had first separated from her I had not found it possible to have her picture exposed in the room in which I lived, but later I found that it added a certain warmth to my life, and enabled me to link up the various epochs of my existence if I could have at hand the reminder of what once had been. One of the most poignant reminders of my wife had been the improvised medicine chest, the shoe shining kit, the collection of more or less valuable papers, that she had gathered together for me just prior to our separation, and upon which she had written directions in her pitiful little childish hand. That pathetic little attempt to do everything possible for me that she could before the inevitable break has not even yet wholly lost the emotion that is connected with it, but the thought of it is much less likely now to throw me into a severe conflict.

The first really acceptable love object was possibly a substitute for the missing wife, and the possibility of transference, or of rebound, would seem to be indicated by the fact that I fell in love with her very quickly, almost at once, and by the fact that she was physically not dissimilar to my wife. Yet she was enough of a self-evident value that such would not necessarily be the case. I saw her in a setting that was somewhat conducive to romance, and she was socially, culturally, and physically sufficiently different from my wife that I was able to tell myself that there was here no question of a rebound, but a love affair that stood on its own feet. The affair ended when the girl rather suddenly married another man, but I was not greatly disappointed. After that my affection gradually shifted to my wife again. This was assisted by her assuming a more receptive attitude toward it, although she still refused to live with me.

This narrative illustrates the slow steps by which the associations centering around the absent love object are gradually dissolved. It also shows what part subsequent love affairs, even the transitory ones, may have in the readjustment of the love life. This man's affair, partaking as it did of the nature of a rebound and a compulsion, was followed by a return of his affections to the absent wife, but it represented a step toward a final freeing of himself from her. There is produced in this process, if it goes on without undue complication, somewhere along the line a fusion of love objects, as evidenced by a fusion of images and a confusion of names. The product may be thought of as a generalized love object, retrogressive, introverted, and probably tracing to the mother as the archetype. In this stage there may be actual confusion of identity, fusion of faces, combinations of names, so that one thinks, "This is so-and-so or so-and-so" or "Now just who is this?" Sometimes it appears that where the emotions centering around the mate have been confused and conflicting, the name of the mate comes to be a name that is given to the confusion, and returns to the lips when the confusion raises again, even though it is a second wife who arouses it.

This fusion of images, apparently a necessary step on the road to establishing a real transference of one's affection, should be carefully differentiated from the extroverted rationalization that expresses itself in the words, "All women serve the same purpose,"—which is also connected usually with the more or less conscious attempt to cheapen sex. This latter is more definitely self-protective, and denotes a considerable inner involvement with the love object from whom it is intended to defend one's self; it is only protective armor. When one is once en route to freedom, some very interesting little reactions crop out, whether due to repression which operates suddenly, or to use of which one suddenly becomes aware. A man while talking to the writer had occasion to take his wife's picture out of his pocketbook. He handed it over to him with some comment concerning her attractiveness. When the proper remarks had been passed and the picture had been returned to him, he glanced at it in passing. "Do you know," he said musingly, "it seems strange to me now that I could ever have lived with this woman? Unreal, unbelievable." Occasionally also when one looks at a picture he feels the world to be fading out, is only conscious of it as something existent in the fringes of his consciousness, and he lives again in the world of the past, become once more suddenly alive and the scene of a booming and buzzing confusion.

The man whose narrative has been quoted was assisted by a habit of facing his difficulties with a fair degree of frankness. When there is a certain amount of repression, things connected with such a complex may retain their affective power much longer. A woman whose husband left her four years before said:

"There are lots of things that still call back my husband to me. Just this morning I was in church and I happened to look at the program and saw a certain date, a date on which a church reception is scheduled to be held. Something went through me; a very painful sensation. Suddenly I felt all choked up inside and I thought I was going to cry. It was the same day of the year that my husband left me, four years ago, and it all came back to me just like that. I can't understand that, because under no circumstances would I ever go back to him. If he ever came to me and asked me to go back and live with him I think I'd commit suicide.

"My husband used to call up and put on an English accent like George Arliss. George Arliss was his favorite actor. He would talk that way for a while, and he could disguise his voice so well that I would nearly always be fooled. The other night someone called and asked for somebody, a Mrs. So-and-so. Then he asked whether this was such and such a number, but when I told him it wasn't he didn't hang up right away, but tried to keep talking. I cried after that. I had a terrible shock and thought about it for days. I kept wondering if it really was my husband who called, and it worried me. I couldn't imagine what he might be intending to do next."

The thought of going back to the former mate is often reinforced by cogent arguments which have a basis in reality. Psychologically, those who have lived together understand each other better than any other persons are likely to do. And people remain, as has been seen, affectionally bound to each other, and for a multitude of reasons. Economically and socially people remain tied for many years, in spite of their best efforts to extricate themselves. So inconsiderable a thing as the possession of a house and the furniture in it may argue powerfully for the resumption of the former relationship as contrasted with the formation of a new one. These lines of argument are often made to seem very convincing, when, the bitterness of the break having worn away, people come to think that they did not after all have very good cause for their separation, and begin to yearn once more for the old accustomed chains. So people think when old love makes return, forcing them disjoined under her brazen yoke once more!

But the arguments against the resumption of the relation are not less powerful. First, since people rarely acquire a very deep understanding of the causes of their matrimonial break, thinking only of incidents, objective causes of friction, and not comprehending at all the deadly struggle of personalities which was involved therein, there is but little likelihood that in a second marriage the same troubles would not arise as in the first. People will be more careful the second time, and will avoid some of their more obvious mistakes, but they cannot avoid being also more self-conscious, and consciousness of self is ever opposed to real emotional fusion with the loved one. People often think that they have learned much by their misfortunes, but since to learn from these requires a very thorough understanding of one's own personality trends and their repercussions and intricate patterns of influence on other personalities, the writer thinks that they rarely have learned much that will be helpful in making the same marriage work a second time. Nothing short of a complete overhauling, such as a psychoanalyst might give to a patient with whom he spent much time, certainly no mere decision to be good, no throwing of a different element of the personality into control, no conversion, can be adequate for the needs of the occasion.

But if people have acquired a thorough understanding of the causes of their difficulty, and have sufficiently revamped their personalities to enable them to adjust to each other, it is by no means settled that they ought therefore go back together. Their marriage may have lost its assets. It has lost, for one thing, privacy. He who gets a divorce must unfortunately take the world into his confidence. He has announced that he and his wife can not get along, and has asked the verdict of a candid world. He has committed himself on the matter and can not go back to her without reversing his decision, which is always hard,—*stare decisis* represents not only a principle of law but a fundamental trait of human nature. If he does go back, after making such an announcement, he lives then like a goldfish in an aquarium. He can never effectively draw the curtain again. Nor can he ever feel free from the feeling that people are asking, "Well, I wonder how they are getting along now?" Few marriages could endure long without privacy and the confidence of others in their security.

Let us suppose that these assets by some miracle have been saved, what is the situation then? One is able to relax his defenses in married love as contrasted with that which is not so formalized because of a feeling of security. That asset too is gone, at least for one of the partners, for the one who did not wish the marriage broken; if both parties wished it so, then neither can feel secure again. Aside from the disturbing incidents of the break,—we are here assuming that the very difficult task of putting these out of mind in such a way that they can do no harm and engender no hate has been accomplished—it is very likely that the emotional rapport of the pair, the feeling of being in intimate touch with each other and of mutual interchange of material, intellectual, and emotional resources, has been severely damaged. For a time, at least, the free giving and taking of intimacy have been discontinued. People have lost the habit of telling their secrets at the midnight hour. Can they reëstablish it? With all this, the physical and emotional bond which we call love has had an excellent opportunity to deteriorate, though it may have preserved a fair exterior it can still be rotten on the inside, it has had an opportunity to be differently defined in such a way that taking it up on the old basis is made impossible,—absence may make the heart grow fonder but it also makes people forget how to live with each other. Aside from the fact that the home has lost its privacy, and its assets, this simple fact that people may unconsciously have grown apart, may have changed so that each no longer represents the longed for person-that-was, constitutes a powerful argument against remarriage with the same mate.

But there is real reason for hesitating in the decisions to take a second mate and cast the old aside forever. Where one has contracted a second marriage without being sufficiently free of the first, the results may well be disastrous. Stekel has analyzed a case of impotence in which the main causative factor seemed to be a repressed love for the former wife. A case which has come to the attention of the writer is that of a woman who repressed her love for her first husband during a particularly trying period, rendering herself psychically completely inaccessible to him, apparently turning against him finally and completely. In her second marriage, contracted very shortly after her divorce, she was completely frigid, and was never at all *en rapport* with her second husband. Years afterward the love for her first husband came to the surface. Of course there was repression in both these cases, and that may account for part of the effect of the persisting attachments to the former mates, as well as account for the persistence of the attachments.

And there are no doubt a good many cases in these days when access to the divorce courts is so frequently had when the best advice that could be given to the former partners would be that they should go back together and learn to adjust their lives to the necessities of the married state. But having said this, we must immediately qualify it, for there are at least as many possibilities of error in this direction as in the other. Serious persons hesitate to counsel others to break up their marriages, they should remember that it is just as serious a matter to advise them to go back to a marriage that has already been broken up. Only where people obviously divorced in haste on account of circumstances that are not likely to recur again, or where after the break both seem to have developed greatly in insight and to have retained their mutual affection almost intact, should this advice be given—and these are rare cases—in all others the counsel of wisdom would be that the persons involved should finally accept the decision of the facts, however unwelcome, and say that since they have tried to get along together and have nevertheless failed, they must take this as diagnostic of an essential weakness in their relationship.[2]

---

[2] A very revelatory series of dreams showing the conflict between old and new love objects was brought in to the investigator by a male subject. In this series he has apparently discussed in symbolic form the same things which had been the themes of his conscious ruminations, and has arrived at almost the same conclusions. The dreams, as they were written out by the subject, follow:

1   I said that I always tried to make myself interesting to people by doing what they liked to do. I saw a dog copulating. When he withdrew his penis the end of it was split in two halves.

2   I was buying a roller coaster wagon. The one which I bought had very high wheels. There were some smaller models lying about which I did not take. The front end of the wagon was peculiarly constructed in that the tongue engaged between two outstretched projections.

3   A friend of mine was trundling along a motorcycle. It had two flat tires. It was going over rough ground. He boasted of the number of miles he could go on a gallon of gas. I heard some noise of the engine going. Perhaps he got on it and rode away.

4   I was in a strange city. Some one was with me who lived there; I went to a place similar to a roadhouse and purchased a meal. I thought it was not quite right and I feared its expensiveness. I ordered ham and eggs and something else, which may have been spinach. The proprietor and the waiter were very obsequious. I thought they sold liquor there too. I thought this food would make me sick and was surprised to find that it did not.

5   I am in a large place resembling a hotel in which I once lived with my wife. I think of the people in the two ends as being compared with regard to something, perhaps their financial ratings, something competitive anyhow. There has been a murder or a death in one of the basement rooms by a bursting radiator. A married couple have died, at any rate. In the room opening out of it is a Chinese laundry. I go into the laundry. I wonder whether or not this will hurt his business. The Chinaman holds up my two unironed shirts, one with red stripes and one with blue, and I find them run together. I complain, and he shows me that it has happened to others also. I am still unsatisfied with his explanation.

It seems to be a series of choice dreams, bringing out in disguised form the arguments for and against each other, and moving toward decision, although not, in this series, apparently settling the matter, or settling it only tentatively.

Briefly, we have throughout a symbolic thinking out and a working out in terms of distant associations and unverbalized thoughts of the main problems of this subject's mental life. He is

Many times it happens that one is so bound up with the former mate that release is only to be had through the intervention of psychoanalytic mechanisms. The theory is that where the attachment to a certain person is ambivalent, both love and hate being present in fairly equal quantities, and where the conflict is not faced frankly, either the love or the hate not being admitted, the normal movement of the affections is interfered with and any change in the love life is prevented. But one may by talking to some sympathetic and meaningful person release these emotions, obtaining what the psychoanalysts call a catharsis. Associated with catharsis, building itself up at the same time, is transference, a mechanism whereby the emotions released by catharsis attach themselves to the listener. Thus catharsis depends upon transference and transference depends upon catharsis.

Transference is both an opportunity and a danger to the divorced person. Transference and catharsis present a way out, and one which he should not neg-

---

trying to decide between his former wife and his callipygian mistress. He thinks, (1) "Well, I have reason to be worried about my love life, on the counts of impotence and attractiveness, but I think I can get around that by adopting a policy of doing things for the other person rather than for myself. (2) But I've got to decide between these two women. On the whole, I think I'll take the mistress, intercourse with her is very delightful, and she has other points as well. (3) But maybe the thing for me to do is to remain single after all. It has its advantages, in the way of economy especially, though I must admit that I think that is rather for other people than for myself. (4) Now when I go to New York, of course, my friends will all try to get me married off, but women I would meet there might not satisfy or might be very expensive. And I also might have to go through a period of rather low-grade promiscuity until I get settled. (5) Anyhow I'm not going back to my wife. It would be too difficult in living with all the unfortunate memories, besides, things have not really been ironed out. I know she says it would be the same in another marriage, but I do not accept her version of this thing."

lect, but the existence of uncatharticated emotion ready to be tapped in such fashion constitutes a danger to him. It makes him peculiarly liable to be swept off his feet and is likely to cause him to form unsuitable attachments through the mechanism of transference. Designing women have known for many generations, of course, that they might acquire power over the man who has suffered a misfortune in his love life by allowing him to talk of it. It should also be noted that the existence of unrecognized conflicts in the mind of the divorced person renders him liable to the peculiarly unfortunate phenomenon of love at first sight, which is always pathological, partaking of the character of a compulsion, and which rarely turns out well.

It is necessary for the divorcé to release the affects bound up with the absent mate and then to reorganize them around a second love object, which must be made emotionally equal to the first. It is preferable that the analyst and the love object be different persons, otherwise the analyzed one may be enchained by the transference to an otherwise unsuitable person. In addition, the psychoanalytic rapport may give rise to innumerable complications in close association.

Sinclair Lewis' *Dodsworth* is an excellent literary study of the reconstruction of the love life after divorce. One is led to believe that it is subjectively autobiographical, although it is probably not objectively so. Dodsworth's history seems to fit into our categories. He had a sex affair with Nante before his high-level affair with Edith. The affair with Nante played a very real part in his rehabilitation, and he left it considerably cheered. He was first driven to Edith by loneliness and sorrow over Fran's defection. Little by little he told her his troubles, and he built up a transference; that is, by talking to her he became dependent on her. She helped him to become conscious of a long-standing resentment against Fran, an emotion which, unrecognized and unexpressed, had hindered his readjustment. Expressing his revolt at last, he was released from his subjection to his former wife, and acquired a new conception of his own rôle.

But if he played a new rôle now, he did not cease to play the old one too. Conscious of his affection for and dependence upon Edith, he was not aware that he was no longer tied to Fran. There ensued a period of comparison between the two women; the conflict was precipitated by Fran's desire to return to his roof. Pity for Fran, the habit of years, and the belief that he still loved her drew him back to her. He found Fran as attractive as ever, but he was unwilling to fit into the accustomed niche. He had lost the habit of subjection, and—the emotions which had previously made freedom seem well lost for love. He had, furthermore, recast his judgment of Fran more completely than he himself realized. This, too, is typical; when we come to see a person at long-range, without the disturbing factor of love the outline may remain the same but the shading is different. He returned to Edith, this time for good, the comparison having been at length ended in Edith's favor. She had not Fran's glitter, but she was her equal and he loved her more. Fran could settle her own problems. (Readers of *Dodsworth* will have no difficulty in tracing out in the story the mechanism of alienation and various other mechanisms which we have treated here.)

When the choice has been made, the emotional

participation of the divorcé in his second marriage depends in large part upon the completeness of the transference which he is able to make. This transference depends upon liberation from the psychological *enclos* in which he was involved with his first mate; certainly the absence of repressions and opportunity for the release of affects by catharsis are necessary conditions of such liberation, but the writer is by no means sure that other, and to him unknown, factors are involved as well. Enslavement to the first mate aside, the defense reactions which are frequently produced by a matrimonial break are likely to continue to affect unfavorably one's relations with the opposite sex, so that even in marriage it is difficult to let the bars as completely down as was done for the first mate. (This occasionally seems to cause one to embrace a second love object which is relatively meaningless, because, being unattractive, it is therefore harmless.) The defense reactions are of course complicated and reinforced if love for the first mate persists, and they in turn help it to endure, for they preclude giving it a real competitor. Ability to form a second attachment of equal value with the first is sometimes lessened by age, since the strength of the sex urge has so diminished that a relationship with a member of the opposite sex has less capital to start with than the previous one had. Pathological adjustments of personality, as the development of homosexual trends after divorce, or a protest against them, might also very unfortunately affect a second marriage.

The second mate is of course sometimes chosen before the first is cast aside. That may, or may not mean that certain problems of adjustment have been avoided; the case is not so clear as one might think, for these too rapid choices may reveal a breathless eagerness arising from a deep sense of insecurity. To those who are too tolerant to be censorious, this jumping back into the bramble bush, though the avowed purpose be to achieve the restoration of one's vision, may seem funny.

The husband-to-be of the divorcé-to-be has a certain funny-paper humor for the spectators. He makes his appearance in Reno from one day to three months before the granting of the decree. I remember one afternoon sitting in a booth having my hair washed and observing across the way a great mound of a woman submitting luxuriously to what seemed like a tiny lawn-mower being run over her face and shoulders which were shining with grease.

"Whatever is being done to her?" I asked.

"That's a contouration facial," my shampooer answered, with the hauteur of the initiated.

At that instant a small and elderly man edged down the narrow passage and outside the now closely curtained booth opposite he paused and called softly: "Yoo-hoo."

An arm swept back the curtain, the mammoth lady smiled, and the small gentleman tenderly leaned over and kissed her cold-creamed cheek, and murmured, "See you later, darling," and was gone.

I caught my operator grinning. "Yesterday he gave her a permanent wave and to-day the facial. This morning she got her divorce, and to-night they get married."

To me this was a romance founded on realism, and I prophesy that they will live happy ever afterward.[3]

It has been said that the marriages of people who have been once divorced are happier than those of others. The writer does not wish to be understood as endorsing that statement, because there are too many things to be said on *a priori* grounds against it, and

---

[3] Grace Hegger Lewis, "Just What Is Reno Like," *Scribner's,* January, 1929, p. 44. From *Scribner's Magazine* by permission. Copyright, 1928, by Charles Scribner's Sons.

too many cases which belie it, but it may serve to reveal to us another side of the picture. There are many persons, indeed, who marry without love, —the writer has studied some of these. Apparently such marriages represent rebellion against a member of one's own family, perhaps the patriarch on whom one is fixated. There is less probability that one will do this a second time. There are other cases in which the first marriage was so bad that any comparison must inevitably favor the second. Let us subtract all such cases from our reckoning, and make due allowances for those in which people are not really happy but are trying very hard to seem so.

We have shown that an unhappy marriage which ends in divorce may have disastrous effects upon personality, which may prevent successful adjustment in a second marriage. If the affects are not liberated from the first mate, the second will be in a very difficult position. Security-seeking mechanisms, too, thrown into a dominant position by the one marital experience, may have a not obvious but nevertheless profound influence. One who has lost his normal biological self-confidence may betray the fear of losing his second mate by an increased clinging to her, and by giving her a very demanding sort of affection; with certain mates these traits must operate to his disadvantage.

But divorced persons do marry and do live happily with their second mates. And among the acquaintances of us all are exemplars enough to enable us to say that sometimes, on account of insight that they have dearly bought, tolerance that they have hardly won, and progressive liberation from their infantile love objects, people love better for having had a little practice.

CHAPTER SEVEN

Pride and the Divorcé; Salve for Old Wounds

IT is a peculiarity of pride that the more it is wounded the stronger it grows; it waxes fat with starvation. The moralist may insist that pride goes before a fall, but it is the concern of the scientist to point out that it also comes after. Thus it comes about that of all persons the most proud are those who have the most of which to be ashamed. The delicate tendrils of the divorcé's ego feelings have been sorely damaged; they were damaged because they were delicate and they are delicate because they were damaged; the divorcé was hurt because he was prideful and he is prideful because he was hurt.

The wounds that divorce inflicts upon self-respect make it a harrowing experience for the best integrated, even though the pains of love denied enter into the picture not at all. It is doubly trying, perhaps, because of the fact that the people who usually get divorces are the sort of people who are already more than normally concerned with problems of their own status, whether they were so when first married, or have become so as a result of connubial conflict. To be sure the sufferings of pride are more easily endured if they are not complicated by the pangs of unrequited love, but in concrete cases it is often impossible to separate the two motives of love and pride, and incidents must be somewhat arbitrarily classified as illustrating either the one or the other. The ego-drives, it should be noted, are likely to be more subtly manifested than are the impulses of love, and there is accordingly a greater opportunity for error in tracing them out.

It has been said that people rarely just agree to disagree and that one person usually takes a more active rôle in dissolving the relationship than does the other. Reconstruction presents different problems for those who have taken the active, and those who have taken the passive rôle. A wife told her husband one morning that she was in love with another man, and wished to have a divorce in order that she might marry him. He was much taken aback, but finally consented. In the case of this man the primary problem of reconstruction was learning to live with the fact that he had failed in an important function of his life, and this problem characterizes the conflicts of many persons similarly situated. For the wife the major problem was that of a return to respectability, and this necessity is more keenly realized than it seems to be. For both these people there were elements of pride in the situation.

A more extreme illustration of the damage done to the self-respect of the discarded one was the following: A woman was rejected by her husband under peculiarly humiliating circumstances. She had occasion to visit the house in which she had formerly lived with him, a friend who had taken some responsibility in aiding her to adjust accompanied her. Approaching the house she started for the back door. The friend asked why she did not go in the front door, and she replied, "Well, I'm really not

good enough to go in the front door...." a symbolic expression of her self-abasement. The problems
of adjustment of the person who is thus discarded
are likely to be more severe at the time of the break,
although final readjustment may be relatively easier
and more complete than that of the more ruthless
partner. The very trying situation at the time of the
break leads occasionally to very interesting phenomena. In one case the problem was solved suddenly
by a hysteric birth and rebirth, by some writing,
wish-fulfilling in its nature, which just had to be
done, and by partial dissociation so that the woman
later could not believe that it was really she who had
for eighteen years been the wife of so-and-so. In
another case the person apparently became rather
suddenly aware that the transition had been made,
although the process of reconstruction had in fact
been gradual.

These cases where the one mate or the other,
apparently without justification, breaks up the marriage, are rarely as simple as they seem. They often
represent on the side of the person who takes the
lead a long-standing rebellion which has but slowly
come to light, and on the side of the other a desire
to maintain the *status quo,* and perhaps to keep the
other person in his subordinate position. The judgment of the community, based only on overt acts,
and having no connection with the inner realities of
the marriage, is likely to be quite wrong.

Occasional newspaper accounts tell of the revolt
of a model husband. For ten, twenty, or more years
he has been the very impersonation and incarnation
of all the husbandly virtues, but one day he puts his
affairs in order and entrains for parts unknown, or
runs off with his secretary, or, more courageously,

files suit for divorce. In a recent Chicago case papers were filed by a husband who for twenty-three years had done all the housework, prepared the meals, washed the dishes, done the shopping, and turned over his weekly pay check faithfully to his wife. On one occasion his wife twice threw away the supplies which he had bought for their Christmas dinner, and he was forced to eat in a restaurant. In other less simple cases the smoothness and apparent good feeling in a marriage are obtained by the subjection of either husband or wife; when these marriages break up, the friends of the pair are mystified because they "always thought they got along so well."

The problem of pride is more subtly involved where there has been in the marriage a definite dominance-subordination relationship. If the marriage is broken chiefly by the efforts of the subordinated one, a special case of the situation mentioned above may be produced. The break represents rebellion, readjustment on the one side involves a feeling of satisfaction over a successful revolt, complicated by the pangs of conscience; on the other side it is necessary to assimilate the two facts that one has lost an important battle for prestige and been spurned as a love object. If, however, the marriage has been broken by the much loved person who dominated the other person, readjustment for the master involves only a return to respectability, while for the servant it becomes a very baffling, almost a hopeless problem.

Jung has noted that there is likely to arise in marriage a relationship which may be described as that of container and contained. It is here thought of, though Jung does not explicitly so describe it, as a special form of dominance-subordination relationship. Breaking a relationship of this sort has effects which may be differentiated from those of any other interruption of marital life. It may be well before using Jung's concepts in interpretation of our own particular sort of phenomena to let him elaborate them:

"Discrepancies in tempo, on the one side, and the range of the mental personality, on the other, produce the typical difficulty, which exhibits its full force at the critical moment.

"I do not wish to leave the impression that by great 'range of mental personality' I always mean particularly rich or big natures. This is not the case. I mean rather a certain intricacy of structure, a stone with many facets, as compared to a simple cube. They are many-sided natures, as a rule problematic, burdened with hereditary units which are hard to reconcile. Adaptation to such natures and their adaptation to simpler natures will always be difficult. Persons with such somewhat dissociated natures generally have the gift of splitting off incompatible habits of character for some length of time, and thus apparently becoming simple; or else their versatility, the changeful character will prove their special charm. The other may easily lose himself in such somewhat mazy natures, that is to say, he finds so many possibilities of experience in them that his personal interest is fully employed. It may not always be in an agreeable way, for he will often be occupied in tracing the other through all manner of deviations. Nevertheless, so many experiences are possible that the simpler personality is surrounded by them, even captivated; it gets immersed in the larger personality; it cannot see beyond it. This is quite the rule: a woman, mentally, fully contained in her husband; a man, emotionally, fully contained in his wife. This might be termed the problem of the contained and the container." [1]

---

[1] Jung, C. G., *Marriage as a Psychological Relationship,* in Keyserling, Herman Alexander, *The Book of Marriage,* New York, Harcourt, Brace and Company, 1926, pp. 354 *ff.*

The mate who exceeds the other in the rapidity of his reactions, and whose decisions are based upon a consideration of the largest number of factors, will tend to assume the rôle of the container, while the other becomes the contained. The relationship is also conditioned by the relative strength of the physical needs of the pair.

The speed of mental reactions is important. When domestic mastery is at issue, the race is after all usually to the swift. The person whose mind moves swiftly manages to keep several steps ahead of his antagonist, anticipates his moves, and defeats him before he has a chance to mobilize his resources. The quick thinker has more to say and says it with less hesitation, seizes an opening more rapidly, gets angry more easily, and bewilders his opponent by a succession of attitudes and moods. It should not be thought that this is a purely intellectual process, for a rapid change of moods and a facile mobilization of emotional resources is of great value in holding the attention of a mate or in beating him into submission. The good rule of domestic strategy is that he gains the victory who "gets there firstest with the mostest men."

Unpredictability may likewise be an advantage. A despot whose cruelty is steady and relentless is likely to be less feared than a whimsical one. Just so no wife can keep her husband dancing attendance so well as she who shows herself capricious. Shakespeare realized this when he made Cleopatra choose her moods by the principle of contraries. Unpredictability, from the standpoint of another person, may arise because one is several steps ahead of that other in his thought processes, because one bases his decision upon wider grounds, or because one has

dissociated a number of his impulses, so that he cannot understand or organize himself. Such a person
acts quickly because he does not think thoroughly.
A slower person, although better organized, may
well be engulfed in such an infinitely mutable and
mazy personality. The resultant preoccupation with
the other's moods need not, as Jung has noted, be
pleasant, and it may be questioned whether it is ever
so. *The Atmosphere of Love* is centered around the
problem of the shifting of the rôles of container and
contained among three persons; who shall be container or contained is determined in that story, apparently, by relative unpredictability and difficulty of
control.

A third trait of mind that is of importance in this
connection is the number of factors upon which decision is usually based. The person who is able to
base his decision upon the widest range of factors,
and to organize himself most completely into his
decision, will usually prevail. The chess player who
can organize in his mind the largest number of plays
must always win. A great range of mentality may
conduce to slowness, in which case the one advantage
must be balanced against the other. The slower and
better organized person may suffer through endless
verbal barrages and be hard put to it to parry the
flashing thrusts that are made at him, but he can
defend himself at length and if he wishes he can
conduct the discussion in a manner wholly incomprehensible to his more superficial mate. We should also
note that the stability of this type of personality is
a great mental advantage. Various combinations are
possible. The mate with speedy reactions may as like
as not win all the battles and lose all the wars to the
slower and better organized mate. Or one mate may

win the mastery of the other by one quality or another, say by greater facility in the organization of emotional resources for combat, in plain words, by a quick temper, and force the other person to simplify his personality artificially through the mechanism of repression. The subordinated one is thus cudgelled into the rôle of the contained.

Whatever the reason, the container holds the interest of the contained, and the contained does not always hold the interest of the container. The contained is wholly bound up in the marriage, makes most of the sacrifices to keep it intact,—in short, submits. The container does not find the same complete emotional fulfillment in marriage, therefore he is always "looking out the window." A workable compromise, as has been suggested, is that whereby the wife is intellectually contained in the husband and the husband is emotionally contained in the wife.

The container, needing to be understood, needing a love object who can hold his attention, needing, in other words, to be organized from without, will usually, after some unsuccessful attempts to force his mate to play the opposite rôle, take the initiative in breaking up the marriage. After divorce the problems of container and contained are still different. The container has lost, probably, a tractable and somewhat dull mate, and he may come in time to realize that as such she had her points. The contained has lost his life, the boundless and perplexing individual within whom all his possibilities of feeling and sensation were carried and contained. The container may reorganize his personality in such a way as to find unity within himself. Or the contained, complicated by the process of divorcing, may develop those qualities whose lack the container previously deplored. A case comes to mind in which the container wife enforced a severance. Coming later to be more at one with herself she made some overtures of reconciliation, as divorced persons frequently do, but found the contained husband, previously simple, now become so complicated and tortuous a personality that she could no longer control his responses. An endless dissertation might be written upon the struggle to contain and the necessity of being contained, which, coexisting in one and the same person, combine to produce an everlasting thwart.

It does not seem to do great violence to the facts to regard this relationship as a variant of the dominance-subordination relationship. The fact that the dominant mate who has on the surface every reason to be satisfied with a marriage but whose interest is not absorbed by the relationship frequently takes the lead in severing a relationship may be explained in terms of these concepts; motivation for the rebellion of the simpler personality is also made more clear. A background for the understanding of some surprising reversals is also furnished; thus dominant women, who profess later to have always wished for the sweet pleasures of submission, sometimes find their love and respect for their husbands greatly increased when these latter have taken the lead in breaking up the marriage, and have on that one point been triumphant. (One such woman, after her husband had quite cruelly disavowed her, said, "Well, the one thing about my husband that I most admire and respect is that he has fought this through and won his battle. I never thought he was man enough to do it.") This revival of respect for the rejected mate may take place on quite other grounds; as the simple nature is made more complex by a crisis in the marriage, so the complex is made more simple, and the container may discover at last, though usually too late, those unplumbed depths and those problematic responses that he so long sought in vain. A new light is also thrown upon the sophistication of simple folk after they have been divorced, as well as upon the fact that complicated personalities, reverting to simplicity, sometimes identify themselves at last with the moral code of their fathers and long for the simplicities of conjugal love.

Other things both inside and outside the divorcé condition the extent to which his pride is involved in the marital break. The nature of the break is of course quite important. If one is able to put the blame entirely on the other person he may avoid much of the injury to his self-feelings; the woman who seemed of all those studied to have assimilated her divorce most easily was married to a sadist who subsequently had a sanity hearing. If one endorses the conventional moral code, adultery becomes a final and definitive cause for divorce, and one need look no further but may lay all the blame at the door of the mate; this is helpful as far as it goes, but is sometimes offset by the fact that adultery in the mate strikes us in a peculiarly sensitive spot. Identification with the moral order is not an asset if one feels that one has been one's self to blame. Publicity, although not odious to some people, and pleasing in some obscure way to many who profess to abhor it, may greatly exacerbate the injuries to one's dignity. How much one feels the disgrace of being divorced depends also in part upon how much one has identified himself with the married state (and this may be connected with the previously noted distinction between the container and the contained). It has also been noted that sometimes the reason for the delay in breaking up the marriage is shame before one's friends over the fact that two people have not been congenial. This affects the extent to which one's pride is involved, also.

Something important occurs in the mind of the divorced person when he hears that his former mate has remarried. Before it has always been possible to think of the divorce as tentative, as a feeling out and experimentation with various possibilities. But when the thing has been sealed by another marriage, there is no going back. That would occasion regret only to those who are emotionally involved in their former mates, but the thing is likely to have other implications which hurt the pride of all. A man has been cast away because he did not come up to his wife's matrimonial requirements; as long as she remains unmarried he is able to say that her requirements are unreasonable and perhaps to solace himself with the thought that she will never find another man who will suit her as well. But when she marries, his successor has been found. Perhaps the man she marries is of a distinctly lower order than her first husband, socially, economically, intellectually, in the opinion of previous incumbent, and the first feels himself disgraced at having such a successor. And, it must be added, it not infrequently happens that those who are tired of the demands of a too complex mate sometimes err the second time by selecting one who is too simple. If divorce is followed immediately by remarriage, it is made to seem that the first husband was unable to hold his wife in the face of the superior attractiveness of the second, that he did not measure up to the same high standards as his second candidate. Marriage, too, carries with it certain property rights, or, better, there are certain elements of property feeling in the love relationship, and although we may formally disavow these, we find it hard to give them up entirely. But when there has been a second marriage, we can think of these no more.

Thoughtless and unintended damage is done to many persons who already have trouble enough by makers of jests and clever young reporters in search of copy. There is much in the marital woes of others that appeals to the risibilities of people who like broad humor, but it can well be imagined that people to whom divorce is at best a crisis of anguish and humiliation will suffer immeasurably from being made the subject of a ribald jest. The following clever story, for instance, obtained a rather widespread publication:

MARRIAGE IS "ON ROCKS"

HUSBAND ARRESTED WHEN HE THROWS STONES AT HIS WIFE'S HOUSE

(...)—The marital life of Mr. and Mrs. (John Blank) of this city was termed "rocky" in divorce proceedings filed Monday but the rest of this story is about rocks, too. Friends visiting Mrs. (Blank) after court recessed were told: "Our romance just went on the rocks."

At that moment a fusillade of assorted rocks and bricks crashed against the walls of the house. Rushing to the windows the guests saw Mr. (Blank), a rock clutched in either hand, being led away by policemen.

"I'll show her what it means to put our marriage on the rocks," he muttered.

Without going into wearisome detail, we can say that the possibilities for wounds to the self-feelings are manifold in any case of divorcement. These wounds may be thought of as falling into one or the other of two classes: (1) Those which are primary, arising from the situation itself, and (2) those which arise from the way in which a person is treated, or thinks that he is treated, in view of his divorced situation.

The little prideful actions of divorced persons are so various and so devious that classification is difficult. For the purposes of this treatment, we have divided the actions which seem to have the function of permitting one to assimilate wounds to one's dignity, or of restoring one's self-respect into three classes: (1) Those where one's thoughts run over the old situations, (2) Defense reactions operative in the present, and (3) Compensatory drives. It will be seen that the time basis of these is furnished by the familiar categories of the past, the present, and the future. Actions or thoughts of the first sort enable one to work over the past, in part at least neutralizing its bad effects. Actions of the second sort, defense reactions proper, prevent further wounding in the present, either by preventing a revival of old conflicts or by warding off further blows like the first. Compensatory drives may be thought of as pertaining chiefly to future adjustments. It is not intended to emphasize any such distinctions; they are simply made in order to enable the material covered in this chapter to be classified.

(1) One way of assimilating the past is to reconstruct it in phantasy in such a way that it can be more pleasantly thought of. This in time may become a source of real distortion in our memories; in some cases the writer was forced to conclude that the subjects of these studies gave him very much

rationalized and reëdited accounts of their experiences, certainly in no case was this completely corrected out. Just as the little boy going home from the baseball game in which he has not done well may conjure up imaginary experiences in which he shines much more brightly, the person who has had disappointments in his marital life sometimes works the whole thing over in his mind and achieves a much more satisfactory result.

A woman who was made the subject of somewhat extended study wrote out the story of her married life, casting it in the literary mold of allegory, while she was experiencing the first agonies of the break with her husband. This was in the form of a story, *Christian's Crises,* and a sequel to it. The allegories recapitulated the whole story of her marriage. In this story her own rôle was idealized, she gave herself a complimentary name and wrote of herself as doing generous, wise things. Her rival was given the unsavory name of Mrs. Real Stench, a play upon her initials and the vowels in her name. The husband was made to reject this other woman finally and emphatically, although there was no reason in the facts of the case for thinking that he had done so. The story was buttressed by biblical quotations so thoroughly that sometimes the quotations took up more space than the story. This writing partook almost of the character of unconscious writing; it was something that just had to get written; when the woman awoke in the morning those characters and their adventures had to be recorded. (The desire, by the way, to write a book about the unusual experiences of one's divorce is a very common one.)

The narratives mentioned above are perhaps worth more detailed attention. They typify admirably phantasy reconstruction of the past. The woman who wrote the words that follow was discarded, cast off, repudiated; the job was done thoroughly and ruthlessly. Yet in her narrative she is in the end victorious. The first of these stories, *Christian's Crises,* was dedicated, not without humor, to The Only Woman My Father Ever Loved. The reproach is obvious. In Chapter Nineteen the villainess was introduced:

"St. Matthew 18:7 to 14. Woe unto the world because of offenses! for it must needs be that offenses come; but woe to that man by whom the offense cometh! Wherefore if thy hand or thy foot offend thee, cut them off, and cast them from thee: it is better for thee to enter into life halt or maimed, rather than having two hands or two feet to be cast into everlasting fire. And if thine eye offend thee, pluck it out, and cast it from thee: it is better for thee to enter into life with one eye, rather than having two eyes to be cast into hell fire. Take heed that ye despise not one of these little ones; for I say unto you, that in heaven their angels do always behold the face of my Father which is in heaven. For the Son of man is come to save that which was lost. How think ye? if a man have a hundred sheep, and one of them be gone astray, doth he not leave the ninety and nine, and goeth into the mountains, and seeketh that which is gone astray? And if so be that he find it, verily I say unto you, he rejoiceth more of that sheep, than of the ninety and nine which went not astray. Even so it is not the will of your Father which is in heaven, that one of these little ones should perish.

"Among the Doctor's patients was a young lady by the name of Mrs. Real Stench.

"Lady had never been jealous of her husband. From her first faith in him had grown confidence that was like adamant stone.

"Christian appreciated this trust and returned it in kind.

"Mrs. Stench was a great gossip. Each trip to the office brought lots of news.

"Christian told his wife the tales and she warned, 'Beware of tattlers.' Use as your motto, 'Bring here no tattle in, nor take none out.'

"There are intuitions, imaginations, and hallucinations. The range of the swing of the pendulum from the one to the other is as wide as the scope from Sanity to Insanity.

"By intuition, Lady one day had a faint view of fangs in Mrs. Stench. She said nothing but let time prove them fangs. They developed into claws that dug into Christian's very vitals.

"The ailment was chronic and so the weed had soil in which to grow.

"Two and one-half years passed and one day a man came to tell Lady all about the scandal connecting her husband's name with that of the scarlet woman. Lady would not listen to him but bade him Begone.

"In all of the difficulties in life the girl had kept up her courage but this day she almost swooned. She ran to her Bible for help and there she read Job 4:3 to 12. Behold, thou hast instructed many, and thou hast strengthened the weak hands. Thy words have upholden him that was falling, and thou hast strengthened the feeble knees. But now it is come upon thee, and thou faintest; it toucheth thee, and thou art troubled. Is not this thy fear, thy confidence, thy hope, and the uprightness of thy ways? Remember, I pray thee, who ever perished, being innocent? or where were the righteous cut off? Even as I have seen, they that plow iniquity, and sow wickedness, reap the same. By the blast of God they perish, and by the breath of his nostrils are they consumed. The roaring of the lion, and the voice of the fierce lion, and the teeth of the young lions, are broken. The old lion perisheth for lack of prey, and the stout lion's whelps are scattered abroad. Now a thing was secretly brought to me, and mine ear received a little thereof.

"In a flash her poise was restored."

At the beginning of Chapter Twenty a quotation from

St. Matthew 18:15 to 20 is given. "Moreover if thy brother shall trespass against thee, go and tell him his fault between thee and him alone: if he shall hear thee, thou hast gained thy brother." There is more. The story goes on.

"A few months more and Lady began to see claws all too clearly. She was still confident of her husband. What could she do to end the evil influence being exerted?

"Many a prayer she raised was only, 'Show me the way, show me the way, show me the way.'

"Vacation time came. A trip was planned. Now came Crisis Four.

"The Waits had no children. Nevertheless, EVERY WOMAN MUST SUFFER TRAVAIL.

"While away from home it was easier to think sanely and see clearly.

"From the anguish and agony of a night and a day, twins were born. They were FORGIVENESS AND SELF-CONTROL.

"The Waits returned to their home. The plan was now clear to Lady. She was driven by a MOTIVE not her own.

"She went to see Mrs. Stench. The first visit almost persuaded Lady that her sight had deceived her.

"She called the second time. Between the first and second interviews, she had her ideas confirmed. This time she KNEW.

"The brass veneer on Mrs. Stench melted. She confessed. Her power of evil was ended.

"Deuteronomy 32:36. For the Lord shall judge his people and repent himself for his servants, when he seeth that their power is gone, and there is none shut up, or left."

On this happy note the story entitled *Christian's Crises* comes to a close.

In the next story the physician is made to give a final answer to the villainess. The answer which he gives in this story is the exact opposite to the answer which he really gave:

"All the threads remaining are tied into a bundle. 'I'll have one last fling and I am determined it shall ensnare him,' she says to herself.

"A hurried visit to the physician's office is made. 'Doctor, you know my ailment is chronic. I insist that you take me to a specialist,' says Mrs. Stench.

" 'All right,' replies the man, 'when shall we go?'

"The date is set for the trip. The remaining threads MUST STRANGLE.

"Doctor Wait and Mrs. Stench are on their way to consult the specialist.

"Mrs. Stench cries, 'DOCTOR? I MUST HAVE YOU. I CANNOT LIVE WITHOUT YOU.'

"The physician rises in all his dignity and hisses, 'AND YOU'LL NOT HAVE ME.' "

It is thought that this narrative may furnish documentation of a fairly common type of phantasy reworking of past events. It is throughout the writing of conflict. An interesting compartmentalization is indicated by the fact that nothing is detracted from the sweetness of forgiveness by the fact that Mrs. Stench retains her unwholesome name thereafter. She is forgiven, but she remains a villainess still. The husband is completely exculpated, and here the narrative is sharply contradicted by fact.

It is not only one's own rôle that is recast, but that of the love object as well. In accordance with their own internal needs, divorced persons work out a favorably or unfavorably idealized version of the love object, who becomes then either god or devil, rarely remaining just a person. A woman whose husband was and is a quite mediocre artist still nourishes the belief that he is a genius with a mission in the world. He has in fact not risen above the status of the commercial illustrator, but she still delights in displaying his productions as art in its highest form. This is complicated in her case by the hope that he will take her back sometime. Occasionally we have mixed forms of thought, composed of reasoning, rationalization, and wishful thinking, in which the love object is at once idealized and subtly disparaged. "He's all right, he's fine, but he's just weak, and any woman can do anything that she wants to with him. You see, he's just a little boy at heart." A woman who felt that her husband had wronged her wrote an essay in which she passionately defended Lafcadio Hearn, assimilating the husband to that character, and thereby at once defending, idealizing, and disparaging him. The husband in this instance was only mildly enthusiastic. Occasionally the desire to go on loving is so intense that one takes the blame entirely upon himself (perhaps because this solution leaves the door open to reconciliation).

One of the prime motives, however, in this working over of the past is self-exculpation. The mixed motives of the writer of the following passage will be apparent, but the dominant mood seems to be self-defense, although the moral he draws is that since he did not deserve to be treated in this way the wife should return to him.

"Besides the ache of unsatisfied desire, there was added a very considerable sense of injustice. I was rather bitter about the thing that my wife had done to me. I was perfectly certain that it was something which I in no way deserved. I used to carry on interminable conversations with my absent wife, arguing, begging, pleading, whining, cajoling, and trying out internally every kind of persuasive device. 'Don't you see,' I would say, 'that I really didn't deserve this? Wasn't I always a good husband to you? Now I want to ask you just one question, and if you say no I will be silent forevermore, and that is this: Do you think that I was a bad husband? Weren't we happy most of the time? Didn't I do everything for you that I possibly could? Didn't I buy you anything that you wanted that we could possibly afford? Yes, I was jealous, I had my faults. But then do you think that they were great enough to justify you in leaving me flat? Do you think it's right to leave me alone in the world like this, with nobody that gives a damn whether I live or die? Do you? What pleasure can it give you to hurt me this way, I'd like to know. Why do you do it? Do you think you're doing the right thing by running me half crazy like this? How can I ever face the world with a terrible thing like this tagged on me? I tell you I can't stand it. It's too terrible and I don't deserve it. You don't think yourself that I deserve it. You don't realize what you are doing to me. You can't realize it. Oh, please try, please don't do this to me. Let's go back together and let bygones be bygones. Just come back to me and I will be so nice to you that all this unpleasantness will fade away and you will soon forget it. Please, please, please give me another chance. I am asking for my life, and for yours.' But she was many miles away, and did not hear my protesting voice, which would be sure to break at just the right moment in this tense, internal appeal. Everywhere that I went I continued this conversation, which became a sort of continued story that somehow repeated itself forever. I was able to put some of it in my letters, but my thoughts would always travel faster than my pen, and I did not succeed very well in preserving the spontaneity of the dialogue. I suppose that this assumed such very prominent proportions because my wife and I had been arguing out the matter of the separation for some months before we actually separated. I formed a habit of talking like that and couldn't stop."

A more subtle instance of the same self-justification mechanism was the following, culled from the letters of a woman about to divorce her husband:

"I read a significant book, *Love Lies Dreaming,* by C. E. Forester, a library book. Try and get it. You will learn things you should have done. The man waits, *always,* and in the end he wins. You never handled me like that. Now you must give me plenty of rope. It isn't you that I object to, it is marriage itself."

In a preceding chapter we have discussed the various attempts to reassert control over the absent mate. These have also a relation to the restoration of one's ego feelings. In case one cannot enforce a response by any of the techniques mentioned, the bare assertion that one has been able to do so is sometimes made to serve the same purpose. It is deeply gratifying to think that the other person has seen his mistake, and either wants to come back, or is going to want to do so. If one cannot really believe this, one can get phantasy gratification by saying it anyhow. It has also the function of saving one's face if there is a reconciliation. A negro whose not very legal wife had left him a few days before told of meeting her. "She wanted to know should she come back or not. I told her, 'Now I didn't tell you to leave, you never asked me nothin' about it. Now I ain't tellin' you to come back. You suit yo'self.' " A few months later this man was arrested for attempting to coerce the return of his wife by firing a gun at her when she was on a ferryboat with a number of white people, so that it seems that his statement may have had the character of wishful thinking. A bootlegger whose wife had recently left him said, "Well, my wife wants to come back. I saw her the other day. I guess she realizes. I guess she'd like to come back to an old reliable concern. Well, I told her that if she'd fix up the shanty the way it was when she left it I'd let her come back. I had this place fixed up pretty swell, you know, and she took the stuff out. Oh, no, of course she can't do it, she hasn't got anything." Instances might be multiplied, but the point is obvious.

It is pretty much of a truism in scientific circles to say that one is always helped by talking out his troubles with an understanding listener. Not to talk about a personal calamity is usually also to react to it insufficiently, and the experience may be spoken of as repressed. We might very well deal with the topics of repression and catharsis in this connection, but it has seemed better to postpone these to the chapter on mental conflict. Repressions have also an influence on one's system of social relationships, and will be mentioned in that connection also.

CHAPTER EIGHT

Pride and the Divorcé: Defense and Compensation

A VARIED and interesting lot of defense reactions are to be found among divorced persons. These may be divided into those which have the function of protecting the person in the present time, by defending him against the setting off of old complexes or against injuries which might be done him because of his change of status, and those which are intended to prevent a recurrence of his unfortunate experiences, to prevent him, as it were, from baring his breast to further wounds. Here again no rigid classification can be made; we shall simply speak from one point of view for a while and then approach the problem from a different angle. Defense reactions of the latter sort will be given special consideration in the chapter on mental conflicts.

As sympathy is costly to the person who gives it, it is likewise trying to the person who receives it. When the proffer of sympathy is linked with the desire to give advice, it is likely to be experienced by some perverse people as unpleasant.

"Yes, it is certain that my vanity was deeply wounded by my wife's desertion. I would look at the men whose wives had stuck by them and I would compare them with myself.

I would ask myself, 'What's wrong with me? Why couldn't I hold my wife if so-and-so could hold his?' It used to hurt me to think that the other men around me had a number of women who were in love with them and in whom they were nevertheless not very interested. I used to find the conversation of these Don Juans very distressing. They would always want to show me photographs of the women they knew, or tell me about all their conquests. I didn't like that at all.

"My friends just would pour out their advice and sympathy. This advice and sympathy was well-meant, as I know, but I did not particularly like it nevertheless. It always came to the same point, that perhaps there was something the matter with the sex life of my wife and myself, or that perhaps I was not potent enough for her, or that maybe I didn't understand some elementary things about having intercourse. All that pained me very deeply.

"These very well-meaning persons would urge me to tell them all, and would hint that perhaps they could tell me after I had finished something that would help me. I knew that they would not be able to tell me anything, but I wanted their sympathy too, and I always hoped that perhaps some one would contribute something that would help. I usually needed very little urging to get me started. I would give a pretty frank and complete story as far as I then could, and I would know what was coming. My friend would ask one or two questions, and then he would say, 'Now that sounds like a case in which the woman was not satisfied. Are you sure that you are all right? Did you pay sufficient attention to the satisfaction of your wife's desires? Were you selfish, or did you look out for her too? Did you always take time to prepare her for the act? You know that's necessary. Now a fellow has to look out for those things. That's the man's business. . . . Another thing is if the man is brutal about it, that disgusts a woman. They say there are more marriages spoiled on the wedding night than any other time. Sometimes it is little better than legalized rape. Of course then the woman never does get roused. Now I have heard of cases when women did not get to know there was such a thing as sexual feeling for women till they were grandmothers. Think of that.' They would tell me all that and a lot more; I had to take it. I would sit there and think, 'Why you fool, I know more about it than you do.' I know that these people who were making so free with their advice had not had as much experience as I had.

"Well, I learned to protect myself against that. I would tell my story. Yes, I suppose it did get more abbreviated. I know it did. Then, before the other fellow had a chance to get in his say, I would say, 'Now I know what you think but it's not so. I am potent enough for anybody. In fact, I'm what you would call a wheel horse. I was always considerate of my wife's desires, and I tried harder to satisfy her than to satisfy myself. There was a sex difficulty but my wife went to the very best doctors and they could not do anything about it. Now no simple little rule is going to have so very much effect.' Yet for all that I used to wonder just what could be the matter with me that I was not able to hold my wife's affections."

A woman whose husband had left her under circumstances which won her friends peculiarly to her and alienated them from her husband described the defenses which she evolved as follows:

"I was cursed with over-sympathetic friends. While it was all very recent in my mind I needed their active sympathy, and was not ashamed to cry in their presence. That soon passed away and I could have wished they didn't know so much. They were always wanting to sympathize and that came to be a great drain upon me. I knew what they were thinking: 'Poor girl. She loves him so! She'll never be the same again. Her life is ruined. She has been treated shamefully. We'll let her know where we stand all right.' I didn't want their sympathy any more and I didn't want them to hate my husband. So I treated my friends, after those first few months, very politely, and I'm afraid, very distantly. For the rest, I cultivated a hard bright cheerfulness and an air of efficiency which dried up sympathy at its source. From a pose, the thing got to be a habit with me. It was a good habit, and helped more than anything else to build up my morale."

A very common reaction, one which is generally frowned upon by the more sportsmanlike members of the community, is that of belittling the former love object. It sometimes assumes very important proportions, and may be associated with a belittling of love and matrimony in general, or with belittling of the entire opposite sex.

Epithets as applied to the missing mate sometimes help to free one of him. By causing him to categorize unfavorably, they detract from his emotional importance, and have also the function of putting the blame for the break upon the other partner. In fact, there are those who do not think that a divorcé has reached a proper state of poise with regard to his former mate until he comes habitually to employ uncomplimentary expressions in referring to her. This is of course quite wrong, for as long as the need to use such expressions is felt, there would seem to be an underlying need for the person. What these expressions indicate is not that the complex organized around the absent mate has gone, but that one is fighting it down, in other words that one has repressed.

Epithets become important in another way. The severance of a marriage relation is likely to be preceded by a period of quarreling, in which one is likely to have his bad points called to his attention by the application of the proper epithet. What is said to one at such a time, especially since it is made the handle upon which important decisions are caused to hang, is likely to sink very deep, which means that during the rest of the person's life he will be very much interested in proving that it was not so. There is here often a delayed reaction, the trait designated by the epithet being retained until after the break and then unostentatiously dropped. This sort of reaction accounts in part for many of the striking reversals that occur in the readjustment of personality after divorce. Thus a man who had been called stingy and accused of non-support became a spendthrift in the years immediately following the divorce. A man whose sister had needed his attention, and had got it, somewhat to the detriment of his own family, while his marriage was breaking up, reacted against the sister afterwards. A woman who before her divorce had not been very enthusiastic about the conventional mores became so afterwards. A woman who had once refused to go on certain "parties" with her husband because there was a bit of indiscriminate kissing, came afterwards to be an enthusiastic promoter of such amusements, savoring every refinement of sensuality until she measured up, almost, to the antique standard for public women.

Apparently what occurs is that the old personality organizes for the purpose of meeting the crisis, and that organization is not abandoned while pressure exists from the outside, but immediately the crisis has passed the old personality disintegrates, sloughing its supposedly undesirable traits, and a new self is put in the dominant position. Following is an excerpt from a letter of a divorced woman. It seems that the positions of the former husband and wife have been reversed with regard to their adherence to conventional morality, for during their marriage the wife had been an advocate of a liberal code and the husband a stickler for the conventions; this was a cardinal point of controversy between them. The wife has just learned that her former husband has been involved in an extra-marital affair.

"Dear God, how I despised the man who interfered between us and how much higher I rated you by contrast because I was sure it was a trait you didn't have. And you say, 'saw fit to divorce you without a definite explanation.' No explanation? Saw fit to divorce you because of the type of man who didn't think that when a woman married it was for better or for worse and that thereafter it was *hands off* no matter *what* the circumstances. Slimy type—sometimes such a one bases his attentions on pity for the woman, sometimes on the fact of knowing her before marriage, sometimes on friendship and liking, and sometimes he offers no excuse. The latter is the only one who deserves any credit. Oh, well, why lecture? It is nearly impossible to pass on to some one else a lesson you have learned yourself."

The word *divorcé* is a label which but few people are willing to bear. One may, by wearing it flauntingly, deprive it of some of its odium, as one may obtain recompense for its unsavory connotation by accentuating the sophistication that is supposed to go with it. This making the most of the rôle varies from a mere assurance that one is able to cope with his unhappiness to a seizing upon and elaboration of the rôle of the sophisticate. The man who says, "Oh, I'm all right, I get along. I've got a little redheaded girl and I see her every so often and we have a nice time. I'm all right," is simply fending off sympathy while the man who elaborates the rôle and talks about his numerous "concubines" and the satisfactoriness of his life with them is making an active bid for the envy and admiration of the community.

Externally the problem of integration and organization after a crisis is always to find a new rôle on the basis of which one may reorganize his social life. This is in part a very healthy mode of adjustment, and the only one by which personality may be changed, but when there comes to be too large an element of the inner playing of rôles and too small an actual readjustment of one's social relations, we speak of a living by fictions, which may usually be thought of as pathological. A case in which a male divorcé made a rather healthy change of rôle, reverting from a self-pitying rôle which had been played during marriage to a different rôle which he had played at a previous time in his life, seems in point:

"I made a good many more friends after this visit than I had before, perhaps because my wife's refusal to come with me had convinced me that it was necessary for me to learn to stand on my own feet again. During the entire period of my married life, I had allowed the outside contacts to be made by my wife; now I had to learn to make my own friends or do without any. I rediscovered my talent for people. It is true that during the earlier period I had made friends with the men with whom I was thrown into close contact by my work, but I did not really extend the circle, nor think it necessary to do so, until after my wife's final and definite refusal to come with me. It is hard to evaluate the influence of these friends that I made, but there is no question that it was more decisive at this time than at any previous time in my life.

"During marriage I had been accustomed to pity myself a great deal, and had used that as a technique of getting what I wanted. Now this all had to be changed. One of the men who influenced me was of the cheerful care-free sort. He used the technique of flattery in his social relationships. I was always immensely cheered by my talks with him and I feel that he was influential in getting me to accept a cheerful rôle myself. It seemed to operate in this way, that when I was in his company I felt acceptable and worth while; this was a type of verbal interchange in which no one was worsted and in which no one came off second best; in addition it identified me with certain desirable rôles and I felt that I must play them out. I discovered new possibilities of spontaneity and cheerfulness, and gradually identified myself with that aspect of my personality. This was not a wholly new rôle for me, but rather a reversion to a rôle which I had played for many years previous to my marriage."

When the ego feelings are damaged, compensatory drives result. They have the function of neutralizing unpleasant feelings concerning one's status.[1] The sort of compensatory drive that is developed will depend upon one's entire personality as expressed throughout his previous life, and, we must not forget, upon his opportunities. Some examples follow:

A mining engineer, separated from his wife for a period of years but still emotionally tied to her, developed the hard-exterior type of adjustment. As a friend of his remarked, "With him it was 'Goddamn this,' and 'Aw, to hell with that,' all day long." He made no directly derogatory remarks concerning his wife or concerning marriage, saying merely, "I'm married but I'm not working at it." Drinking was a very prominent part of his life. He would sometimes engage in drinking bouts six nights a week. His desire to impress one with the fact that

---

[1] Defense reactions which it has been considered best to discuss elsewhere are (1) those concerned with concealing the fact of the divorce or its implications from the public, (2) the development of a general sensitivity to slights, and (3) the development of parapathiac combination locks to prevent the recurrence of the unfortunate experience. The first two of these are discussed in the chapter on the complication of social relationships by divorce, and the third will be postponed to the chapter on mental conflict.

he took great pleasure in this activity led one to suspect that perhaps there was something else which was quite unfulfilled which he wished to hide. Gambling was also an outlet in which he was very much interested. We call particular attention to his habits, for by these and by his arrangements for sex satisfaction he also solved some of his status difficulties. He took great pride in the fact that he had always about him a large number of women, and in the fact that they were willing to submit to considerable inconvenience and to work for the privilege of being his mistresses. He used to say, "Well, I'm going to have that damned phone taken out. I've just got so I don't answer it." He took great delight in telling of the large number of his mistresses, all of whom were endowed with peculiar ability to "keep the bed hot." On Sundays he did not get out of bed, but used the day to rest and recover from the week's dissipation. On this day his "women" would assemble and bring in food for him. Some of these women, it should be noted, were of a distinctly lower type than those with whom he had been accustomed to associate and some of them came to see him solely because of his generosity with his liquor, but they served to enhance his ego nevertheless. He did not merely use these women to fetch and carry because he was proud, but he was able to hold up his head because he could use them in this menial way. This combination of egotistic and sexual gratification is not an unusual adjustment. It is notable also that there were involved in this case the adjustments of resort to alcohol, a somewhat frenzied social activity, and gambling. The diagnostic guess that this man was still emotionally involved with his wife has since been corroborated by the fact that he has gone back with her, since "there was nothing else to do."

Work has been mentioned as a substitute for sex, but not discussed or documented; an access of interest in one's work is also to be understood as a reaction to wounded pride. A redirection of the life energy into the channels of work is evident in the following excerpt from the life history of a divorced man:

"My work, interesting enough in itself, was made to serve in part as a substitute for my lost love life. The many social contacts that it afforded, although they were transient and of no great moment to me or to anyone else, gave me a very good release, and I soon found myself looking forward to them from week to week. I cultivated a more friendly attitude toward the people with whom my work put me in contact than I had had before, and I found that my work could be made the vehicle of considerable personal expression.

"Whether I was simply rationalizing a process already finished in the unconscious, or whether I worked it out through bona fide logical processes I cannot say, but I used to reason like this: 'My work is the only place where I can invest my time and my interest and—myself. I have tried love. It was a poor investment. For years my life, my every thought centered around the woman whom I loved. Everything that I did was thought of with reference to her, what she would say, whether she would approve or disapprove, whether it would call out from her the much desired love response or one of the feared and dreaded tantrums. I used to spend much of my thought on the problem of making her happy and keeping her so. I used to be engrossed in the problem of keeping her happy. All that is gone, and I have nothing to show for it except my poor lost soul wandering around in hell. Nothing remains in the form of results for all those years except the very small fragment of myself that I invested in my work. It has brought rich returns. Everything else has been lost. My work, that is the only thing that matters. It is the only thing that pays. It is the only thing that lasts. I must turn to it.' And turn to it I did....

"I discovered an aptitude for thoroughness and meticulous working out of details that I had not thought that I possessed. I grew more and more desirous of discussing everything from my own particular point of view, and of carefully differentiating that point of view from that maintained by anyone else. (Sic!) How much of our scientific advance is due to this refining and differentiating of a point of view thought of in a personal fashion! I learned a new language, and took great pleasure in parading my proficiency in that tongue. I did not often omit to mention how easily that proficiency had been acquired. It was long before I was able to evaluate praise; rather I seized every morsel that was given me and took from it every bit of nourishment that was to be had. (Sic!) Since these morsels were not few, my work helped me very much over the difficult time. The interesting hours of work, hours of activity and self-realization, stood out the more by contrast with the dark hours of idleness."

Penance may be thought of as a compensatory drive. Admitting the truth of the charges made against one, or admitting it in part, one attempts to make amends by mortifying the flesh. A typical adjustment of this sort was that of the woman who said, "When I do penance I do it thoroughly. I haven't worn silk underthings since my husband and I separated. I haven't bought a single good dress, and that was a year ago."

The observant Mrs. Lewis has described behavior that was probably similarly motivated among the women "residents" of Reno.

One almost unvarying development of a week's sojourn in Reno is the shyly expressed desire to economize by even the most extravagant.

"I can see no reason for keeping my maid here. I think

I'll send her back, give up the two bedrooms, and use that funny let-down thing. I hear they are quite comfortable. ...You know I used to rather like to cook. Coffee and toast in the morning I could certainly achieve, and even an egg for lunch. I think this would be a marvelous place to diet.... As a matter of fact I brought only my oldest clothes, and I am going to wear them all out and leave them behind when I go. I think I'll even go light on the lipstick and give the poor old face a rest."—"Just What Is Reno Like," Grace Hegger Lewis, *Scribner's*, January, 1929, p. 39. From *Scribner's Magazine* by permission. Copyright, 1928, by Charles Scribner's Sons.

Let us not forget how Hosea, hero, if hero he was, of a bold Old Testament scandal, profited, as it were, by his experience.

"A man usually accounts it a disgrace and a misfortune if his wife does not keep faith with him. Such did they think it in ancient Israel, and such, no doubt, did Hosea consider it when Gomer betrayed him. But if it was a disgrace, in his case it was no misfortune, for out of the agonies of his cuckoldom came the prophesying that gave him his place in the everlasting pages of history. He had done a goodish bit of prophesying before his marriage; perhaps that helps to account for the fact that two people with such utterly different outlooks upon the world as he and Gomer ever happened to take up with each other, for she too was without standing in her own community. Nor did he, even while living in a solid and uninspired domesticity with the wife of his bosom, entirely suppress the soothsaying faculty; he gave to the children which his wife bore him symbolic names, names intended to convey a message to Israel and to cast a doubt, ever so faint, upon their own paternity. But somehow he had never managed to say anything that had the authentic ring of prophecy about it and none knew it better than he.

"Gomer was the making of him. He lost a wife and found a figure of speech; Israel was a harlot and Jehovah was her husband, wronged but forgiving, and ready to take her back to his bosom if she would but repent. By the metaphor Hosea is remembered: thus did the faithless Gomer indirectly do for him what a score of more virtuous women could not have done. He was not the first man to be betrayed into the remembrance of posterity, nor yet the last. He did not go down the gory road of Bathsheba's first husband, nor did he play the more common rôle of the *mari complaisant* or stay to take his revenge or collect damages. The chief benefits, for him, were psychological. Divorcing his wife, he was metamorphosed into an attitude. It was so much of an effort to settle the question of Gomer and her lovers that his mind was frozen forever into a habit of thought, hence these prophecies. When later he needed further inspiration, he sought it in the same way, for he knew now what rôle suited him best. He indulged the flesh to mortify the spirit that from his mouth could come forth the sayings of the prophets." [2]

Those with a taste for learning of the sort will remember that "Milton wrote his treatise on divorce as a result of his troubles with his seventeen-year-old wife, and when he was accused of being the leading spirit in a new sect, the Divorcers, he wrote his noble Areopagitica to prove his right to say what he thought fit, and incidentally to establish the advantage of a free press in the promotion of Truth." [3]

---

[2] Unpublished manuscript.
[3] Robinson, J. H.; *The Mind in the Making;* New York; Harper & Brothers; 1921; p. 46.

People still seek the consolations of religion or embrace some new philosophy which gives promise of enabling its disciples to attain a certain undivided-ness of self. If it is religion to which one turns for sorrow's surcease, the more soothing brands, such as Christian Science, are very popular, although the more emotional sects, with their conversion phenomena, and many opportunities for the expression of "free-floating affects," have a certain vogue as well. Religion or philosophy may demand forgiveness of one's enemies. If that forgiveness is not granted, we have interesting inconsistencies as that of the amiable Christian Scientist woman who could dispense with doctors, reaching here some heights of heroism, but could never even consider forgiving "that old sow from Chicago" who took her husband from her. If one does forgive, it may be by repressing hostility, which will have deleterious effects upon the personality. This discussion should not obscure the fact that an adjustment probably fully as common as turning to religion is repudiation of it.

Divorcés of both sexes, women a bit more than men, pay more than the usual amount of attention to the fashions. There are numerous reasons, some obvious and some complicated. There is direct compensation by dress for the inner hurt, arising perhaps after a period of lethargy or penance in which slovenliness or extreme simplicity was the rule. This direct compensation might be characterized as an attempt to achieve happiness directly by being well-dressed; as dress is ordinarily more important to women than to men, the attempt has more chance of success. (We pass over the somewhat greater probability of a strong narcisstic dash in the woman.) Then there is the desire to hide the inner misery behind a gay and enviable exterior. If one hopes for a reconciliation with his former mate, and continues to organize his life around the slim chance that one will take place rather than around the large one that it will not, he may dress well in the hope that she will see him and be pleased. If one has turned away from the thought of reconciliation, and gone husband-hunting or wife-seeking, he finds that he must compete with persons somewhat younger than himself and without a failure on their records. It would therefore be folly to overlook whatever advantage might be gained from dress. Perhaps most important is the fact that one ceases to be old-fashioned. When life is smooth and easy in accustomed grooves, and a man is satisfied with the feelings in his breast and the thoughts in his head, the man and his life are protected by some magic preservative against the inroads of time and change. When one dates, it is as of a time when he was happy, a time which he has preserved overlong in its externals, a time when he was strong and life was good, but when the evil days come there must be change in externals. (What has been said here of dress applies as well to moral codes in the old and the new fashions, although in discussing moral codes we should not forget that one's point of view varies as he has or has not a stake in the moral order, as he has an ox to be gored or not.)

Occasionally the ego comes to be exalted by the very things that laid it low. One may come to think that his difficulties had their roots in his special abilities, in which case they must be accepted as an inevitable part of one's self. This may be illustrated by the following letter in which penitence, sorrow, and pride are seen disputing for mastery:

"When I stop to think too deeply I believe that I have a fatal curse laid upon me. Inside of me I have the right ideals and the right abilities—strength and fearlessness and unselfishness and sympathy. But I attract men and they are almost always hurt by that attraction and then I am hurt also and then I draw still further away from them and it goes in a vicious circle. Sometimes I look at a woman like Mrs. Blank and envy her. Only one man ever made love to her and she can worship the ground he walks on. On the other hand, Mr. Blank never experiences any high moments married to some one like her, never having been made love to, her giving is anxious and pitiful. And now that I have written this I can see that both sides have some good and some bad points and that nothing can be perfect."

Not infrequently the answer, when it comes, is in terms of courage. Elaborate codes in which courage is the main virtue are occasionally evolved; the life of the person is organized around that one virtue seen to be necessary and displayed with pride. We will bring this discussion to a close by citing one instance:

"For a while courage was a special virtue with me. The situation demanded it, and only through making a special fetish of it could I live. I remember telling certain people who had, relatively, had but little trouble, although it is true that I thought they had fewer personal assets with which to combat it, that I had had my troubles and had conquered them, because I had found that none of them was as bad in realization as it was in anticipation. To one man quivering for fear that he might not make good and would therefore lose his job, I said, 'A year ago there were three things that I was afraid of—that I would lose my job, that I would lose my wife, that I would lose my sex morals. I might very well fear to lose my job. It was a good job. It paid good money, and there was a lot of dignity connected with it. I did not want to lose it before I was ready to give it up. I lost it. What happened? I found another. No, not such a good one, but a job, and I have lived. I will come through in time. I feared to lose my wife. Well, I might. I loved her and thought that she was wonderful; I lost her. Well, what happened? I went through hell. But I am alive, and I am here now and I can smile and laugh at it all now. I lost my sex morals. What does it matter? I have conquered my troubles by having them. I had them all at once. I hope I got them all over with, but if there are more around the corner I will know what to do with them. I am not afraid of anything else that may happen to me now, because I know that whatever happens I will still live and will come some day to taste a sort of happiness once more. Courage! That's all that's necessary. Take heart from me."

That was said in the spirit of Henley, dramatic courage beneath the buffeting of fate and the persecutions of an outrageous fortune. Others, with a talent for or a habit of complaint, assimilate themselves to Carthage's queen, assume a dramatic self-pity, and furnish material for a new literature of lamentation. It is hard to see just how pity for oneself is a matter of pride, yet it seems certain that it should be so classified. One may be directly proud of success, however that be defined. Failing to achieve success, he may pride himself upon some incidental quality, such as courage, making of it a *summum bonum,* and there would be few who would wish to prove him wrong. Deprived of these positive consolations, he may still find solace in negative attitudes. Self-pity is an excuse for unsuccess and takes away the responsibility for failure. There are not many who say to themselves that the fault is not in their stars but in themselves. Then, if one may not arouse the admiration of people by success or courage, he may at least occupy their attention by exciting their pity. In like manner is self-conscious villainy begot. Whom the gods favor they make great, but he whom they have persecuted must also be, for good or ill, important.

CHAPTER NINE

The Complication of Social Relationships

EVEN those people to whom regret over love that has burned its fitful flame and turned to ashes is but a passing fancy, and who suffer less from injuries to their self-esteem than they would from a pain in their stomachs, must yet find divorce expensive. One of the greatest costs of divorce inheres in the fact that it immeasurably increases the complexity of one's existence; it complicates both the person and his system of social relationships; by complicating the one it complicates the other—a reciprocal interaction which is apparently unavoidable. The end result is a tangle of people, attitudes, and institutions fit to mystify an Einstein; by its side the deceiver's web and the tempter's snare are alike simple geometric structures.

Inherent in the situation of the person who has been divorced are things enough to make his system of relationships more intricate, his contacts with other persons less direct and simple, totally without the intervention of any of his own personal complications arising from the fact of divorce. The rôle of the divorcé is a very real thing—a rôle which one may, it is true, not accept, but which one must nevertheless either accept or arrange to avoid. There is the fact, in itself simple, that people expect from divorced persons responses which are not simple but subtle and sophisticated, and this leads to the development of a social structure around the divorcé much more intricate than it would otherwise be.

Among the things external to himself with which the divorcé must reckon as complicating every situation in which he is involved is gossip, which is, it is true, a greater problem in the small town than it is in the city, but which remains nevertheless a potent factor in determining the nature of human relationships everywhere. A case in point is that of a girl whose home was in a small town of the South. She married a wealthy young man who happened to be a sadist, and much publicity centered around the circumstances of their married life and their subsequent divorce. She was, in addition, the first person who had ever been divorced in the small town in which she lived. She describes her experiences in the following narrative: (In the first part of the story she is living away from her husband, but has not yet obtained a divorce. This takes place at a summer resort, also a small town in the South.)

"I got frequent glimpses of Henry that summer, both in my home town and in the summer resort. One time I was walking down the street with a boy I had known for years when suddenly a car pulled up by the side of the street and a man jumped out and held a gun at the boy's stomach. It was Henry. The boy didn't know what was up, just stood there with his hands part way up as if he were not sure whether or not it was a joke. He said, 'Put down your gun, brother, I don't want to talk to you with that gun in your hands.' Henry said, 'What chance would I have without the gun?' The boy was a big fellow. I finally smoothed it over and got Henry back in the car.

"Henry came to the same summer resort in the mountains where we had been spending our summers. He took a big place just on the outskirts of town. He did a number of crazy things. Once we heard a noise downstairs and went down and saw the window being closed. The next morning there was a case of champagne on the porch with a note from Henry saying that he wanted us to have it, that he knew how hard it was to get up where we were, that he was afraid that it might be stolen and had tried to put it in the house for us. All of which may have been true, I do not know. Then Henry threatened to shoot on sight any young man seen with me that summer. The boys heard about it and took a great pleasure in teasing him. They didn't think he would really shoot, you know. It pleased them especially if I were some place with my mother, and they could talk to me then, and he could not possibly object.

"The editor of the newspaper was more or less friendly to Henry, perhaps because of some business about a franchise in which they were both interested. I got a lot of publicity through that. There would be breaks in the middle of an editorial in which some smart cracks would be pulled about me or my affair. I think it was the editor of that paper who finally wrote it all up for the city papers.

"I was getting pretty bitter about it all by this time. I had had enough of being hounded and made miserable. I had reached a state where any further compromise was out of the question. I had Henry put under bonds to keep the peace, but you can imagine what that would amount to with him. I saw that I would have to get a divorce in order to be able to live my own life. When he heard that I was thinking of divorce Henry sent a letter promising to settle some money on me, but it did not seem best to pay any attention to it. Not that I would have refused the money, if he really wanted to give it to me, but my attorneys thought it might affect my legal situation unfavorably.

"The suit for divorce came off in the fall. . . . I appeared on the stand for myself and my husband's chauffeur appeared for him. My husband did not go on the stand. When they put me on the stand my attorney said to me, 'Now, Mrs. Robinson, just go ahead and give us a general summary of your married life.' I said, 'But I couldn't. You'll have to ask me questions.' Then I started in talking and I talked for six hours. . . .

"I went home then to live with my parents. My divorce was the first one there had ever been in that little southern town, and of course there were all kinds of difficulties involved in my staying there. Your real friends won't ask any questions, the others will all be interested in knowing the gossip and will say, 'oh, how interesting. You must tell me all about it some time.' While I was at home there were no young men there and I was not interested in those that were there. Once in a while I would go with some old friends to football games at the University of Texas or something like that. Occasionally I would run into some boys that I knew and they would take me for a ride or would take me to a picture show or just stand around and talk to me for a while. Not very much social life.

"People knew I was not happy and there was a terrible lot of gossip about that as well as about everything else. People seemed to seize upon everything that I did to talk about it. If I happened to be at the picture show with some harmless, unattractive boy the next day someone would call up my mother and say, 'you know, there's a lot of talk around town about Jane and so-and-so. You'd better have her entertain her friends at home where everybody won't see them, because people are talking a lot.' People would even whisper behind my back in the show. Some of the most outlandish stories got out. One was that Henry had thrown me off a yacht and made me swim to shore one night. That was one thing he never did do. When I was written up in the city papers, the story was right across the page from that of a woman who tried to kill her husband with a revolver. The newspaper dealer helped us there. He just bundled up all those papers and sent them to my father with a bill for seven dollars and something.

"My mother was wonderful to me through it all. She certainly showed a lot of sense through the whole thing. I used to talk to her about my trouble and her sympathy helped. I used to talk to her about Henry, not using his name, just referring to him by the pronoun. I would be in the other room, and then I would think of something else that he did, and I would go in and say, 'Yes, mother, and he did so-and-so.' My mother would laugh about that. She would say I was a little bit cracked on the subject. But she used to tell me, 'If you do right, nothing but right can come of it. Let them say what they want. I don't intend to do everything to please the people in this town.' And about the people who were doing the talking, she would say, 'My own relatives. It's my own relatives that are doing the talking.' You see they would talk about me and then call up and tell mother that people were gossiping. My mother is very broadminded for a woman who has spent all her life in a little town like that.

"Finally I made my plans to go away and study. You see, I just couldn't live there any longer."

The undefined status of the person who is married but not living with the mate leads to many difficulties. In the case above, the problem was rendered a bit more urgent by the physical presence of the husband and his active participation in the situation, but the problem is there in any case. There are always grave questions as to how one should act with his friends, what should be his attitude toward them, where he should go with them, what he should tell the people about him concerning his marital affairs. The extent to which he should be included in social affairs, or to which he should allow himself to become involved—these are likely to be serious questions. Thus, self-exculpation does not arise wholly from internal necessity, but sometimes also from the knowledge that one is on trial. There is the further fact that the curiosity of one's acquaintances is greatly increased by the fact that his marital status is undefined.

It should not be forgotten that gossip is often motivated. One of the most unfortunate things about a divorce is that one is exposed to his enemies while it is in process. He lives for a long time in a position which is open to attack from all sides, and they are rare who are too gallant to take advantage of such an opportunity to injure an enemy or a rival. If those who do not like a man are clever, they may alienate his friends by taking advantage of the mistakes he makes while his emotions are not at one. In professional circles, the fact that one is having or has had a divorce furnishes a handle by which his enemies and professional rivals can take hold of him. A recurrent mechanism is that by which people who are themselves gossiping pass on their tales with the comment, "There's a lot of talk about so-and-so." (A word of caution is perhaps in order. We should not take at its face value the statement, "Gossip has ruined my life," for such a belief is more likely than not mere rationalization. It is a mistake of emphasis.)

Complications arise where there is nothing more than simple and uncomplicated divorce, but in the more unusual cases there result intricacies not capable of being entangled by any calculus which we now know. Cases occur, for instance, where husbands and wives are traded. What do the amenities demand in such instances? The writer knows of such a case which was further complicated by the fact of children born to both men by both women; in this tangled situation all was apparently arranged so that everybody was happy, and more than the amenities were preserved, the exceptionally close rapport between the families being prolonged to the second generation; but what all this required by way of inner adjustment, or what it cost in terms of psychological travail, the writer does not know.

In a recent murder trial a unique living arrangement came to light. A man named Carr, a former Philadelphia policeman, was divorced by his wife some years ago. The wife remarried, but Carr did not. When Carr was unable to find work and needed a home, the second husband took him into his home. When Carr was indicted for the murder of his benefactor, his own son testified against him. In an Omaha divorce case the former husband was named as a corespondent, but he insisted that although he had lived in the same house with his former wife after her separation, his only object was to help her financially by paying board. He had, he said, attempted to reconcile his former wife and her second husband.

A husband and wife who had frequently separated over a period of years, but who seemed nevertheless to have a great deal of affection for each other, finally broke up and the wife sought a divorce. The previous separations had been at the instance of the wife, who had periodically run away from home with other men; in this final separation she divorced her husband and married the new love. The husband sought another wife and put the first one definitely behind him. This second wife had also been married before, and had a child to whom he became much attached. The first wife, tiring of her second mate, returned to her husband, who refused to repudiate his wife, but could not be entirely cold to his first wife's pleas. She took an apartment close to the one in which he lives with his second wife, and he divides his time between the two households.

Sometimes one marries twice into the same family. Even where the opportunity to do this is given by death, complications arise, but where it is divorce which furnishes the occasion, the complications are multiplied. This is true even where the highest of motives prompt both parties to the second marriage, as in the case of the man who marries the woman whom his brother has treated shamefully.

If there are children by both marriages in any of these double-decked households, the business of life grows very complex, but children by themselves complicate things sufficiently. The bitterness of divorce is often increased by a struggle over the custody of the child. When that is settled, the tendency of the child to sympathize a bit with the parent who does not have custody of it, and to look forward to the occasional visits, may bring heartbreak to the more responsible parent. Situations replete with tragedy are not uncommon; the father who, coming to the bedside of the son whom he thought to be dying, heard himself cursed and reviled with all the boy's none too plentiful strength, must have gone away with a feeling that his life was somehow awry. Children learn to take their little vengeances in their own way, as did the boy who purchased silk stockings and expensive perfumes for his mother on the charge account which his father maintained for him. What should the parent who has been deemed more worthy to have the custody of the child tell that child concerning the absent mate? Ah, that is a question not to be answered lightly, and the answer cannot yet be given in terms of morality, or sportsmanship, or psychology. (This is the essential problem of Ibsen's

Ghosts. Should the child be allowed to learn what kind of man his father was?)

Often, there comes about as a response to both inner and outer compulsions a turning to one's own, and a throwing into a dominant position in consciousness of the thought that blood is thicker than water. When a stranger lays us low, it is our relatives who pick us up and nurse us back to life and health. With marriage the parents have lost some of their emotional importance, if a proper transference of love has been made, and this no doubt is as it should be, but the one who has ceased to be married is aided in his readjustment if, for a time at least, the parental images are there and willing to receive again his love. This is the parent's opportunity to remedy the damage which he has perhaps indirectly done to the child, by incapacitating him for marriage. It is of course also his chance to arrest an alienation between parent and child, and to reëstablish rapport. Whether it is wise that parents should intervene is another matter, and must be decided on other grounds.

In case the divorced person, usually young, and in this case usually a woman, goes back to live under the ancestral roof, complications again arise. If the parents do not sympathize, a double conflict arises; if they do sympathize, they do so at the risk of producing an unnecessary break. The attempt to reassert control over the child who has been a man is fraught with comic as well as tragic complications, as is the attempt to regulate the sex life of the daughter who has no husband but is not a virgin. And the family slave who returns to his home may at length resent the yoke which he has hitherto considered light.

And there are such things as suits for alienation of affections.

In-laws are not always inimical; if they were, the divorced would be saved a certain amount of perplexity. It sometimes happens, however, that a man extends the scriptural injunction that he should cleave unto his wife in preference to his parents even to the wife's family, and where this happens there are likely to arise in case of divorce some most puzzling problems of human relationships. Occasionally even the closest relatives of the woman will remain partisans of the husband during and after the period of separation and divorce, proving that water may acquire a viscosity exceeding that of blood, but this is rarely the case except where there is involved a considerable antagonism toward the wife, and is even then only possible at the expense of decisive conflict. Nevertheless, in several of the cases studied, the wife or husband continued the closest contact with the parents-in-law after the relation with the spouse had been severed. On *a priori* grounds it looms up as a much greater possibility that one should keep as intimates the more distant relatives of the divorced wife or husband, and this is found to be in fact the case. The same statements hold good with modifications for the friends whom one met through the divorced mate.

Marriage and divorce are apt to take place entirely within the confines of some small group in which the person lives most intensely. (In general, the existence of such a group tends to make marriage more permanent, but there are many small groups in which divorce is something of a folkway, being permitted and even considered smart.) If several members of such a group have married within it, divorced, and then married a second time within it, the most amazing complications ensue. It used to be said, for instance, that hostesses of the 400 needed an excellent knowledge of history in order to be able to seat their guests at table in a manner that would be satisfactory to all; the object of this care was to keep the separate members of a riven couple from coming into too close contact. It is true that the animosity which match-making hostesses excite is as nothing as compared to that which they may arouse by too obvious attempts at reconciliation of people who have decided for reasons of their own to separate. Perhaps the greatest complications arise not where the former husband and wife are inimical, there is no moral issue here, but where there is still life in the embers of love; and this becomes a problem of paramount importance if there has been a remarriage. These difficulties in the adjustment of one's social life within a small group account in part for the frequency of the complete break with all the past and all the people in it.

The complication of internal problems by an external carry-over of the old liaison is often strikingly and painfully in evidence. A man and his wife had separated under circumstances which conduced to bitterness on both sides and which led a considerable number of the home town people to sympathize with the woman. Partly on the strength of this very general sympathy for her, she was elected to a high office in a secret society of which she was a member. This meant that she would get a large number of telephone calls, but through some confusion in the telephone directory, those who intended to call her usually got her ex-husband's office. In exasperation he finally told one person who had so called, "I am Mrs. Green's *former* husband. I get calls for that woman all day long. I don't know where you can get her but for God's sake don't call me. This is the wrong number."

A marriage lives in the minds of men when it is legally dead. When people have had many friends in their marital state, the task of informing the friends of the break may string out over half a lifetime. While a break is recent, one sometimes experiences the keenest revivals of regret when he is asked, "And how is Mrs. so-and-so?" or reminded of some trivial incident that occurred during marriage, or when some chance meeting ends with the polite request, "Well, give my best to your wife." A man told of being unable to present a letter of introduction because it said: "This will introduce Mr. so-and-so, and his wife"; he would not use it because to do so would have involved answering embarrassing questions and would have allowed his former friends to learn of his divorced condition.

Alimony and arrangements for the custody of the children, with the customary privilege of visitation which is accorded to the other parent, are also important as ensuring the continuance of contacts between former husbands and wives. An acquaintance of the writer, still apparently a bit in love with his ex-wife, must by order of the court allow her to see her children when she wishes. Out of consideration for her, he acts as chauffeur for her and the children on those occasions. He then feels, he says, "like a chauffeur"—a psychic arrangement to make tolerable a socially imposed situation.

There is of course a very obvious relationship between these external changes and certain inner ones. The personality changes of divorcés are due in part to the fact that they must rearrange their system of social relationships. Sometimes they break completely with their former friends, and must form their whole set of acquaintances anew; where this is done it is a means of avoiding other complications whose nature has been briefly indicated. But when one is friendless, he enters the group that is easiest to get in, and this helps to account for the prevalence of the Bohemian mode of adjustment among divorcés. In all cases one assigns new values to his friends; people who have been meaningful before are avoided, and those who have been previously not significant are taken up and made important. Sometimes one takes up a person whom one has previously declined to know.

"I got in touch with a French girl that I had met some years before. At the time that I had met her I did not think that she was the sort of person I wanted to go around with, and neither did my husband. But when I got so very lonely I finally decided to call her up. I called her and told her that I was divorced from my husband and was living alone. She was glad to hear from me and came right over that same evening. She began to take me on parties. You see, I had never been on what you call a party before. My husband had done that for me, he had kept me out of touch with everything of that sort. I met lots of men, but most of them seemed very crude to me. My husband had at least not been like that."

If the things that we have mentioned so far as making for complication in the system of relations in which the divorcé is involved are mainly of external origin, there are other factors, no less important hidden deep within the breast of the person himself. If one takes an inventory, as many divorced persons have done, he must find many changes in his internal constitution. True, these changes are not all in the nature of losses; many persons have felt that they came through their troubles refined and improved by the ordeal. And not all these inner changes are such as to produce a greater complexity in one's social relationships; there are some, such as the growth of courage and the throwing off of restraint and fear, that are of the essence of simplicity. But the general weight of the experience is on the side of sophistication rather than that of naïveté, and in most things the divorcé finds that his responses have become more circuitous, that he is more likely than he used to be to gain his ends by indirection.

One of the traits which the divorcé has which increases the complexity of his relations to other people, which makes those other people have to handle him more deftly than they would handle persons of a different sort, is sensitivity. This fact, together with its relation to the mechanism of projection, is well illustrated by the following excerpt from a case record.

Certain things about which subject is sensitive are as follows. If any of the girls where she works make "double dates" in which she is not included she feels it very strongly. It happens, too, that she is occasionally not invited to parties to which she thinks she should be invited, and this, too, hurts. Other incidents give support to the supposition that there may be herein involved a projection mechanism. At a small informal gathering she very much wished to reveal to another person in the group the fact that she was divorced, but hesitated for a long time for fear that her escort would not wish it known that he was going out with a divorced woman. The escort, it happened was a fairly well-liberated young man, having reached that stage in liberation where he was proud of his broad-mindedness. Further, after she had revealed to the investigator her unconventional amours she seemed very sure that he disapproved, or that he would "look down on her." This could be classed definitely as projection.

(When this subject was made aware of her inferiority drives and of her projection mechanisms whereby she put into the heads of others thoughts which were really only in her own mind, her social relationships considerably improved.)

Defense reactions in general have been discussed more or less in full in the previous chapter. It should be noted here that every one of these has an effect upon the contacts which one makes with other people. There is, for instance, among men, the matter of ruthlessness toward the opposite sex, which may come about whenever one's ego feelings have been injured because of love.

By an exaggeration of this type of reaction, coupled with a perhaps unspoken desire to get even with the members of the opposite sex, or at least the notion that they do not play fair, further complicated by a philosophy of promiscuity, and perhaps by strong sex needs, we find the divorced person often arriving at a place where his personal mores are widely separated from those of the group. This makes him incomprehensible and unpredictable to those who would otherwise be his friends, and in many cases produces severe complications. If those with whom he lives experience the conventional mores as subjectively real, they will find the excuse of another person that he does not endorse them in their current form a halting one. Or the divorcé may be thrown into association with the sort of people who express advanced ideas with regard to the relations of the sexes, but are shocked and surprised to learn that anyone puts these ideas into

practice. A similar reason for misunderstanding between a divorced person and those who are about him
is his technique of sexual adjustment. As married
persons find themselves unable to keep up in conversation the reserves that are considered best among
single persons, so divorced persons, having experienced the whole gamut of sexual expression, sometimes find polite pretense wearing, and the inhibitions of society unwelcome. In the mere matter of
the technique of effecting a sexual adjustment, the
person who has been married, since he has not been
accustomed to wooing his love anew in every separate instance and has therefore lost his knowledge of
or patience with the process, may jump several preliminary stages considered necessary, and may
therefore be thought crude.

One who has suffered a great injury may be led to
acts of protest which lose him the confidence, if not
the affection, of even the closest friends. A doctor,
for instance, who goes on a two-year spree, cannot
hope to retain his practice, however easy his friends
may find it to condone his inebriety. A minister, too,
who has lost his professional standing because of
divorce, and has taken up certain radical activities
and beliefs in the hope that these may furnish some
relief for his internal tensions, cannot for long retain
the esteem of the good people of the church.

Not infrequently one's ego necessities become so
aggravated by divorce that his entire life seems to
be organized around the ego drive in its crudest
form. Such a person is unwilling to deny himself any
ego gratification at the expense of others, unwilling
to forego any jest which may be hurtful to the dignity of another. Driven by the cruel pains within
himself, he takes an aggressive rôle in all his rela-

tions with others, and does not hesitate to sacrifice them to his own vanity. Naturally such a person is hated. If he later assimilates the experience of divorce more completely, and obtains insight into his actions, he comes to regret his childish intolerance. In any case, the people who are driven to hate him usually take their revenge. A newspaper man told the following story of his personal relations after divorce:

"Just after my divorce I was very unhappy and very troubled in my own mind, but I tried to hide this from all but my closest friends. Toward them I was perhaps more than ever devoted, because of my increased dependence on them, but toward all others, and especially toward people whom I did not like, or people whom I did not consider very intelligent, I was very intolerant and often abusive.

"There was a kid in the advertising department named Red W——. If you've ever been around a newspaper you know that the reporters don't think very much of the solicitors of advertising and the people in the advertising department don't like the reporters. The advertising people think the reporters are crazy and wild, and the reporters think the advertising people are dumb. Of course I had to take up the old feud and make it personal.

"Red was a very good sort of boy. Just a plug horse, nothing brilliant about him before or since. No fight in him, though, and he never had anything much to say for himself. He was about my age, or just a little older. I singled him out for a sort of special persecution. I crucified him in the name of the advertising department of the newspaper. He was very religious, so I did a lot of very blasphemous swearing in his presence. He was very moral, so I would catch him in the midst of a group of people and would walk up and slap him on the back and make some vulgar remark. I accused him of being a sly dog and not letting any of us know of his crimes. I would take lunch with him just to get off a lot of wise-cracks at his expense. A few of them went over his head, but he got the drift anyhow.

"He hated me, and the time came when he took his revenge in the most natural way in the world. I wanted a certain position which depended in part upon his immediate superior, who liked and trusted Red because he was decent and honest. This man asked Red about me, and Red said that I was noisy and vulgar, and that lots of people didn't like me. I was very indignant for a while but a friend pointed out that I had given Red every reason to dislike me, and I had to admit that it was true. I tried to make amends, but it was too late, and I guess Red still thinks me a pretty bad lot."

Employers often feel that they have a certain stake in the matrimonial affairs of their subordinates. There is some justification for this feudal attitude, for the prestige of many concerns depends in part upon the confidence of the public in the personal integrity of their employees. Where it is not justified by business statistics, the interest of the employer in the employee's wife and family is a human failing, but it is one which the subordinate is very likely to resent, taking the moving picture attitude, "You can buy my services, but my private life is my own." If employer and employee are members of the same social set, so that the employer knows the divorced wife and likes her, her husband is likely to suffer a loss of prestige in the eyes of his superior, and with it may go his chance of preferment. Peculiarly strained is the situation when the chief, believing, rightly or wrongly, that he has a right to know the important developments in the personal life of those who work for him, finds that one of his trusted subordinates has been lacking in frankness in his relations with him.

The necessity of concealment is of prime importance in the lives of many divorced persons, whether
it be concealment of things that are within them,
perhaps concealment from themselves as well as
from others, or concealment of the events of their
lives. Sometimes, in response to these inner and outer
needs, a pretense is elaborated until it becomes a
way of life. One may carry this on for years, and
then when the pretense is at length found out, the
disclosure is the more shocking because it has been
so long delayed.

All will remember, for instance, the intense public
interest in the recent tragedy in which the wife of a
certain great baseball player was involved. A woman
who had been living with a Boston dentist, and who
had been known as his wife, burned to death, and it
was learned from pictures and from some letters that
the woman was none other than the wife of the celebrated athlete. Although there had been frequent
rumors that all was not well in the household of the
star, the extent of the alienation had been concealed,
perhaps with the connivance of friendly newspaper
men. When the story broke it was all the better for
having been so long in preparation; on the morrow
the details were on everybody's tongue. Many things
about their life which had previously seemed mys-
terious then became intelligible, and columns of
news were published in all the papers.

Motivated in part by a desire not to injure the
earning power of the husband, this pair had for years
kept up a pretense of domestic life. In their pretense
many dramatic gestures figured; when either was ill,
the other went to the hospital and sat by the bedside
with every appearance of concern. There were little

semi-public acts of conjugal affection, all of which were made to seem later merely a part of the show. To be sure, the performance was not so convincing that people did not suspect that something was wrong behind the scenes. But when the rumors began to fly thickest, there was always a new subterfuge, pathetic, halting, and insincere, but enough to quiet suspicion. The whole life of the pair came to be like a performance in a play, a pathetic attempt to make the truth a lie, a thing of comic excuse and shabby fraud.

That was perhaps the most sensational affair of the sort in recent years, but others break into the public prints from time to time. There was, for instance, the case of a very famous playwright, who, lack of candor having apparently become a habit with him, was arrested while on an innocent visit to the Orient because he acted suspiciously, i.e., because he acted as if he were trying to conceal something. This when the time was near when he should put aside his second wife, while the third, already spoken for, awaited her turn.

There is justification for the circumspection and secrecy of the divorced in the fact that the newspapers are more than willing to exploit their adventures as news. There are a certain number of divorced persons who commit sensational crimes or adopt bizarre and unusual solutions to their personal problems. It would be an error in reporting if the fact that the persons involved in such cases had recently been divorced were not mentioned. But the words *divorce, divorced, divorcé, estranged wife, estranged husband,* etc., are catch-words, and are used to give significance to many stories which would not otherwise be considered important enough to print. But while journalism gains by such use of words, the people most concerned sometimes suffer disproportionately. For, excepting a few publicity-seekers whose twisted minds bring them frequently and unprofitably into the public view, divorced persons want privacy in which to work out their own problems.

The past, which one has attempted to put forever behind him, is sometimes rather cruelly exploited by those who have a point to gain. There may be important psychological effects when it is suddenly revived. This was strikingly illustrated by a story in a recent issue of the Philadelphia *Evening Public Ledger*.

FAINTS IN COURT ON SEEING
FIRST WIFE HE DENIED HAVING

A $10,000 damage suit was ended sensationally in Camden Circuit Court to-day, when the plaintiff, suddenly confronted by his first wife after he had denied a previous marriage, collapsed on the witness stand crying: "I don't want them to bring up my past."

The name of the first wife, who was whisked into the courtroom while the claimant, Frank T. Praria, Camden deep-sea diver, was discussing the case with his lawyer, was not revealed. The woman left hastily with her mother immediately after Judge Jess ordered the case nonsuited. Praria admitted he had not seen the surprise witness for fifteen years.

Praria frequently has come into the limelight. At the time of the S-4 submarine disaster he blamed government divers for the loss of life in the tragedy and later was called before a Congressional Investigating Committee.

SUIT FOLLOWED BUS ACCIDENT

As a result of alleged injuries received a year ago when a Penn-Jersey bus was stopped suddenly, Praria sued the company for $10,000 damages.

When the case came up for trial Frank K. Lloyd, counsel for the bus company, opened his examination of Praria with inquiries regarding his domestic life. He asked Praria how many times he had been married. The diver said once. Lloyd then motioned to a woman seated in the rear of the room and told her to stand up.

The lawyer asked Praria if the woman was his wife. Praria identified her as his wife, who before her marriage, he said, was Katharine Sink.

Praria flatly denied any other marriage. Lloyd then produced a letter signed "Your devoted wife, Clara." It had been mailed from Charleston, S. C.

HIS FIRST WIFE BROUGHT IN

"Did you ever receive such a letter?" Lloyd asked.

Praria admitted he had. A moment later Praria was startled when an elderly woman walked into the courtroom. Praria was asked if he knew her.

"Yes, that is Mrs. Skerret, my mother-in-law, the mother of my first wife," he admitted, and then added, "I'd like to talk to my lawyer."

This request was granted and Praria and Joseph Wilson, his counsel, went into an anteroom. At this moment the first wife was introduced into the case. An attractive woman was brought into the courtroom and took a seat facing the witness chair.

Praria came back and resumed the witness stand. Apparently he did not see the new figure in the case.

"Do you know this woman?" asked Lloyd.

Startled, Praria looked where the lawyer pointed.

"Yes—my first wife," replied Praria. "I haven't seen her in fifteen years."

He then slumped in the seat, burying his head in his arms.

It was five minutes before the case could continue. At the mention of the first wife, Mrs. Praria, 2nd, half rose in her chair, and then, taking her child, got up and left the room.

"Stop the suit," said Praria to his counsel. "I don't want them to bring up my past."

Judge Jess reminded the man that he had committed perjury in saying he had been married only once.

"Yes, why bring that up?" replied Praria.

The case was ordered non-suited and Judge Jess instructed that the County Prosecutor be given a copy of the proceedings to determine if a perjury charge is to be pressed.

Judging from the effect of the introduction of the surprise witness upon this man, apparently he had not only hidden the past from others, but from himself as well; in technical language, he had repressed knowledge of it. His desire to keep such knowledge from others no doubt rooted in his unwillingness to accept that part of his past as part of himself. Thus an old, unassimilated experience arose fifteen years later to confront him with tragic results.

The reactions of the people in these more extreme cases are paralleled by those of divorcés everywhere. People do not want their divorce to get in the newspapers, and much of the injury to one's pride comes from the danger of, if not the actuality of, unfavorable publicity. Secret divorces, and the prolongation of the externals of marriage, pathetic attempts to keep it all out of the newspapers, to hide it from the prying world, these recur again and again.

Sometimes there is some one person, or group of persons, from whom one particularly desires to keep the information. More often this is from hate rather than from love, yet either motivation is possible. The parents of the divorced person are thus often the last ones to hear of the break. If there is any particular person who one feels will be gratified by such news, then every effort will be made to conceal the facts from that individual. Thus one divorced woman, whose mother had years before counseled her against the marriage, did not break the news of the divorce to her mother for years after it had occurred, and kept up the little pretense as long as she could. In a marriage of rebellion, and the result of the present investigation would be that such marriages are somewhat more likely than others to be unwise, this is peculiarly likely to be the case. Or it may be that the persons whose knowledge of the affair would be regarded as most damaging are outside the family; in this case people have been known to move out of town and go on sending joint Christmas cards to their inimical friends for some years. And the question which is then ever alive is: How much do they know?

An elaborate pretense may have other objects than mere concealment. A divorced woman who has a marriageable daughter must at the very least do double duty in furnishing a genteel background for her and must not only display the daughter's charms, but also gloss over many things which might detract from them in the eyes of desirable suitors.

A woman who a few years ago was involved in a sensational and hotly contested divorce action now has it as her central purpose in life to marry her daughter well. About this main purpose she has organized her life and her personality.

She continually, but very adroitly, parades her social position. She mentions famous people whom she knows, and makes clear the intimacy of her connection with them. She has read the right books and seen the right plays. Her house is a model of refinement and accepted good taste. She has become a lion hunter; it has been remarked that when she was a girl she was a sincere enthusiast, while now she is a calculating person—a calculating, but not a selfish woman, for she makes a return for all kindnesses.

She is always charming to eligible young men, sparing no personal cost. She keeps open house for them; they may come when they will and they may stay overnight if they wish. (This last privilege is intended to offset the relatively inaccessible location of the home.) For herself, she adopts the rôle of the genteel Bohemian. She drinks a bit, and gives to the young men the understanding sympathy of a woman of the world. But with all this goes always a suggestion of the daughter's naïveté. The girl herself is studiedly and carefully naïve; perhaps, the mother and daughter somewhat overdo this.

The former husband is mentioned casually in various social groups, in such a way as to suggest a complete assimilation of the experience and a complete objectivity toward him. If she is questioned, she can say with the utmost poise and dignity, "I'd rather not talk about that." Her rationalization of her marital break—since she was once a Catholic, this was an experience difficult to accept—is that a spiritual woman should never marry an athletic and animalistic man; since the husband is a scholarly and refined person, this would hardly seem to fit the facts of the case.

Financial stringency in such a household as the one described above can give birth to a whole species of complications of a similar nature.

In discussing the complication of social relationships by divorce we have in fact but brushed the surface. For these tangled social relations are on the obverse side of every subjective difficulty, and these subjective difficulties are the subject matter of this entire work. More particularly, we have omitted to discuss the complication of social relationships which takes place as a simple result of prejudice against divorced persons, thinking that this might be included in the less simple cases.

CHAPTER TEN

Economic Consequences of Divorce

A MAN who has no real fear of making that journey so renowned in song and story, the trip over the hills to the poorhouse, may yet when he comes to get a divorce find worry over matters of economics frequently and unpleasantly present in his thoughts. In many cases, no doubt, this concern over income is, in accordance with the by now familiar displacement mechanism, made to serve as a substitute for a deeper anxiety which is not faced and admitted as such, yet there are possibilities enough of injury to one's business or profession to justify one in looking at the future with a certain dread of what it may bring forth.

The creation-day difference between male and female is of course present here as elsewhere. Divorce injures a man in his business primarily by affecting his system of social relationships, so that he loses standing, loses the confidence of his clientele, and loses friends and connections. But a woman must often learn for the first time to bear the burden of her own support; this is the more difficult because she has left an occupation so highly specialized that it unfitted her for any other. The man has more to lose professionally, but he also has more with which to work in reëstablishing himself. Both men and women are handicapped by the fact that they must make far-reaching readjustments at a time when adaptability is lowered by preoccupation with internal problems. Where there are preëstablished channels of activity, with habits of self-expression in a certain kind of work well established, the inner tensions, giving rise to compensatory drives, may be of great economic utility, but this is probably not the usual case.

For a divorced woman not provided for by alimony or inheritance the problem of learning to pay her own way is likely to be for a time the subject of the deepest concern. She must often take up some sort of occupation which will pay her an immediate salary, she has neither time nor money to invest in a long-term career; this shuts out many possibilities. More than likely she has been trained only for matrimony; matrimony is a specialized profession, and women who take that way of life must lose some of their adaptability. If she was professionally trained, she has very likely lost touch with her profession; at any rate she must start all over again. She is not, and has perhaps never been, habituated to self-support; she does not know her way around in the workaday world. Besides, she is worried, worried about her marital break, and worried about how she is going to live.

Often we cannot but be amazed at the singleness of purpose with which women whose marriages have broken, or are in process of breaking, plunge into work. A woman who was faced after six years of marriage with the problem of learning to earn her own living tells of the experience:

"One of my biggest worries during those first few months, both before I gave up my apartment and after, was wondering whether or not I would be able to make my money meet my needs. You see, I'd never been out on my own before, and

I didn't know how I was going to come out. Of course, I'd seen all this coming about six months before the break, and I'd gone to school and prepared myself for self-support but still I didn't know whether or not I was going to make both ends meet.

"Well, the day my husband walked out of the house I cried all day and all night. I expected him to come back, though. He had left once before at the end of our fourth year together. This time he didn't come back. I called him up Monday and asked him what he expected me to live on. He said he'd give me fifteen dollars, which he did,—for about six weeks, and then he had to be reminded that he'd made the promise. I wasn't bitter about the money. I didn't want his money.

"For three months after my husband left I went to school every evening and worked all day. I made no friends, and had only the few that I had had before. There were no men friends. I was all alone those three months. At the end of the three months I moved into a new neighborhood, changed the environment and changed everything that might remind me of the old life. I went to live with some other people who were very nice to me. For a while I turned to my work and I got along well with it. I worked all day and went to school in the evenings. It gave me something to do and something to think about.

"Finally I got a lawyer and he got my divorce for me. The judge said that I was entitled to twenty-five dollars a week alimony, but since we had settled on fifteen dollars a week as a sum that was agreeable to both parties he would make it just that. I got it irregularly for a year or so but I never pushed him very hard for it and finally he quit paying anything at all."

A Spanish woman, once married to an American, now makes her living by giving Spanish lessons to a private clientele. With her the process of learning to make a living was complicated by a language handicap and the fact that she was not a native of this country. She also had a child for whose support she would have to take the responsibility. In her case the process of establishing herself economically and the break-up of her home went on concurrently.

"My husband's trade? Ah, that's the thing. I have told you what his background was. He left school when he was eleven years old. He had just drifted around the world, and had done a little of everything. I will always have affection for him. I suppose I dominated him. The best part of myself I have given him and I cannot take it back. I never gave him cross words. I'll tell you how long I was happy. My happiness rested on the fact that when I first came over here I was helpless. My husband was the one who knew things and I was alone in this strange country. I did not know English and did not know what kind of English he was speaking.

"That second year I went home on a visit. When I got back into the old environment I realized what a change it had been. I still had affection for him, though. All the way over on the boat I was thinking, 'Oh, what I shall feel when I see him,' but I felt—absolutely nothing. It was that way that night, too. He asked me, 'Margaret, what is the matter?' I could not tell him. I said, 'It is because I am so happy to see you.' The next day I realized that he had not been working. I thought, 'Well, if he won't work, I will.' I wanted to teach. I had wanted to teach all my life, perhaps because I am a little bit bossy....

... "Well, I finally got a job in a kindergarten school in a suburb. Not much, but it was a start. It only paid ten dollars a month, and I had to pay five of it for someone to take care of my boy and I had to pay carfare. I used to get sick on the trolley car; it was a long ride and the car was stuffy. But it was a job, and it was experience in handling American children, and I thought I might get a better one later.

"Well, along toward spring an offer came from the —— school to work for them. They don't pay very much and you are there from morning till night, from eight in the morning until night, but I wanted to get started. I talked to my dear husband— Yes, I'm being sarcastic, and he said, 'No, your place is here at home.' You see, we had gone to housekeeping. We had a little place, hardly any furniture and my money had paid for most of that. A little gas stove, we had paid a dollar and a half for it, I think. My husband was working then and was making twenty-five dollars a week. He gave me six dollars a week to run the house. You can imagine how much we could buy with that. We bought one-half pound of butter a week. If we ran out of butter before pay-day we had to eat our bread without butter until then. You have no idea what I went through for him. Such a contrast to what I had been used to at home. But I never wrote a word of that home. I wrote home that everything was fine and that we were getting along well.

"In May I went to the —— school and I made a little money and worked hard all summer trying to get enough together so that we could furnish a house. I got a job in a different suburb that paid twenty dollars a month and that helped. In February we left the house, that I had furnished, and went to boarding. The rent was too expensive. I was beginning then to give some private lessons, and that helped with expenses.

"The next year I got $1,200 for teaching. That was beginning to be a salary. I gave some private lessons, too, and made in all about $1,800 that year. But my husband did not work from January till May. That was our fourth year of marriage.

"The next year I did better, but I found that the more I made the less my husband worked. In addition I found my husband empty. He was nice, but dreadfully empty. I began to think that I could not be his wife. I explained to him that I could not. In January I told him. He would not believe me because he knew how I loved him. I do not regret that I loved him.

"... (Six months later she left her husband and established herself in an apartment with her son.) I was alone till January and didn't know a soul. You see, when I had left my husband I had broken with all his friends. I worked from morning till night. I took every bit of work I could get; I was so afraid that I might not be able to make both ends meet. I had an eight o'clock class in the evening. At nine the people would go and I would sit in that chair and sometimes I would cry."

These accounts will perhaps serve to show how important the matter of learning to earn one's income may be. Sometimes women compelled to face this situation show a surprising amount of generalship. Houses are rented, rooms are changed around in such a way as to make possible another guest, a latent talent for business arrangements is discovered.

But there are cases in which there are no assets to utilize. Those who have read *Family Disorganization* will remember the case of Miriam Donovan.[1] This case was paralleled by one known to the writer, that of a French girl who, divorcing her husband, was induced to become the mistress of an elderly, but well-to-do American. Here there was no such tragic dénouement, for the girl subsequently made a very advantageous marriage. In another case a woman who had been living in a luxurious home went to a private school as a serving maid. Here she was compelled to work long hours for low wages, whereas before she had employed a maid to do her work and had spent her afternoons riding around in her car, but strangely enough she seemed happier when earning her bread literally by the sweat of her brow. Often the difficulties of learning to make their own way drive women to contract second marriages whose unsuitability contributes much to the essential tragedy of their lives. Especially is there inducement for the woman to go back to the old trade if she has children dependent upon her.

---

[1] Mowrer, *op. cit.,* pp. 230 ff.

A woman who is able to return to the parental home is apparently better off, but in fact perhaps no more fortunate than her sister who must fight it out alone. In many cases it was this home which produced the traits which incapacitated the woman for life and marriage; these will be accentuated and conflict perhaps made more severe if after her divorce she returns to it. She must also often go through a double conflict about her divorce, one within herself, and the other in the minds of her parents. And she must once again learn to accept money from her parents, a thing which requires a flexibility of the neck which some women do not possess.

Often the women who win through independently must bear the scars of their struggle during the rest of their lives. An attitude of playing safe may be engendered, for instance, which will prevent her from entering wholeheartedly into a second marriage. Mindful of certain economic difficulties which she had had, such a woman remarked: "Well, I must play safe. I must have a raincoat the next time I get caught in a storm." Sometimes the parents are blamed for the fact that they have not permitted the daughters to fit themselves for a career of their own; one amazing young woman thought her husband at fault because he had not, during their marriage, given her a college education. Or the work that a woman must do may involve a lowering of her dignity which she does not soon forget. Immediately after her separation from her husband a certain young woman worked in a cheap department store. Four years later she had a dream which reflected her anxiety not to be classified as a shopgirl.

But the fate of the left-over ladies who do not

find another niche into which they may fit, who do not reëstablish themselves as self-respecting members of a working world, is perhaps more dire than that of those who reëstablish themselves, but with difficulty. Margaret Culkin Banning has described the hapless plight of these women in a recent article in *Harper's*. Mrs. Banning's felicitous language may well be reproduced here:

"Suppose it all does come true. There is a reputable school of Ingleside thought which refuses to credit such a possibility, but suppose, none the less, that marriage does come to be regarded as a short-term lease on a relationship, and that men and women look at it dispassionately, and at each other even more so. What is going to happen to all the left-over wives, the scrapped ones, the women set adrift after temporary anchorage, the women whose youth has passed and whose youth was their chief value in exchange—the extra ladies? That is what bothers me. . . .

"The economic problem involved in turning a great many more women out of marriage, which was the only occupation for which they were even comparatively trained, was recognized. . . .

"They are too old to learn and too healthy to die. . . . Now and then a latent talent, a re-shaped mind, a strengthened soul, breaks through the fog and finds direction lessening the waste. The rest of them will have to be scrapped, and we might as well face it." [2]

When we turn to the men we find different problems, but no less important. The man is already established, as a rule, and his problem is to keep from losing what he has. We are not here speaking of expenses, such as lawyer's fees, court costs, etc. which are often almost ruinous, nor of such continu-

[2] Margaret Culkin Banning, "Extra Ladies," *Harper's Magazine*, Harper Brothers, New York, October, 1928, Vol. 57, pp. 557 *ff*. By permission from *Harper's Magazine*.

ing drains as alimony, but of such things as affect the income which a man receives from his business or profession. The effects are in general such as would ensue from the complication of a man's system of social relationships. There are some professions, for instance teaching and the ministry, in which a man is seriously injured by the existence of any marital maladjustment, whether the fault be his or that of his wife; in fact, by some inverse logic, we may forgive a man for what he does himself, regarding certain transgressions as the foibles of the male, but condemn him completely for what his wife does. The break with former friends on account of divorce may lead to the loss of valuable business connections. Always, too, where the divorce has given rise to serious subjective problems, there is the possibility that a man's professional skill is actually reduced. Also, it happens that a man is led by his internal necessities to do things which are considered unwise or reprehensible by the community at large, and these will react unfavorably upon him. Some of these factors were present in the following case:

A young physician was established in a French parish on the outskirts of Chicago. Although himself of English extraction, he had been reared among the French, understood them well, and had built up a very lucrative practice.

He went occasionally to visit his parents in Kentucky. While there he met a young woman whom he had known for a long time, had a number of engagements with her, and ended by seducing her, without much difficulty, he says. This young woman claimed to be pregnant, and the doctor took her word as to her condition. They were married.

While the young doctor and wife were on the train going to Chicago, the wife said, "Well, I guess I've got you now. I might as well tell you I put one over on you. I'm not pregnant at all." The doctor was enraged, and refused to live with his newly-wed wife. Since he remained obdurate, the wife returned to her home. It had been agreed that they were to take no immediate steps toward a divorce, but were to keep their marriage a secret.

One day the doctor entertained a friend from home. In the course of the conversation, the friend said, "I notice you don't come down our way any more. Well, you're lucky, that girl you were running around with is having intercourse with everybody in town." The young doctor replied, "That woman is my wife." The friend replied, "I am sorry. If I had known I should not have said what I did, but it is true." This incident decided the doctor to get a divorce.

But his wife was not willing to be divorced, and there was a struggle. Although morally certain that grounds for divorce existed, the doctor was unable to get acceptable evidence. Since the case was contested, and was heard in Chicago, it received considerable publicity, and the doctor began to lose practice, for his patients were Catholic, and orthodox.

Grown bitter over the fact that she had not been given an opportunity to demonstrate her talents as a home-maker, the wife seized upon an opportunity which presented itself to injure her husband in his profession. She also was Catholic, and she gave to the newspapers a statement that her Catholicism was the real reason why her husband was divorcing her, that the religious conflict was in fact back of it all. This statement came to the eyes of the doctor's Catholic clientele; he was denounced by the priest, and was ruined.

What remained of his professional standing in that community was destroyed by his own indiscretion, for he now made the so common answer to unfair treatment; he took to drink. In his own words, he "went on a two-year toot." This completed the ruin.

After two years he took hold. He removed to another part of the city, took up a specialty, and because of his very real ability was ultimately able to establish himself again.

One of the most pathetic cases which have come to the attention of the writer was that of a preacher who, having allowed his wife to divorce him on the grounds of cruelty, was thereafter forever denied the habiliments of the ordained. Forced out of the ministry, he turned to other lines of activity, but it was some ten years before he could be said to have reëstablished himself, and the intervening years were spent in the most grueling labor. In his case, as in the preceding one, the matter was somewhat complicated by his own actions, for he turned to radical beliefs and activities which still further alienated from him the orthodox religionists. But these actions are part of our problem, for they arise from a compelling inner necessity produced by divorce.

Sometimes the effects are not so striking. Professional men often weather the storm and sustain no damage at all, but it is a period of insecurity, and one in which anything may happen. The professions differ, of course, in this matter. A lawyer may not find his usefulness greatly reduced by an uncomplicated divorce, but if it comes out that his wife has made a fool of him or he slips in his law, he may suffer considerably. A doctor in general practice will do well to present an irreproachable front to the world, for he comes into very close contact with the families of his patients, but a specialist need not preserve so spotless a record. School teachers will not find that a divorce ordinarily adds to their acceptability to prospective employers and they may find that it takes away from their security of tenure. College professors may get divorces provided the thing is done quietly, but there must be no breath of scandal; every year there are added one or two to the number of those former denizens of the academic world who are forced because of their implication in some scandal to turn from the instruction of the young to other pursuits in which they would not be, presumably, so dangerous to the community.

Often there are effects of divorce of which we are quite unaware. Divorced persons find their applications for insurance sometimes mysteriously rejected. They have been adjudged "bad moral risks." Or divorced persons find themselves mysteriously passed over while others are advanced. When one has a divorce, "every day is judgment day."

Women have more difficulty in readjusting themselves economically after divorce, and have difficulty more frequently than do men. The answer which a crude justice has given is to take money away from the man and give it to the woman. This is alimony. Originating as a means of meting out approximate justice in rare and difficult cases, alimony has come to be a social problem. Permanent alimony is granted in about fifteen per cent of all the divorce cases in the United States. The details are shown in the accompanying table:

Year and party to which divorce was granted	Total divorces	Alimony granted number	%
1922			
All cases	130,251	19,144	14.7
Divorces granted to husband	41,946	3,299	7.9
Divorces granted to wife ...	88,305	15,845	17.9
1916			
All cases	107,544	16,492	15.3
Divorces granted to husband	33,393	1,564	4.7
Divorces granted to wife ...	74,151	14,928	20.1
1887 to 1906			
All cases	930,271	86,559	9.3
Divorces granted to husband	309,912	6,354	2.1
Divorces granted to wife ...	620,359	80,205	12.9

Divorces for which facts as to alimony were returned.[3]

[3] The table above is a reproduction of table 22, of the Special Report of the Census Bureau, Marriage and Divorce, 1922.

Certain statements concerning the table should also be noted: "The statistics concerning alimony related only to permanent alimony secured as an incident to the divorce suit. They do not include alimony secured by a separate and distinct action brought for that purpose, and to that extent, therefore, do not include all the cases in which permanent alimony was considered by the courts. . . . As stated in a former report, it should be explained in connection with this table and the others concerning alimony that the classification 'Granted to husband' and 'Granted to wife' is determined, not in accordance with the party to which alimony is granted, but in accordance with the party to which the divorce is granted. It is not unusual for alimony to be granted to the wife, although the husband sues for and obtains the divorce; but it is very unusual for the husband to obtain alimony from the wife, as in most States the wife is under no legal obligation to support the husband. Where alimony is granted, therefore, it almost always is to the wife." [4]

The widest variations exist in the practice with regard to alimony. Quoting the census report again, "In 1922, of the divorces granted to the husband, the proportion in which alimony was granted varied from .3% in Louisiana to 29.2% in Wisconsin, while in the cases of divorces granted to the wife, the variation was from .3% in Pennsylvania to 54.7% in Wisconsin. Similar variations are shown in the percentages for 1916. These wide variations may be accounted for largely by differences in statutory provisions, in pleading, and in practice." [5]

---

[4] *Ibid.*, p. 29.
[5] *Ibid.*, p. 30.

There is considerable regional variation with regard to the granting of alimony. In the Pacific States (Washington, Oregon, and California), alimony is granted in 21.9% of all divorces. In the West South Central States (Arkansas, Louisiana, Oklahoma, and Texas) it is granted in 4.3% of all the cases. The States with the highest alimony rates are: Wisconsin (48.2%), Utah (40.5%), and Minnesota (30.6%). The States in which alimony is least often granted are: Pennsylvania (.5%), Texas (.7%), Delaware (.9%), North Carolina (1.9%), and Louisiana (2.3%).

At one time alimony was more or less strictly limited to cases in which the divorce was granted by reason of a fault of the husband, but as we have seen this is no longer so. The lack of a satisfactory rule as to when alimony should be granted is to be deplored. Likewise there is confusion as to the amount of alimony that should be given. A rule that is seemingly abandoned was that the wife might not take for her own support alone more than a third of the husband's income. Opinion is divided as to the proper measure of alimony. Some lawyers argue that the wife should be given enough to live on comfortably and no more, others that she should receive enough to support her in the manner to which she was accustomed during her marriage, and yet others think that she should have no alimony at all if she is financially independent.

The fabulous sums paid out in alimony by our millionaires make interesting reading. Some astounding figures are quoted. Sebastian Kresge, ten cent store magnate, has twice been mulcted for large sums, the first wife receiving, it is said, $25,000,000 when she sued for divorce in 1924, and the second receiving some $10,000,000 after four years of married life with him. The international dispute of Orator Francis Woodward and his wife was ended by his giving to her and his children by her, according to the newspaper report, the sum of $3,150,000. A few renowned beauties have become enormously rich by a succession of marriages, each followed by alimony paid in lump sum. There was that fairly well-known lady, Peggy Hopkins Joyce, who named $1,000,000 dollars as the sum which she should require of J. Stanley Joyce, but was dismissed by a niggardly jury with a mere $880,000. This sum did not, it is true, include certain gifts of jewelry which her husband had supplied; the estimated value of these is said to be around a half a million. Ganna Walska received a $300,000 trust fund when she parted from her first husband, a mansion in New York City from her second husband, the late Dr. Joseph Franckel, and has received many golden gifts from her fourth husband, Harold McCormick.

Some specialist in the fatty degeneration of the soul may some day come to fame by explaining the personal bankruptcies of the very solvent. The extraordinary fragility and instability of familial relations among this group must certainly be noted by those who wish to write the social history of our times. In part it is to be accounted for by a novel concept of marriage which has gained acceptance in this sub-group. This concept involves a repudiation of conventional moral standards as to the relation of the sexes. The family is thus simply and finally a property institution. A young woman of vast wealth whose changes of husbands had made her notorious on two continents was asked why she took husbands instead of lovers. She replied, "The only reason any of us in our family get married is because we want our children to be legitimate, for purposes of inheritance, you understand."

Men do not always pay alimony cheerfully. Daily we read of sensational struggles over arrears of alimony, huge sums which have accumulated through years, or the protests of alimony martyrs who choose to languish in jail, giving up their own lives completely, rather than pay their ex-wives the price of their freedom. Sam Reid was California's most distinguished conscientious objector to alimony. Rather than accede to the demand of the court that he pay alimony to his former wife, who had now remarried, and whom he did not consider a fit person to have the custody of his child, he remained for three long years in the jail of the little town of Willows. He was finally rescued by the American Legion, albeit somewhat against his will, for he did not wish the money of his friends to be paid out on account of his wife.

A man who had spent eight months in jail to stalemate his wife in a suit for non-support was interviewed by the writer. His story follows:

Four years ago this man was a prosperous tradesman in a small city in New York. Now he is employed as a night watchman in a factory in New York City,—a position which he has held for the last three years.

Twenty-five years in all intervened between his wedding ceremony and the final decree of the court which severed him from his wife. He was known as a "home man," and lived very really in the relationship with his wife. He took great pride in the efficiency of the household, and says yet that there is no better housekeeper in the world than his wife. He could "feed a dozen visitors without going out of the house." There were two children, both now almost grown.

But after the first ten years the man began to suspect his wife of adultery. In discussing some incident which came up at that time, he said, "I think you're a whore, but I can't prove it." Although his wife enjoyed an enviable reputation in the city in which they made their home, he never gave over his suspicions, and his life came to center around the problem of finding out whether or not they were justified. This lasted almost fifteen years,—small wonder that the man has acquired a considerable personality distortion in consequence.

There was a boarder who was particularly suspected by this jealous husband. He tried by spying to catch his wife and the boarder in a compromising position, but for years did not succeed, although his suspicions remained unabated. He was at first very hostile toward the boarder, and did not hide his suspicions. Then he decided that he would make more progress if he changed his social technique. He therefore became this man's great friend, his very special chum, thinking by this means to throw him off his guard, thinking also perhaps that this last card of friendship could be played to save his home.

His ruse worked. He caught his wife and her paramour in a situation whose meaning could not be denied. This occurred one day when he had remained at home on a pretense of illness. But although he himself was convinced he had no proof which he could offer in court, and his wife's splendid reputation would suffice to give the lie to his unsupported accusation. Nevertheless, he left his home and refused to have anything further to do with his wife.

The wife sued him for non-support. What he had to say in his own defense sounded weak, and the court could do nothing else than issue an order. After some months in which, with the connivance of friendly officials, he escaped arrest, he was caught and sent to jail.

There he stayed eight months. He was perfectly determined to live out the rest of his life behind the bars rather than pay out money to his wife, after the offenses which he knew that she had committed against the marital code. She was perfectly determined that she would have the money or keep him in jail until he died. An impasse.

The keeper of the jail, who was his friend, made him head cook. Always conscientious, and possessed of considerable culinary talent, he tried to perform his duties well. He prides himself on the fact that while he was cook no supplies came into the jail which were not in good condition. In addition, he varied the prison diet with vegetables and other foods supplied by his friends on the outside. In all this he had the approval of the jailer. Naturally of a charitable, as well as stubborn, disposition, he found many persons in jail to befriend, and was rewarded by deep emotional attachments on the part of many of the underworld characters.

His deliverance was effected by a state trooper who was a close friend. This man watched the wife closely, and at the proper time saw that the required number of witnesses were at hand. On the strength of affidavits of these witnesses he was released; a friendly judge having induced the wife to withdraw her action rather than engage in a pitched battle. The husband then, for the sake of the good name of the woman who had so long been his wife and who was the mother of his children, allowed her to get the divorce. There was no alimony.

He was free but he had lost his business, and he had lost his standing in the community, having become identified with persons who were on the wrong side of the moral ledger of the community, having come to be "a jail bird." He removed to the city somewhat discouraged and took the first job which was offered, making no effort to reëstablish himself otherwise. He still had some money, which he kept. After three years he is beginning to build up again, and now holds two positions, with the intention of saving enough money to start out for himself once more.

When the alimony is paid, it often adds much to the man's difficulties of readjustment, whether it be paid willingly or with reluctance. A certain college professor, leaving the wife of his youth, has turned over to her and the children his entire salary, with the intention of living only upon the small income which he gets from his writings; he has been able to do this only by radically curtailing his standard of living. A bank official with an income of three hundred dollars a month gives his wife half of that for her support and that of the two children, certainly not too liberal an allowance, but one which leaves him but little, for he must pay over fifty dollars a month as carrying charges upon his home. In this latter case this economic handicap has led to certain irregularities with a married woman, much to his regret.

The struggle over alimony, and the struggle to pay it, but recently culminated in the suicide of a prominent Chicago artist. This man, whom we shall call Arthur Smith, first gained notice by photographing his wife and child, mostly in the nude. At the time of his divorce from his first wife, she alleged that he had an income of about $20,000 a year, and he agreed to pay her $50 a week. He married again on the day of his divorce, but found it increasingly difficult to pay alimony and to support his second wife. The exactions of the first wife contributed most to making his life with the second difficult, and in the end she too divorced him. He gave her a sum of money, estimated by newspaper writers at $15,000, in lieu of alimony. Torn by love for his second wife and the financial demands of the first, he at length committed suicide, using both poison and a revolver.

Smith left a long typewritten letter in which he gave the details of his story. He had never, he said, loved his first wife, Tess, but had felt, "just the de-

sire of possession which she aroused by her vitality."
He had had with her "ten years of hell." After the
divorce he had expected relief, but he found that life
continued to be difficult, largely because of the alimony which he had agreed to pay. He charged that
the court fight over money wrecked his second marriage. "Jane" (the second wife) "became unhappy
and irritable. I came home unhappy and worried,
thus making Jane unhappy. It was Tess back of
this, her constant dogging me ruined my second home
and caused separation, which was uncalled for.
Nothing seems to matter to Tess as long as she
accomplished her purpose, her desire for possession,
destruction."

His letter continued: "To-day I am without an
asset. Without a home, broke, everything taken from
me. Her greed, her desire for possession has again
taken hold. What a mercenary woman, no regard
for love, romance, life, things beautiful, nothing, just
possession, a greedy want, wants everything she can
lay her hands on. And the most horrible part, she
wants to make a slave of me as before." He spoke
more favorably of his second wife, Jane. "I love her
like no man ever loved a woman, truly and sincerely
I wanted her. I needed her, she was everything to
me. Why did I ever let her go?" Addressing her, he
said, "I'm sorry I caused you any unhappiness.
Please forgive me. I love you too much—too de-
votedly—good God, what a love! I loved too hard
and long—good-by, good luck—God bless you all.
I forgive everyone—please forgive me. Please."

The fight over Arthur Smith continued after his
death. Tess, the first wife, charged that he had not
really committed suicide, but had been murdered,
and that the letter blaming her for his misfortunes

was a forgery. Police thought that this charge might be prompted by a desire to collect a life insurance policy which would not be good in case of suicide, and did not consider it seriously. A new angle of the case was the testimony of a prominent clergyman that he had effected a reconciliation between the estranged pair, who were shortly to be remarried.

The second wife came out of her seclusion to give her side of the story to the press. She told a vivid tale. She charged that Tess had hounded her "Art." until the day of his death and that both she and Tess had heard again and again Smith's threats to kill himself. She told of his unhappiness with his first wife, declaring that he had tried in every way to avoid a break with her. When it came, he signed over to her all the property he possessed and agreed to pay fifty dollars a week alimony. His life with the second wife had been made wretched by the exactions of the first. "Do you know," she asked, "that he and I lived in a hall bedroom for an entire year after we were married in order to meet those alimony payments? And do you know that after I separated from him and came here and left him the few furnishings we had been able to get together for the house we were trying to buy in the suburbs, that she took those furnishings when he could not meet the payments? She not only wanted him but she wanted everything he had or was. What happiness we had together we snatched between her court proceedings and the scenes she made in the studio. She ruined his happiness with me and she ruined his business. She set detectives upon us. They came even when we dined in hotels as guests of friends demanding how we could eat in expensive places when we could not pay alimony. I knew she would never let him alone and I believed I would help him get on his feet if I separated from him. We were friends to the end. He loved me. He gave me every proof of it."

The struggle over this *felo de se* continued until his body was laid in its grave. For a time his body lay unclaimed; then the first wife offered to pay for the funeral if the second were not allowed to attend. But she came, nevertheless, and quietly looked on at the dramatic scene staged by the first Mrs. Smith. In the funeral sermon, delivered by the clergyman who had already figured as a friend of the first Mrs. Smith, no mention was made of the second wife.

Any analysis of the psychological elements of so complex a case would have to be very tentative unless many more facts were available. The nature of the struggle between the first and second wives, however, comes out very clearly, and is perhaps not dissimilar to that which arises in thousands of less extreme cases where a man still pays alimony to the wife he has put away after he has taken another. The collection of alimony assumes in the eyes of the first wife a disproportionate importance. It is an end in itself and an instrument. It is an end financially and as a symbol of security, it is an instrument of dominance, of revenge, a curtailment of the happiness of the second wife. The desire to collect alimony is not all greed; it is a sign sometimes of reluctance to relinquish control over the once-loved mate. That is not to say that the desire to kill the goose of the golden eggs is wholly absent. It would take a second Solomon to decide where, in this complex welter of human motives, the love ends and the hate begins, or to evaluate justly the claims of the two women upon the man who is pulled to pieces between them.

Undoubtedly there are many cases in which human happiness is best attained by an arrangement whereby a man supports his wife after he no longer lives with her. It is always hard for a woman who has been married to learn to earn her own living, and after she has reached a certain age it becomes almost impossible. And the fate of such a left-over lady, even when she has no economic worry, is hapless enough at best. But there is a growing school of thought which condemns alimony. Miriam Allen de Ford, herself a divorcé who refused alimony, has stated that case clearly; it may be well to listen to her remarks before we close our chapter:

Most of us marry because we are in love, because we expect and hope to spend the rest of our lives with the beloved object; and if we find out, after years of disappointment and struggle against disillusionment, that we were blinded by emotion, and that the mate we chose is not the mate for us, it is with a rending of ourselves which leaves a permanent scar that we decide a clean operation is better than a festering disease. But this is just as true of men as it is of women; and why should the men be so heavily penalized for our common frailty? The viewpoint of the fanatic to whom all divorce is loathsome is of course comprehensible; but that of the person who allows divorce and yet makes alimony a necessary concomitant is beyond the understanding of those of us—women as well as men—who have progressed beyond the ideology of the days of the burning of heretics and nonconformists.

The situation is one which women alone can remedy. As with nearly every other aspect of feminism, the main fault lies in the lack of self-respect of women themselves—even though that lack of self-respect may ultimately be traced back to the environmental conditions of the past. . . .

Mrs. Banning and many others would say: But what of the woman who married young, in the transition days when many girls were trained for nothing but matrimony, who now in middle age must somehow adapt herself to a world where only youth is welcome? ... I am even willing to advocate a temporary alimony for the sake of training these poor misfit wives to take their stand with other self-maintaining adults; just as I concede alimony to the aged, the ill, and those burdened with the care of small children. It is the lying down forever on the soft cushion of another's captured couch that I deplore....

It is, however, interesting to note that in the only country where divorce by mutual consent, or even by desire of one of the parties concerned, is the rule, alimony also is determined solely by the need of either the man or the woman, and denied if neither has that actual physical need. It may well be that the continued payment of blood-money to healthy, competent divorcées will never entirely cease until this country has in this respect at least caught up with Russia. Until that time comes, the gradual discontinuance of the alimony system as practiced at present can come only by making it unpopular and disgraceful, instead of popular and honorable. What women need to develop is what Racine calls "being jealous of an austere pride." When that has become their second nature, not even motherhood will persuade wives to accept from their abandoned husbands more than the bare support of their children—perhaps if they are able to maintain their families and the children are exclusively in their custody, not even that.[6]

---

[6] Miriam Allen de Ford, "Why Take Alimony," *The Nation,* April 24, 1929, Vol. 128, No. 3329, pp. 504-5. By permission from *The Nation.*

CHAPTER ELEVEN

Conflicts That Persist

OLD dog Tray could get a bad name, but he could never have "a past." That is reserved for beings with a "moral consciousness." We humans assimilate our past, and that is what makes us human, but there are as many hindrances to the assimilation of experience as there are disorders of digestion. This is the paradox: That we are human because we remember, but because we are human we wish to forget. De Leon and the decrepit hedonist may long to lave in the waters of youth, and to take leave of the afflictions of insidious age, but he who would help mankind must discover the true location of that half-remembered river whose waters gave forgetfulness,—he must seek Lethe, that mythical river where memory went in and came not out.

But short of the journey, awful and ineluctable, to that undiscovered country from whose bourne no traveler returns, there is no forgetfulness for us who think and dream and die. If we cannot forget, the best that we can do is to pretend that we do not remember. This occurs when the ego, that part of us that dwells in that inner chamber, so tortuously inaccessible, where we worship each our own high god, does not wish to admit the existence of an impulse, an image, or an emotion; bare refusal on the part of the ego to admit the unwelcome guest sets up *conflict,* and if the ego is more or less successful in excluding the intruder from consciousness, *repression* occurs.

A certain amount of conflict is intrinsic in life that is human. We are; we are as others; we are animals who have developed consciousness and social life; we live together, but apart; we live each for himself but all for the others; these are facts with which we must live, abrogating more grandiose pretensions. Neurosis is an attempt to escape these facts in order to dwell among more pleasant illusions. The Pharisee's prayer, classic example of smugness, was not without its element of pathos, for it represented not only conscious belief that he was not as other men, but unconscious recognition of the fact that he was; only the gods may smile; we may not, for if we laugh we are Pharisees ourselves. The gods that gave us life put rigid restrictions upon our utilization of the gift. We must learn to accept the universe and ourselves as part of it. We must admit that we are only the step-children of destiny, and find in the end resignation,—peaceful resignation to the fact that we are born of woman, to the fact that we must die.

But if we must all have conflicts, and solve them, or live bedeviled by them till we die, there are some of us who have more of them than others, and times when inner dissension is specially divisive and sanguinary. The divorcé must put the past behind, and learn to live in the present. He must get away from himself and be no longer what he was. There has been a sharp break in his life, and he must sharply readjust to it. Conflict arises because adjustments that have been made in the past are no longer possible; we deal with such conflicts by repressing memories and impulses welling out of the self-that-was. Conflict arises also from the fact that certain adjustments adopted in the present are not satisfactory, and we deal with these by repressing the dissatisfaction. This unwise, but tempting, solution by repression, may operate to cause a continuance of unadjustment. In a previous chapter we have discussed the conflicts arising from the early necessities of reorganization; here we are discussing those which come after, representing more long-continued strife. The early conflicts flame, the later smolder.

Some subtle changes in the quality and tempo of the divorcé's personality will remain to tell of his experiences long after the hammer marks of fate have ceased to be hot upon him. Though he achieves at length a smooth and convincing ensemble, some interior stress and strain, some bitter memory, some attitude, some hate, some pose, some fear will still be left to remind him of the old struggle. Divorce brings experiences that sting for a while but are forgotten like the pangs of childbirth, but it carries with it also a various assortment of duller aches and pains that are meant to last a lifetime.

Sex starvation, produced by the rude interruption of the love life, is gone in an instant; yet in a way it lasts forever too. Especially do its effects persist if one is led by it to accept satisfactions which have no meaning. When divorced people attempt to conquer sex by degrading it, as they sometimes do, and habituate themselves to love that is all carnality, they pay an exorbitant price for their immunity from love that is all meaning. The blood of the lamb may wash away our sins but it can never remove the memory of grossness, or overcome the little reser-

vation of the ego that stands between the devotee of
the flesh-pots and the delights of idealism. Nor can
any kindness melt away entirely the walls that are
built around the ego after it has been wounded by
divorce. Not for many years does the divorcé,
though he be simplicity itself, overcome the effects
of the various tension points in the system of social
relationships in which he lives during and after divorce. Marriage, too, necessitates certain emotional
adjustments which, once made, are not easily un-
done; dominance, subordination, impotence, frigidity, guilt or unfaithfulness may be carried on after
the necessity for them has ceased. The luxurious indulgences of a marriage may outlast the marriage.
As the crisis of divorce is long looked forward to,
and great effort is made to mobilize one's resources
to meet it, so it is looked back upon. Doubt about
the advisability of and the justification for the step
remain when the ink of the decree is fading on yel-
low pages. So reasons, arguments, causes, reproaches,
complaints and accusations must be rehearsed forever. The very adjustments to the fact of the
divorce may in the end be causes of conflict themselves. Bohemianism, leading to overt acts that are
later regretted, promiscuity, leading to physical ex-
haustion and emotional starvation, gayety, implying
the repression of self-pity, inversion and its ten thousand demons, sophistication and all that the pose
demands—of all of them one may grow very weary,
and not, being weary, be able to cast them off. Then
there are the living products of the marriage, the
children begotten in it. Not even the most irrespon-
sible of us are willing wholly to abdicate as parents,
and the thought of the child being reared by the
estranged mate is likely always to be unpleasant and

to produce a certain distortion of the self. With conflicts such as these the divorced person is usually left.

When a conflict is satisfactorily resolved, its influence may be so reduced that it is difficult for the person himself to recall it in all its poignancy and intensity. The person has rounded the corner and straightened his wheels; now we can tell where he has been only by the trail he has left and not by internal evidence. This we have tried to do in preceding chapters by examining the histories of many divorced persons. Of the conflicts that remain, the best evidence is obtained by attempting to uncover definite repressions.

The tale of conflict neither begins nor ends with repressions, but we may obtain insight into the chief schismatic tendencies present in any personality by ascertaining what repressions are there. Certainly we cannot get a complete picture of any person without listing his major repressions and discussing their effects. Often the means by which he finally organizes himself for new life and new action is the utilization of this mechanism; its effect is usually unfortunate, since it does not allow the impulse or the memory against which it is directed to be assimilated in the normal way into the general personal organization. It has been noted, as well, that when an impulse is repressed it not only retains its original strength, but may actually increase in strength.

What the divorcé gives most easily is the carefully edited and highly rationalized account which he has prepared for himself and the general public. The so-called newer psychology has, however, furnished us certain techniques by which we may, if we persist, discover further facts of a very revelatory nature.

Often the material so disclosed is illuminating because it is at variance with the first story that was told. A woman who had apparently told all her story at the end of the second interview recalled the following incident at the next:

"Years ago when my husband was contracting, just before he got into that jam and had to leave town, he had an affair with a thirteen-year-old girl. It all started as an April fool joke. He was dared to kiss her or something like that and he did. Then he used to take her with him when he went riding. Nobody thought very much about it at first, I never did, but there was some gossip about that, too. Well, you know that he left me and went away without telling me where he was going or even that he was going. He went away and came back in a few weeks after we had got it all straightened out. I knew that he had told some men about it, but had not told me, and I resented that, but one day when I was ironing I found a letter in his coat. It was from this little girl. In it was something that told me that he had told her he was going away, even though he hadn't told me. She wanted him to tell her all his troubles. She said, 'Kindness is your very life, and I won't be satisfied till I can live with you.' Well, I took that letter and went over to the girl's parents and told them what kind of parents I thought they were to let a thirteen-year-old girl write that kind of stuff. Well, I put that out of my mind and went back to him. I don't know exactly what effect it had. I guess I decided then and there to be more the boss than ever."

This woman had previously insisted that her husband's reputation before their final break had always been spotless, that there had been no wagging of tongues, and no stirrings of suspicion within herself. This memory was sufficiently repressed that it was only brought to light after considerable probing; yet it adds much to the explanation of the process by which her marriage broke up, and may serve as an example of the sort of thing of which we are speaking.

In another case repressed love, lightly repressed, it is true, was brought to light in a series of three interviews. This young woman had had a post-marital love affair in which she had been deeply involved and had been quite shamefully treated. From her general nervousness,—she was under treatment for her nerves,—from little give-aways, such as the fact that when she spoke of this man she always said that she did not love him and could not possibly love him because he had treated her so badly, the writer divined that she was still in love with her former lover. The subject was requested to bring in her dreams, but she insisted that she never dreamed. When it had been suggested to her that she would dream, she brought in the following: "I dreamed that I was in a very beautiful place which seemed like the scene of some beautiful paintings which I have seen, but it was not the same as any of those. Dave was with me there. I was very much struck by the beauty of it all. The dream was very pleasant." This was interpreted as possibly showing a persistent attachment to this man. This interpretation was inacceptable to her and the point was not pressed.

At a succeeding interview she told the following dream: "I was paddling a canoe through some marshes in New Jersey. I was going to Dave's summer house out there and I was taking him something, some grass or something like that. I had a dreadful time finding my way there, and had to paddle the canoe through all sorts of bypaths. Finally I got there and I went up to the door of his cabin carrying this bunch of grass or whatever it was. I knocked on the door and he came to the door to answer. I showed him what I had brought him. He was not pleased to see me. I was so hurt that I fell on his door-step in a faint." The interpretation of this dream was quite obvious to the subject herself, and she confessed her love for this young man. Her nervous symptoms in the main disappeared after this interview.

It occasionally happens that after one is divorced there is an accumulation of unverbalized hostility toward the former mate. This being unrecognized and unexpressed, that is, repressed, may affect the entire personality unfortunately.

Repressed hostility may operate to produce a typical aboulia, may give rise to certain troublesome compulsions, or may furnish the emotional motivation for displacements. Aboulia is a sort of paralysis of will produced by a conflict in the love life. In cases where aboulia occurs the attitude toward the love object is ambivalent, that is, it is composed of two antithetical attitudes, so that love and hate appear in the complex in nearly equal proportions. The necessities of life require that the hostility be repressed. Although unconscious, the hostile attitudes toward the love object continue to influence behavior. Denied direct expression, they operate to paralyze the expression of the other side of the ambivalence. The result is that the normal affectional outgo is effectually blocked. Since this positive side of the complex is conscious and the negative, or hostile side, is unconscious, the inhibition of the expression of love and the resultant inability to complete acts for which love would furnish a motive is very puzzling. One suffering from aboulia finds it difficult to carry on the most ordinary actions of his love life and next to impossible to reach decisions concerning his love problems. His first reaction is probably to concentrate his attention upon the preliminary stages of decision, but even in these he finds that he can achieve no final results. The theory is that this aboulia produced by the conflict in the love life gradually spreads over the remainder of the personality. Thus is produced the Hamlet-like type of character, the character in which the "native hue of resolution is sicklied o'er with the pale cast of thought." [1]

This typical aboulia is not uncommon among divorced persons; it is easily seen that their situation is one which offers much opportunity for this sort of conflict to arise. A man whose philosophy and notions of sportsmanship did not permit him to express his resentment of the way in which his wife had treated him, both in marriage and out of it, was put in a situation where he had to decide between going back to his wife and going on with a new love. His answer was to play solitaire! But when the underlying resentment of his wife's actions had been brought to consciousness he made his decisions, those connected with his work as well as the decision in his love life, and lost all interest in solitaire.

One of the most common repressions is the identification of one's self with the stereotype of the divorcé. "Now my case was exceptional," says each one as he begins to tell his story. The fact is that one's own case is always slightly different, somehow unusual, in some way set out from the others, so that one does not take his place among all the rest of the divorced persons. Never two people loved

---

[1] For a discussion of the theory of aboulia, see Frink, W. W., *Morbid Fears and Compulsions,* New York, 1918, Dodd, Mead and Co., pp. 176-177.

each other more and were divorced, or loved each other less and were married, or never two lived a shorter or a longer time together, or never were involved in a more complicated situation. This is in accord with the tendency of the neurotic modern to think that his problems are not like those of any other person. This is the reason why one may write as frankly as he will about divorced persons; every divorced reader will make himself an exception and apply the generalizations to the rest. (Where knowledge of the fact that one is divorced, or is going to be divorced, is repressed, such unusual experiences as hysteric birth and rebirth, panoramic views of the future, obsessive visions, etc., may occur when this knowledge reaches consciousness at length.)

The writer found the analysis of dreams, phantasies, and Freudian errors a useful technique, a very sharp-edged tool even in awkward hands. Such analysis frequently not only gave direct clues in itself, but by building up the transference helped to release a flood of information which would not otherwise have been accessible. It will be illuminating to give some of these in full, together with the analysis that was made of them. The following dream was furnished by a male subject:

"I dreamed that I was at my wife's home with a large number of people. We were all in the kitchen discussing how the plates were to be arranged and the pieces of food divided in preparation for the dinner which was to be served. We had chicken and potatoes. My plate and one other were prepared and I started to take them both into the dining room. I think I had a wing of chicken. The food at this stage looked rather appetizing. Just as I went to pick up my plate I noticed a great black bug on my plate. I was filled with disgust. Suddenly the bug jumped out and ran onto the table. I was frightened and horrified. My appetite was ruined. I thought I should not be able to eat, although I knew that everybody would think that I was unduly squeamish. My father-in-law, to reassure me, picked up the bug and put it in his mouth. It pinched his tongue and he winced, admitting that it had bit him. He ate it, but my appetite was not restored."

Asked to associate, the subject explained that he had always been uneasy about the food at his wife's home. His people were German, his wife's Jewish, so that there was a considerable difference in the way in which the food of the two families was prepared, handled, and utilized. He related that during the three years of his marriage he had often sat at their table wondering how he might appear to eat and yet not really do so. He did not on any account wish to let them know that he did not like their good food, because he realized that they were fond of him and attempted in every possible way to please him. He realized in addition that his fears as to cleanliness were groundless.

But there was more to the dream than that. The food was a sexual symbol, the chicken female, the potato male. The subject confided that his wife, although apparently a very delectable love object, had certain psychological peculiarities which were of such a nature as to make married life with her difficult. Hence the black bug.

Then came out a long-standing rebellion against the wife. She was, it seems, domineering, and that was the reason why the subject, although he had often wished to do so, was determined never to return to her. That was the thing that spoiled the relationship. The wife's mother was also given to the use of the less subtle forms of control, and the sub-

ject had often marveled at the fact that his father-
in-law seemed to enjoy his subjection to her. He had
often said, "If I could be like him, then I could live
with my wife and not mind it." Perhaps not suffer
from it, for the father-in-law seemed a very well-
adjusted and happy man. But then he remembered
that occasionally the father-in-law did suffer from
it; sometimes his feelings were so hurt that he would
go away for days to sulk, and to recover his ego
feelings once more. (The bug bit him, and he admitted it.) The net effect of the example was that
the subject's appetite for renewed marital relations
with his former wife was not restored.

This dream was in all probability yet further determined, but this much of the analysis, necessarily
much abbreviated in the presentation, seems quite
clear. In this dream the man's motives for not going
back to his wife are laid bare; in addition, it has the
effect of clinching his conscious decision. These restatement-of-grievance dreams are not uncommon
where return to the former mate is still being considered.

A similar dream was furnished by the same subject:

"I awoke with the name Schwarz on my lips. He
was an elderly German fellow who had been involved
in the Smith case (a celebrated murder case) and
had been made a fool of by the woman. I asked
where he had been, what he had been doing, where
he had been seen last. He had been on a trip in
northern New York, and it was stated again that
he had been in love with the woman in the Smith case
and she had treated him badly. I wondered about his
sex life. My father, apparently the person whom I
had asked, said, 'It was no good. Sobbed right

through the orgasm.' Some reflection was made about the poor way in which this man took care of his health. Something to eat after midnight, a pill, or an 'eccentric sid,' that was his idea of what to do when something was wrong. I had a flash of the unattractive bed in which he was sleeping, and at the same time I thought of it as my bed."

After Schwarz was identified, the analysis of the dream was very simple. Schwarz was the name of the second husband of this man's divorced wife, although he had been unaware of the identification until the process of analysis was begun. The wife and the second husband are belittled on a dozen different counts. Schwarz is seen and imagined as an elderly German fellow whom the subject had known some years before. He recalled that he had once visited this man in his home and had found it very foul smelling because of the fact that a number of unemptied receptacles for holding urine were standing about. In addition, Schwarz was a spiritualist, and occasionally engaged in some table-rapping seances with an unkempt old woman who lived nearby. The subject had at the time been curious about these seances, and had intended to attend one, but had been warned not to do so because they were usually made the occasion of low-grade sexual debauches. This man's divorced wife's husband thus lives in a house that smells from dirty occupancy, there are ghosts there (the former husband), and about it all clusters the aura of low-grade sexual indulgence.

This man had been involved in the Smith case and had been made a fool of by the woman. This was a woman who had poisoned her husband,—the subject confessed to a feeling that his wife had subtly poisoned him. The woman had made a fool of him;

thus the wife's second husband had been cavalierly treated before marriage. So poor Mr. Schwarz is associated with a woman who poisoned her husband and has been badly treated by her. (Murder, or double murder, or death, appeared in other dreams also as a symbol of divorce.)

Before the marriage, Schwarz, still uncertain as to whether he would be accepted or rejected, had been on a trip to northern New York. The latent content did not become altogether clear, because of the haziness of memory as to certain diagnostic details, but it came out that some curiosity existed in the mind of the subject as to the whereabouts of the couple at the present time. The trip to northern New York continues the general belittling, for the subject, whose home was in that region, felt that it was a very undesirable place in which to be.

The father appears in the dream partly because at an earlier time he had figured in the subject's life as a person who gave reassurance and support concerning the divorce, who told him that he was unquestionably better off away from his wife. As to the sex life of the former wife and her second husband, the subject had always been frankly curious. His wife had often been frigid during their marriage, and this was one reason for the curiosity and the belittling tone of that curiosity. As to the sobbing, the subject remembered that the former wife had told a mutual friend that her second husband was more responsive in the sex act, especially at the time of orgasm, than her first had been. The subject admitted an aversion to the making of noises during the sex act (possibly partly self-defensive).

Then the second closely connected flash. The wife's habits of life had always irritated the subject.

She frequently ate after midnight, took many pills and medications in order to keep herself in health. The term "eccentric sid," meaningless in itself, apparently represents a condensation. It had great meaningfulness to the subject and had been emphasized in the dream. The visual image that was associated with it was that of an effervescent salt which the wife had been accustomed to use before retiring. The subject was unable to find the rest of the term, but readily assented to the suggestion of the writer, here the analyst, that the phrase was "eccentric kid," asserting that he had frequently so referred to her while they were married. The something that was wrong, and the general atmosphere of indigestion suggested unsatisfactory sex life and undigested experiences. The unattractive bed, seen in a flash and thought of as the subject's own as well, ends the dream on the same general tone.

Apparently this dream represents an attempt of the subject to restore his pride by belittling his wife and her second mate on all possible counts. The dream seems to have solved something, for the subject awoke with a feeling of renewed integration, and believed that he had made some definite gains. Sometimes these restatement-of-grievance dreams appear in simpler form, as where the wife dreams that she sees her former husband's fly, which is worn threadbare, he being thought of as worn threadbare by promiscuity. The dream of the husband that everyone around him was eating, that his wife was near and ought to bring him food (here cold chicken and pickles), but did not do so, represents a simpler form of the restatement-of-grievance dream, since one of his main grievances against his wife had been the fact that she starved him sexually.

The opposite form of this dream, the restatement
of the accusation of one's self, also occurs. A certain man after his divorce reproached himself for
having brought sorrow to his gay little wife, accus-
ing himself the more in order to escape the realization that she had also made a rather sorry wreck
of his existence. He had, he said in his rather ora-
torical way, "ruined her shimmering little humming
bird's wings in the effort to control their flight," and
had "wrought irreparable damage with his clumsy
hands." Eight years after, when during a period of
several years there had been no communication between his wife and himself, he had the following
dream: "My wife was seated on a couch by the side
of the room, smiling, and dressed in a billowy,
fluffy little gown. I came into the room, and the dress
was immediately deflated." This was treated as a recrudescence of the former self-reproach.

These restatement-of-grievance dreams are possible, apparently, because the impulses to which they
give expression are not, whether because of religious
or moral scruples, or whether from mere sportsmanship, allowed free access to consciousness. Self-pity
over the fact of divorce is likewise often repressed
with the result that it comes out in dreams.

Sometimes there are dreams in which something
is decided or new weight is added to the arguments
on one side or the other so that the decision seems
clearer. A woman dreamed as follows: "We are in
the water. A charred frame of a building which used
to be Blakesley Manor (an apartment house in
which she and her husband once lived) was there.
I recalled that it used to have many mazy rooms, in
which once in a while I got lost. It burned down and
now only the framework remains. It is resting on

stone foundations. Water is all around. I tell about its history. Someone asks, 'Is that all real to you?' I reply that it certainly is. I recall how the floor used occasionally to give way, so that one would almost fall through it, before the building burned. I take hold of the framework and move it off the foundations."

The building is her marriage, which is now destroyed so that nothing but the charred frame remains, and it, though resting on foundations of stone, is in an unfriendly element. She recalls that, although she had once lost herself in it, it gradually went to pieces. Without repudiating it as a memory, she decides to move it from its foundation, completing its destruction.

It would be expected that homosexuality would often rear its head in the dreams of divorced persons. A person who has recently experienced a disappointment in heterosexual love is a little more likely than is another to consider the alternative; as a person without strong heterosexual motivations is more likely than is another to have experienced such a disappointment. At any rate, many dreams occur presenting homosexuality as an alternative either accepted or repudiated, or representing frankly homosexual yearnings.

Symbols which have been found to recur in the dreams of divorcés are: a house, denoting a marriage; the second floor of a house, denoting a second marriage; food, denoting sexual intercourse; a bed, denoting a marriage; death, murder, or fire, denoting divorce; meat, or a wagon, denoting a woman; laundry, scrubbing, cleaning house, etc., symbolizing a necessity of cleaning up, *et al.*

Phantasies have often given clues, although in the

main they are clues which might be had directly from
the conscious mind or clues which are extremely difficult to follow out. Sometimes they are illuminating,
as in the case of the woman whose phantasies centered about her child, thoughts of his possible death,
thoughts of his going away and leaving her, thoughts
of her return to her home under such circumstances
that she would have no money with which to come to
see her boy. The interpretation of this phantasy
along Freudian lines is obvious enough. Frequently
phantasies represent displacements whose basis is
difficult to reveal without complete analytical pro-
cedure. A man had a phantasy, for instance, which
was very meaningful to him over a period of two
years, of killing by refined tortures a man who had
attempted to possess his former wife sexually by
force. There was some basis for real resentment, for
this man's action had apparently helped to bring
about the divorce. The phantasy had some of the
earmarks of an inferiority manifestation, since the
subject laid great stress upon the size and physical
qualifications of the other person, but when it was
discussed as an inferiority manifestation it nevertheless did not lose its meaningfulness to the subject.
However, when this man had brought to consciousness his resentment of certain of his wife's derelictions, the interest in the phantasy disappeared, making it seem that we had here an example of the
familiar mechanism by which the life of the family
is so often preserved at the expense of friendly relations with the group outside; the action of the mechanism was here, of course, carried over into the postdivorce period.

Failures of memory and slips of the tongue or pen
frequently reveal hidden conflicts. A woman related

that while she was at a dinner she was carrying on a conversation and quite suddenly forgot what she was talking about. She was reminded of it, and went on with the conversation. The next day she could not remember at what point in the conversation her memory had failed her. Every means of recalling the incident was employed, but unavailingly. Later it came out that the topic of conversation was quite harmless, and that the forgetting occurred when she saw a woman dressed in an apron preparing to demonstrate some domestic appliances for preparing food. It developed that the domestic side of this woman's nature was so strongly repressed, although still very much alive, that when its revival was threatened, the memory of incidents on both sides of it was temporarily destroyed.

When one is looking backward at a great crisis he may lose track of time, living always in the unforgotten days of his sorrow. A man whose marriage had broken up in September continued to write September at the head of his letters for almost a year, signifying, perhaps, that it was still "September" inside him. A woman who had been definitely repudiated in the spring, frequently wrote or said "Spring," when she meant some other time. Others have reported a general inability to reckon time during the first few months following divorce.

It may happen that the memory and the meaningfulness of a child are repressed, and only with difficulty brought to light. A woman who had been divorced under such circumstances that she lost the custody of her children gained the daughter because of the insistence of the child herself, but lost the son, who preferred the father. She lived for the daughter and forgot that the son existed. She car-

ried her defense against the realization of her persisting affection for her man-child so far as to refuse
to read a book in which the hero's name was the
same as his.

We have seen that fires of conflict smolder long
when the flame has died down, and that one continues to be concerned with repressing the attempt
of the self-that-was to go on functioning after the
divorce, but perhaps the most acute conflicts are over
the adaptations which are effected after the divorce.
One accepts sex on a low basis, or drifts into *faute
de mieux* masturbation, or squints toward homosexuality,—this must throw him into the severest conflict.
One builds up guards against the tendencies which
the situation has revealed, but the guards may, and
often do, interfere with the wholesome reconstruction of his life, and hence more conflict arises. Then
come further compromises, and the compromises
themselves may not be satisfactory. But perhaps the
reader has forgotten the complex reorganizations
with the necessity of which we started, the love life,
the ego feelings, habits, economic life, and social
position; let him go back and pick these up; let him
remember that all these are not separate, but only
analytically separable, that in fact all operate together, with each other and in each other and
through each other and against each other, and that
the existence of mental conflict complicates each type
of conflict—all becomes very complex, too complex
for the human mind, and that is the essence of conflict.

In a case of this sort psychic impotence was a
result of an adaptation reached in the attempt to
readjust after divorce. This man, basically much
enslaved to the conventional mores, had drifted into
a love affair with the wife of his best friend. Im-

potence came as the result of the conflict engendered by the situation. After his divorce he gave his wife and two children two hundred dollars of his salary of three hundred and fifty dollars a month. Out of the amount left him, he paid more than sixty dollars a month as carrying charges on his home,—he would gladly have sold his home but was unable to do so. His position required that he dress well and that he dine often in expensive places. He drifted into the intimate affair of which we have spoken partly as a result of his financial stringency; the woman gave him feminine companionship without cost for entertainment and in addition gave him expensive presents. His involvement in the affair was further conditioned by the fact that this woman, by catering to his every whim, helped to restore his ego feelings to a healthy condition. But though his conscience could be benumbed, it could not be completely stilled, and after a period during which he compensated by over-indulgence for the underlying unease, he became impotent.

The transference mechanism may entrap the best-intentioned into love affairs which are inadvisable on moral and social grounds. Perhaps it is a woman who is already married to whom the divorced man chooses to tell his troubles. Perhaps she also has problems. By the insidious workings of transference they may come to go far with their love affair before it is recognized as such, and after the affectional basis of the association is recognized rationalizations can easily be produced which allow the affair to go on. One case of this sort was further complicated by the existence of a displacement of the conflict from the forbidden to a legitimate affair. Although he was at the time carrying on a blameless affair with a single woman, a young divorcé developed an attachment to a married woman, a woman to whom he had talked concerning his troubles. Terrifically in conflict about being in love with a woman who was already married, he decided that his association with the unmarried woman was wrong and accordingly gave it up !

It may happen that one adopts a cynical philosophy of life which enables him to go on living, but which he has difficulty in reconciling with his previous set of attitudes. In such a case Dr. Jekyll and Mr. Hyde were seen interrupting each other in conversation. A man was talking about love. He was talking sentimentally, his voice was in the upper register, and his tongue lingered with affection upon every syllable. "Well, it's very nice to have some one. I ought to know. Some one who cares about you. Some one to run her dainty little hands over you. Some one with all these little reticences. Some one with all these little affectionate"—Then, with the tone of the underworld, his voice hard and coarse, he almost shouted, "Hell, they're all built the same way." There was obviously a man who was not at one with himself.

But after months in which conflict has flamed and years in which it has smoldered, there comes a time when the fire at length has burned itself out. There are certain reagents, too, by whose beneficent action combustion may be arrested before it has consumed all the resources of the personality. There are certain means by which conflict may be ended, checked, or sequestered. In the chapters on *The Assimilation of Experience and Reorganization* we take up this more constructive process.

CHAPTER TWELVE

The Assimilation of Experience

BEMUSED philosophers, wearing many robes, speaking many tongues, have thought through countless years of the problem of the self and the relation of its experiences to it. Subtleties aplenty, and niceties of logical discrimination, have been produced in their efforts to solve these problems, alluring and evasive, yet the problems themselves are not such as would suggest themselves only to philosophers, for no thoughtful child has passed adolescence without perceiving them, while he was letting his fancy run over the half-verbalized questions which are "the long thoughts of youth." In the lives of the most extroverted of us there are moments of brilliant subjectivity when we ask, "Who am I? What am I? Who are these others? What are they to me? What am I to them? What is all this to me?" This is the personal way of asking, "What is the self? What is its relation to its experiences? How are experiences assimilated to it?" Simple questions, these, but the simplest questions have ever called for the most abstruse answers.

The answer which we offer here will be in terms of such scientific concepts, laws, and generalizations as seem to apply, but we shall not bind ourselves strictly to the most objective sort of scientific explanation, and shall not forswear the aid, if it seems useful, of science's elder brother, metaphysics, at present in bad odor, but mighty in its day. Now as explanation is the art of connecting one thing up with others, and arranging all into a new configuration, it sometimes happens that at the start of an explanation we must introduce a number of new elements, with the result that we appear to be making a problem even more difficult than it was at first. If we seem to be doing this in the explanation which follows, the reader must remember that the end in view is not mystification or complexity, but the simplicity and obviousness that are products of more complete understanding.

The explanation of the peculiar experiences of the divorced is a part of the general problem of the assimilation of experience in general, and this sketch is included in order that we may from a discussion of the more general subject approach the particular one with greater understanding. The method of this short discussion will be frankly eclectic, and the treatment as far as possible non-technical. No attempt will be made to compare the points of view of various schools of psychological and sociological doctrine, or to translate the concepts which will be introduced into the terminology of any one school. Nor can we pause for those little asides, delightful though they be to the academician's heart, in which we evaluate the contribution of this person and that to the point of view which we are developing.

Our notion as to the relation of experience to the self will be different accordingly as we adhere to the doctrine of the instinctivists or incline to think of human nature as inherently plastic. No extended statement of the instinct theory need be vouchsafed here; it should suffice to say that the instinctivists were inclined to explain human nature on the basis of certain complex inherited action patterns which were the cause of human actions. Since the instinctivists believed that most of the important action patterns of mankind were inherited, they needed to concern themselves but little with the effect of experience upon the individual. We use the past tense because it has been pretty well demonstrated that these so-called instincts were nothing more nor less, in most cases, than habit complexes.

A view has gradually been established which gives to the original nature of man greater plasticity, and thus emphasizes experience. We have found that human nature can take on the outlines of a thousand different molds, while yet remaining human. Reformers draw the moral that we can do anything with human nature any time, anywhere. But though human nature is plastic, it is not blank, and it is not passive. We start with no passionless *tabula rasa*. Rather should we think of the human being as assembling and organizing his personality in a dynamic interaction with the environment.

It is sufficient for our present purpose to think of the social group into which the child enters as constituting his environment. This is a methodological device at which no one need take affright; its use is possible only since we are mainly concerned with the social aspects of the person. Let us see how the group enters into the organization of personality. The food habits of the group, for instance, are early acquired. Dog-eaters and cat-eaters, eaters of sheep and eaters of swine, are ancient enemies who have always heaped contumely as well as hate upon each other, and it is recorded that even the very young

participate in the prejudices of their elders. To question the superiority of the pies that mother used to
make is in our country a great heresy, yet there is
reason for suspecting that the prevalent belief in
the excellence of that good woman's cooking is based
only on the fact that she got the child first and
formed his taste. As the sex taboos of the group are
embraced and made subjectively real, the individual
comes to believe in and to practice polyandry,
polygyny, group marriage, promiscuity, chastity,
sacral prostitution, circumcision, subincision, monogamy, divorce, or any other of the thousand things
that people have thought it necessary and desirable
to do with their sex life. One by one the other customs of the group impose themselves, and the child
grows up to be a man not unlike his elders in his
attitude toward the things that one should eat, the
relation of the sexes, his occupation, ideals, aspira-
tions, morality, tastes, and ethics. It is a commonplace of sociology that the mores, the ways in which
we do things, and in which it is thought that we
ought to do them, are self-justifying.[1]

We do not know just what impulses are included
in original nature; we do not know how many they
are, or how strong any one of them is, or what
specifically they lead us to do. Strictly, we never can
know, for no tendency can be known to exist until
it expresses itself in action, and then it is already a
combination of impulse and experience. We do know
that as time goes on original impulses become over-
laid with habit and certain more or less universal
tendencies become apparent. The major trends in
any personality, consisting of both the impulse which

---

[1] See Summer, William G., *Folkways,* Ginn & Co., New York, 1906,
pp. 2-8.

is inherited and the habit which is acquired, determine the nature of the self. The self is continually evolving, and the vicissitudes of life are continually causing it to be cast into new combinations. Of each new combination, however transient, a residuum is left when the self is thrown into a different configuration. All that we have done, and all that we have been, and all that we wish to be are included in the self. Our repudiation of a memory or an impulse makes no difference, it is a part of the self just the same. The self is what we are, not what we wish to be. Dewey has well said concerning habits, "When we are honest with ourselves we acknowledge that a habit has this power because it is so intimately a part of ourselves. It has a hold upon us because we are the habit." [2]

But we like to think of some things which we do as truly representative of ourselves, of our real selves, whereas we instantly repudiate others of our thoughts and actions. Few of us would be willing to be judged by our acts alone, without any consideration of the subjective weighting of those acts. There is thus a self which is self-conscious, a self which sits in judgment on the rest of us, a self which comes to be the central and in fact the ruling part of us, though it is itself but the distillate of our neighbors' acts. As Ellsworth Faris has said, "One's consciousness of one's self arises within a social situation as a result of the way in which one's actions and gestures are defined by the actions and gestures of others. We not only judge ourselves by others, but we literally judge that we are selves as the result of what others do and say. We become human, to

---

[2] Dewey, John, *Human Nature and Conduct,* Henry Holt & Co., New York, 1922, p. 24.

ourselves, when we are met and answered, opposed and blamed, praised and encouraged." [3]

Now self-conscious behavior merges into dramatic behavior, the playing out of rôles, for a rôle may be thought of as a self-conscious attitude toward a social situation. When we add that this tendency of human beings to act out parts is very strong and seemingly universal, we see that there was a vast deal of truth in the Shakespearean aphorism, "All the world's a stage and all the men and women merely players." So important a tendency is this, in the opinion of some sociologists, that they have based their definitions of persons and personality upon it. The person, according to the definition given by one school of sociologists, is the individual, the biological member of the genus homo, who has status in a group.[4] The child is not really human until he acquires a rôle in the group. The same authors define personality in such a way as to emphasize the dramatic tendency in us yet more. "Personality may then be defined as the sum and organization of those traits which determine the rôle of the individual in the group." [5] This definition is in fact often given in a shorter form, "Personality is the sum total of all the rôles one plays in all the groups to which he belongs."

Always a potent factor in the determination of conscious behavior is the individual's conception of his rôle. If one identifies himself positively with a certain rôle, he at first consciously, and perhaps with

---

[3] Faris, Ellsworth, "The Nature of Human Nature," Proceedings of the American Sociological Society, Vol. XX, 1926, p. 16, University of Chicago Press, Chicago.
[4] Park and Burgess, *Introduction to the Science of Sociology*, University of Chicago Press, Chicago, 1921, p. 55.
[5] *Ibid.*, p. 70.

an effort, regulates his conduct in such a way as to live up to the rôle. (This is spoken of sometimes as an identification mechanism.) If he repudiates the rôle, he cannot fail to be led to certain behavior which will constitute more definite proof that the rôle does not fit. One's reaction to a rôle which is assigned to him in any group may thus be positive or negative, but it may be laid down as a general principle that the reaction to the rôle is always significant if the group is significant.

If a rôle is accepted it is incorporated into the personality, and overt habits connected with playing it out are developed. The longer a rôle has been established the less conscious are we of playing it, and this may occur without the intervention of any of the mechanisms described in psychopathology, through the familiar mechanism of habit formation whereby we are not conscious of the functioning of habits which have become inveterate. Likewise the repudiation of rôles may become a well-established and central part of the personality through the same mechanisms, although repression or suppression is a bit more likely to be in evidence here. There is no unhealthiness in living out a rôle, for that is the only way in which we can adjust to a social group and participate in social life, but our judgment must be more unfavorable when rôles become fictions. One who lives by fictions makes his adjustments to an excessive degree within himself; without changing his behavior, he changes his conception of his behavior; the inevitable result is lack of adjustment to reality. Thus the healthy minded person lives by rôles, but the neurotic lives by fictions. When one does this he may, as has been suggested by certain writers, even create the emotions appropriate to his imagined conception of himself and his situation.

In the drama of human life every player writes his own lines, revises them from moment to moment, makes them most intimately his own by reading into them the deepest meaning of himself. Each acted part is thus dynamically elaborated, internalized, made subjectively real, infused with the glow of life. As the person grows up, certain central rôles emerge which have great importance to him. These, organized into a complex about which in turn the rest of the personality is organized, are that central, directive, self-conscious part of the self which we may call the ego, not because that term is particularly descriptive, but because it seems to fit what we have in mind better than any of the other terms now in ordinary use. The ego is highly important in such crucial subjective experiences as choice, effort, and the assimilation of experiences. It accepts certain things, and repudiates others, and mobilizes and directs its forces like a general.

Sometimes the way in which one came to identify himself with certain standards of conduct is forgotten, so that one has the conception of his rôle but does not know where it came from. Or one may, following out a rôle that has been long established, take on a new one which modifies or elaborates it, without being clearly aware of what it is that he is doing. Thus it usually happens that by the time one reaches reflective years he is no longer able to trace out the patterns of causation which affect his choices, and it appears to him that his will is free. He has, as a result of the combined influences of all the groups in which he has lived, come to have an independent soul. Faris has discussed this in his usual lucid and arresting fashion:

The conception which it would be profitable to develop lies in the assumption that out of multiple social relations which clash and conflict in one's experience the phenomenon of individuality appears. The claims of the various social groups and relations and obligations made on a single person must be umpired and arbitrated, and here appears the phenomenon of conscience and that of will. The arbitrament results in a more or less complete organization and ordering of the differing rôles, and this organization of the subjective social attitudes is perhaps the clearest conception of what we call character. The struggles of the tempted and the strivings of courageous men appear, when viewed from the outside, to be the pull of inconsistent groups, and so indeed they are. But to you and me who fight and hold on, who struggle amid discouragement and difficulties, there is always a feeling that the decision is personal and individual. Someone has been the umpire. When the mother says, "Come into the house," and Romeo whispers, "Come out onto the balcony," it is Romeo who prevails, but it is Juliet who decides.

Individuality may, then, from one standpoint, be thought of as character, which is the subjective aspect of the world the individual lives in. The influences are social influences, but they differ in strength and importance. When completely ordered and organized with the conflicting claims of family, friends, clubs, business, patriotism, religion, art and science all ordered, adjudicated, and unified, we have not passed out of the realm of social influence, but we have not remained where the social group, taken separately, can be invoked to explain the behavior. Individuality is a synthesis and ordering of these multitudinous forces.

Here human nature reaches its ultimate development. Henley, lying weak and sick, suffering great pain, called out that he was captain of his soul. To trace back the social antecedents of such a heroic attitude is profitable and germane, but it is never the whole story until we have contemplated this unique soul absolutely unduplicated anywhere in the universe—the result, if you like, of a thousand social influences, but still undubitably individual. It was Henley who uttered that cry. That you and I so recognize him and appreciate him only means that we also have striven. We know him and understand him because of our own constructive, sympathetic imagination. He who admires a masterpiece has a right to say, "I also am an artist." [6]

We have seen that the self represents what we are, while the ego represents what we wish to be or wish to think we are. The self is both objective and subjective, and an estimate of it may be arrived at by a consideration of one's actions and the states of mind which accompany them. The ego is purely subjective, this self within a self by which our actions are weighed and evaluated. The self may be thought of as arising from the simple conditioning of the human animal by environmental stimuli; the ego arises from the playing of rôles and the gradual sifting and selecting of modes of conscious behavior regarded as fitting. Many things within the self are repudiated by the ego; even though they are forced out of consciousness they yet remain a part of us. But the ego is that innermost part of the self which is just as we want it to be because it is our standard of judgment.

Without going to an anthropomorphic extreme, we may say that this self-conscious self sometimes acts as if it were a ruling personality enthroned within the larger self. It arbitrates between conflicting impulses, and casts the deciding vote where decision is difficult. To some impulses it allows free access to the machinery of expression, others it banishes to the limbo of forgetfulness. It stands watch at the portals of thought, and does not allow all

[6] Faris, Ellsworth, "The Nature of Human Nature," Proceedings of the American Sociological Society, 1926, Vol. XX, pp. 28-29, University of Chicago Press, Chicago.

comers to enter. And, like other monarchs, it expends a large amount of the resources at its command to ensure its own continued dominance.

We may think of the human being as an essentially dynamic agent organizing and assembling his personality from materials furnished by the environment. The most important of the materials are furnished by the social groups in which one has his being. In a simple society there are few groups and not conflicting, in our more complicated society there are many groups with diverse heritages, so that wide variation is possible in these functioning mosaics of action patterns which are human beings. The importance which experience assumes if we subscribe to this view of the nature of human nature should be apparent at once. Our experience is important to us because we are our experience, and there is here involved no figure of speech, no metaphor, no paradox. We are our experience because we have grown to be what we are by assimilating our experiences.

If our experiences are part of us then we cannot ever really get rid of them. A fact which we must all sooner or later face is that the past is permanent. We can no more amputate the past than we can amputate day before yesterday's dinner. The dead past cannot bury its dead, because it cannot die. Alone in the universe in the possession of this one quality, the past is indestructible. We may forget certain of our experiences, but we do not cease to carry them with us. This does not mean that the past, if unpleasant, must always weight us down like an incubus which we cannot cast off. Much depends upon the configuration in which things are perceived, and any part of our life has meaning only with reference to the whole of it. We must learn to utilize our past experience; if we succeed, we have in it a resource which cannot be squandered;—a penalty for not learning to utilize it favorably is that it may become a liability from which we cannot escape.

While it is true that in the strict sense of the word experience is always assimilated, a distinction is sometimes drawn practically between experience which is assimilated and that which is not. In this sense the word is employed in speaking of various crucial experiences which may, if incorporated into the personality and utilized in a positive fashion, contribute much to personal growth, but which if not so absorbed make for unhappiness. Divorce and the putting away from one's self of the former marriage partner are such experiences, and as such may be spoken of as assimilated or not according to certain criteria.

We may say that an experience is assimilated in this special sense when the following conditions are relatively fulfilled: (1) Acceptance of the experience by the ego, (2) Dissipation of the affect, or emotion, connected with the experience, (3) A more or less stable rearrangement of the fundamental impulses in whatever pattern is necessitated by the new conditions of life created by the experience, and (4) Rearrangement in such a pattern that all aspects of past experience are utilized positively.

(1) Acceptance by the ego involves first of all a realization that the experience has really taken place. Many mechanisms may be evoked to prevent this realization, from the simple numbness of which people often complain in periods of unpleasantness to dissociation so deep that the memories are only accessible under hypnosis or through psychoanalytic

techniques. Associated with this is the neurotic doubting of reality, or the feeling that although certain things may have happened one was not himself a participant in them. But no experience can be regarded as assimilated until one is perfectly willing to admit its reality in relation to one's self. There must be no repression either of idea content or affect. The divorcé, for instance, who is unwilling to admit his divorced condition, or who shows his inner desire to hide the fact by constantly parading it, cannot be said to have fulfilled this criterion of assimilation.

(2) Immediately after a distressing experience one is likely to experience a considerable emotional turmoil which gradually abates with the mere passage of time. During the period of upheaval the experience which is being assimilated is the one great experience in one's life, but later it comes to be seen in different proportions. This criterion of the disappearance of overt conflict is the only one which people usually apply in discussing the assimilation of a shocking experience. "He has got over it," they say of a man who has ceased to give outward expression to his grief, but it is not true unless the other conditions are also fulfilled. Nor does the untrained eye see all the remnants of affect connected with an experience, for one cannot ordinarily see very far into the hidden portions of the mind without being put in an especially favorable position. The appearance of having put certain experiences completely behind one, and the belief that one has done so, may arise through the operation of the mechanism of repression, yet this is precisely the case in which real assimilation of the experience is most difficult. In many cases, for instance, love, hate, or love and hate tied together in one ambivalent

whole, for the former wife or husband may persist for many years after the break, and persist precisely because these emotions are repressed. Being repressed they not only cannot be drained out and allowed to lose their strength with expression over a period of time but they may actually increase in strength because of the fact of repression. The existence of repressions may lead to certain compensatory behavior which further deludes both the person himself and the casual observer as to the real state of his mind. This is peculiarly so of divorced people, whose experience is of a sort that one is especially likely to run away from or to cover up.

All this is not to say that there is no experience which can have permanent emotional value. A large part of the solution of many emotional problems consists in the admission that they are likely to remain always with us, and in developing a technique for living with them painlessly. The affect connected with any such experience must, however, be sufficiently dissipated that it ceases to be the one experience with which one is constantly preoccupied. In this sense one ceases to be a divorcé when he stops thinking about his divorce. The experience must be sufficiently deprived of its emotional value that it can be fitted into the personal scheme of things, into the life-pattern. One may travel forever in the sight of distant headlands, but as one goes away from them their importance in the circle of vision decreases. We forget because we must, and old experiences are seen in a new perspective over the years, but before this process can go on the mind must be sufficiently liberated from the old experiences to be able to deal with the new.

(3) After certain crises—and this is true especially of the crisis of divorce—the general mode of life must be completely reorganized. There may be many intermediate stages before one reaches a stable form of reorganization. These must be passed through and there must be some indication that the new life organization is relatively stable before we can say that any such experience is really assimilated. People often think, of course, that they have arrived at the end of the line when they have in fact but reached a way station. There is a danger that instead of actually readjusting to the changed conditions of life, by facing our problems and solving them, we will merely arrange to perpetuate our conflicts, settling ourselves to live with them and in them. The difference here between a normal adjustment and one which is not so is one of degree, for it seems likely that we must preserve some of our essential conflicts and contradictions, if we are ourselves to survive. From another point of view, we can never have a really stable life organization, because we must go on living and to live is to adapt and to reorganize; it should be remembered that the difference here indicated is quite relative.

(4) If possible the old experience must be utilized in the new organization in a positive fashion. It is much healthier on the face of it to attempt to utilize all the experience complexes which go to make up one's life than to use some and block others off. To utilize one's experience it is necessary to have a positive attitude toward it; this is an ideal whose realization is not always possible. Sometimes it is attempted by negation, as in the case of the drunkard who becomes an evangelist to others like his former self, and uses his knowledge of the personal

peculiarities of the species to make his appeals more forceful, or in the case of the priest who turns atheist.

Some very fine questions might be raised. There are those who think that they have completely reorganized when they have merely arranged to live permanently in one of what we are forced to call the preliminary stages of reorganization, such as, with regard to the sex life, promiscuity. One might question also whether a stable disorganization might not be a real reorganization on a lower level, a reorganization by reverting to the elemental. We must leave these questions for others.

One may connect with the notion of this ideal assimilation of experiences the psychological ideal of integration. One who has assimilated his past experience will have what the psychologists call integration. He might have his compartmentalizations (arrangements whereby more or less conflicting impulses come to expression in some sort of temporal order) but not his dissociations. The ideals of integration and the complete assimilation and utilization of experience might be said to be united in the case of the man who could truthfully say, "I am loyal to my past because my past is me."

In the past it has been said that character, or personality, is developed in crises. This is to a large measure true, but it is not so completely true as has perhaps been thought, or at least not literally true. It is true that at a time of special crisis our impulses are likely to reform themselves into new and different combinations, and that these new combinations may carry over into the after adjustment. The emphasis, however, upon things leading up to some dramatic climax is not justified. Life in the story books moves swiftly from one dramatic climax to another. Always the emphasis is on what leads up to a climactic experience, whether it be a marriage, a divorce, a death, or a seduction. This emphasis has to a certain extent been copied by the philosophers and the scientists. Life in the story books is like that, but real life as the writer has observed it is never like that. No dramatic experience is ever permitted to stand out like a promontory. One never comes coasting down from the mountain top, for always there is the anti-climax to check one's speed. Always the qualified victory and the not altogether crushing defeat. Either one has taken the sting from defeat before it happens, or he has, anticipating victory, tasted already its sweet rewards. Climax is delusive, merely an effect, begins nothing, ends nothing, decides nothing, and ever on its heels is anti-climax.

All this is not to say that crises are without importance. In a very real sense crises develop us, but we will learn more about the actual mechanisms of character formation if we focus our attention upon the descending rather than the ascending side of climactic development. It is not the grand finale that counts, but the myriad little crises that follow after it. One's behavior in a single great crisis may be no clue to his behavior afterward; if the crisis is a real one, he has to become a different person in adjusting himself to the changed conditions of his life. The old personality speaks for the last time in the crisis, immediately after one begins to develop a new one in meeting the thousand problems of existence.[7]

---

[7] This same conception has apparently been hinted at by Ellsworth Faris in the following passage: "The conception of personality as subjective culture will seem to lead to very real changes of stress

In the process of readjustment after certain far-reaching crises, of which marriage and divorce are types, there is often sudden and pronounced change of the externals of personality, amounting almost to metamorphosis. A change of the social group, or such a readjustment of one's relations within the group that it sets up differently, is a concomitant of such metamorphosis of personality, if it is not the typical situation from which such change results. After peculiarly painful experiences people often conceive the idea that they have changed more completely than in fact they have; this is a way of destroying the continuity of their lives, and robbing their unfortunate experiences of their sting. This sudden change may approach the pathological when it involves the changing of one's name, or a complete break with one's former friends, as is often the case with divorced persons.

Real change of personality is perhaps more limited than the untutored mind is apt to think. Continuity as to externals, continuity of the rôles one plays in the social groups in which he has his being, is secured by two sorts of factors: (1) Such as assure the assumption of similar rôles in the groups to which one may transfer, and (2) such as limit the completeness of the replacement of old associates by new. Assuming that factors of the second sort are not operative, similarity in the new personality, though not actual continuity, might be assured by those permanent traits of the individual as a bio-

---

and emphasis, among which we may venture to include the following: . . . (5) Increased emphasis on, and study of, emotional behavior, and the location of the central problem in those crises where old habits break up and new objects and new attitudes are formed." (Faris, Ellsworth, "The Subjective Aspect of Culture," Proceedings, American Sociological Society, 1925, University of Chicago Press, Chicago, p. 45.

logical and psychological organism which would assure the assumption in the new group of rôles similar to those played in the old.

Sudden changes of front are common after divorce. Fidelity to the marriage partner is replaced
by a flaunting promiscuity, good habits are exchanged for bad, and more rarely bad ones for good,
love is metamorphosed into hate, and idealization is
replaced by bitterness. What people who have experienced such sudden reversals need to know is that
their fundamental drives, their major complexes and
demands for activity are the same after such changes
of emphasis as before. Their complexes have re-
arranged themselves in different connections, but
they have not themselves been changed in any fundamental way. A man does not cease to be enslaved
by religion because he is in revolt against it; only
when the revolt has gone to its uttermost limit, and
religion is neither a positive nor a negative value to
him, can he consider himself free. Neither can the
divorced person call himself free while his rebellion
lasts. Real reconstruction after a divorce, and it is
the opinion of the present writer that this is quite
rare, can only proceed by acceptance and positive
exploitation of the past, which is to be utilized,
however, in a new orientation. Repudiation of the
past always hinders reorganization. It is only possible to be independent of the past by first admitting
that we can never be independent of it, by granting
its importance and attempting to tie it up to the
new organization of personality.

Both because of the emotional importance of his
experiences and because of the publicity connected
with them, the divorcé is more tied to his past than

other persons. The expression applied to divorced persons and others whose life has supposedly contained some lurid chapters, "Oh, he has a past," is of significance to scientists as well as to the old ladies on the porch. It may be desirable to differentiate the channels through which the divorced person's past influences him. We may tentatively include the following:

(1) Through its relation to his psychological organization, i.e., through his assimilation or non-assimilation of his past experiences. We have seen that whether it is accepted or repudiated our past experience nevertheless remains a part of us. That is true, but the sort of effect it has upon us at any time depends much upon our acceptance or rejection of it. If the past is accepted, and an attempt is made to live with it and if possible to utilize it positively, its influence can be made on the whole a favorable one. The old habits can be exploited, and the old identification mechanisms (rôles) allowed free play, but in a personal life-pattern so arranged that benefit instead of harm is derived from them. Repressed memories are more powerful in influencing behavior than those which are allowed to remain conscious; if they are not more powerful they are likely to seem so because they are out of control. Their effect, also, is nearly always bad. To try to forget the past is useless and foolish, and this is the more true the more living with it is difficult; whichever horn of the dilemma is accepted, whether we choose to assimilate it and utilize it, however unpleasant this course may be in itself, or whether we choose to flee from it and leave it unsolved, and unabsorbed, the past will continue to affect us profoundly.

(2) Through its effect upon his social relations. Quite aside from its effect upon one's own psyche, one has to consider the fact that his past is carried over in other people's memories. As we do not wholly die, so we do not wholly cease to be married. The divorcé is treated in accordance with his past even in the most liberated circles. The complication of social relationships, which occurs in the most subtle and intricate fashion, is one of the inevitable sequelæ of divorce. This is true because the past is so obviously there for all to see. In addition, the way in which one has assimilated his marital break, or the fact that he has not assimilated it, will have an effect upon his system of social relationships.

(3) Through the effect of his change of status upon his psychological reorganization. There are certain kinds of behavior, certain kinds of reactions, which we expect of divorced people, and we treat them in such a way as to elicit or to prevent the calling forth of those responses which they are supposedly ready to give. The grass widow is supposed to be merrier than her sister of the sod. A man must weep whom God bereaves, but he whom the judge pronounces no longer a husband must rejoice and be glad. Positive identifications with these rôles, arising from certain internal necessities,—a sort of identification which may in fact reflect nothing very deep, or which may reveal merely the presence of the opposite tendency, but which nevertheless often deceives others and sometimes deceives the person himself—positive identifications are more common than negative ones, but either can be very significant in determining the future behavior of the divorcé, and behavior so determined may operate to hasten or to obstruct readjustment.

The divorcé cannot put his past behind him; he must take it into him. Having his cake, he must eat it, or it will be useless and worse. He must utilize all his experience in a positive and dynamic reorganization.

CHAPTER THIRTEEN

Reorganization

WE promised to show some of our divorced ones drinking in the happy sunshine, arrived at last after many toils and many hazards safely on the infernal shore. To fulfill this promise is a pleasant task and a sweet duty. Yet the ceremony cannot be unattended by sorrow, for, as we take stock of our little band thrown upon the happy shore of hell, we cannot be unmindful of those others who once started bravely on their journey through the land of fire.

This, after all, is no time to bemoan the miseries of stragglers—those who have arrived prove that the journey is not beyond the power of the human being to achieve. We have throughout pointed our efforts directly at this goal, and have ever envisaged organization as the end result of disorganization. To be sure, it is an end result in the ideal sense none too frequently attained, yet it has always been in our mind in the preparation of this volume, and the divagations into the varieties and intricacies of maladjustment have had as one purpose that the sort of adjustment which of all seems most desirable should ultimately be revealed.

It is an amazing farrago of the stuff of life with which we have been concerned. We have seen the human personality reacting to the stress of painful experience. Personality, let us repeat, is no thing, but an adjustment, an adjustment of inner and outer processes expressing themselves on their dynamic fringe as life. Now it follows from this processual and dynamic conception of personality that the adjustment is one which is easily disturbed. Once that has happened, many intermediate stages, requiring the most delicate discrimination for their differentiation, may have to be passed through before the dynamic equilibrium is restored. And in a sense all those intermediary processes are part of the final reorganization. Whether they are to be thought of so depends upon whether there is effected in any case a final reorganization sufficiently stable and satisfactory to be worthy of the name.

The basis of life is altered when a marriage goes. This may be a gradual process, or may take place suddenly, it may occur before the actual legal step of divorce, or after it, it may be a very simple proceeding, or one attended by the greatest emotional and social complications, but it is rarely avoided except in those cases where a home has never been either physically or psychically established. When the conditions of life are changed, personality must change; this is decreed by its very nature. We have been studying the attempts of personalities thus faced with changed conditions of life to readjust themselves. They have readjusted by changing themselves in a dynamic mediation between the new and the old environments.

What is the end result of the process of change initiated by divorce? There is no end result, and a moment's reflection will convince the discerning reader that this is true. For if personality is an adjustment, then there is never any end to its change. We can, then, only discuss processes and mechanisms of adjustment, and there is never a logical stopping place. In a slightly different sense, too, there is never any end, for we continue throughout our lives to react to all the experiences that we have ever had. But let not these carefully worded reservations, so dear to senators and the *homo academicus*, blind us to the fact of which all people of common sense are aware, that a virtual end to the process of readjustment is reached when the divorcé reaches a state in which he thinks and feels and acts more or less as does everybody else.[1]

There is an answer for the reader who happens to be in a hurry, but the one who feels less the press of his quotidianal pursuits may wish a more carefully pondered, and more qualified generalization. When the divorcé has returned to the common breast of humanity, and thinks and talks and acts and dreams just about as does everybody else, so that he can be more significantly described by referring to

---

[1] The anonymous author of *Ex-Wife* has defined an "ex-wife" in words that suggest a similar distinction: "In that lazy space on Sunday, between late breakfast and time to dress for a cocktail party, Lucia, with whom I was sharing an apartment, tried to define 'ex-wife.'

" 'Not every woman who used to be married is one. There are women about whom it is more significant to know that they work at this or that, or like to travel, or go to symphony concerts, than to know that they were once married to someone or other.'

"She looked at me, reflectively. 'You're an ex-wife, Pat, because it is the most important thing to know about you ... explains everything else, that you once were married to a man who left you.'

" 'You're one, too, by that definition. That you once were married to Arch explains most things about you,' I said.

" 'Yes, but I convalesce somewhat. One isn't an ex-wife if one's in love again, or even if one never thinks about one's husband any more.' "

Ex-Wife, Anonymous; Jonathan Cape and Harrison Smith, New York, 1929, p. 5. Reprinted by permission.

him as a conservative or a Campbellite, a radical or a realtor, an efficiency engineer or a drug-store cowboy, how does he, nevertheless, act differently from any of these others of his social type because of the fact that he is a divorcé? A very fine question. . . . Let us give it up—our information is not sufficient to answer it—and only hint that the discerning eye might see in many of these apparently well-adjusted individuals the persistent action of some of the mechanisms which have been described, and that the ear attuned to hear such things might dimly catch the rumblings within their vitals of processes not yet complete.

To the perplexing question, Who has really rehabilitated himself after going through the experience of divorce?, we can give a negative answer and one which will help to explain why satisfactory reorganization is rare, for it will show that the places at which most people have stopped are not the final destinations toward which they started, but way stations at which they have tarried, and tarrying there have forgotten where it was that they were going, if indeed they ever knew. There are so many things to avoid, if one is to assimilate a divorce in a healthy manner, and it is so difficult to avoid some of them, that one who succeeds in working out a thoroughly sane adjustment finds himself in select company.

A formidable list it is, that of the dangers which the divorcé must fend off if he is to be saved. There is a large chance of going wrong in any of the major adjustments which we have mentioned, and only a small chance of going right. The divorcé must have learned not to love his former mate, or if he yet loves her, it must be in a manner which does no harm to his present adjustment, and does not prevent him from giving an equal, or a greater affection to another mate. There is a problem to try the soul of any philosopher;—just how will one solve it? The readiest weapon, repression, is one which must not be used; it gets immediate results, but wins always a Pyrrhic victory. If one has repressed the love of the former mate, a long list of personality maladjustments, impotence, frigidity, general inability to solve one's problems (aboulia), over-reactions, etc., may result from the fact of the repression, and the original problem of the persisting love of the former mate will still remain. There is the matter of promiscuity; we have seen that this is one of the first answers that some divorced persons make to their love problems. This is not only a poor solution, but one which gives rise to more problems than it solves, for it complicates the system of social relationships, and leaves unquenched the fire from which it sprang. The attempt to solve the love problem by turning to work or some narcotizing activity is also rarely successful.

The reconstruction of the ego feelings is a problem which has perhaps even greater possibilities of complication. What attitude must we take toward the old hurts? One cannot allow his mind to run over them forever, yet he must admit their existence and draw upon the experience associated with them as freely as upon any other for the regulation of his future conduct. For here, too, the ever ready tool, repression, must not be used. There is another danger, equally formidable, that one may, in the attempt to avoid exposing his vital parts to further wounds, build up defense reactions which hinder him in going on with his life. These wounds to the self-feelings also usually give rise to some sort of compensatory drive; in the divorcé who has assimilated his experiences well these drives must not be of a sort which hinder his social adjustment. If no new drives are invented to fit the needs of the occasion, then the old ones must not be so overworked that they give way under the strain. And if one has in the course of his divorce or his post-marital life done things which he later came to regret, he must face them too, without denying their existence or minimizing their importance, and learn to utilize them positively in his new life. (It may be laid down as a general rule, however, that one is not integrated until he no longer does things for which he is immediately sorry.)

Our ideal divorcé must have effected a sane reorganization of his habits—habits as details have escaped our attention while we were concentrating upon the major types of personality change, but habits are important too—and he must not have exchanged a set of good habits for bad ones. He must have solved his economic problems but not by over-compensating; we have already mentioned the unsatisfactoriness of work as a substitute for lost love.

And in the reorganization of his system of social relationships the divorcé must have been eminently sane. His new friends must be qualitatively equal to the old. The divorcé must not, compensating for his internal unease, have formed a habit of giving himself ego-gratification at the expense of others, for that is always expensive, and usually more expensive than one realizes. He must have changed the rôles which he plays in the groups in which he lives, yet this must not be done by adjustment altogether internal, else he is living by fictions. He must not have allowed his personal mores, produced in part by the peculiar conditions of his own life, to come to be too sharply in contrast with the collective mores; if this has befallen him he must under pain of calamity more dire than any he has yet experienced hide the fact from the world. Above all, the divorcé must have avoided the projection mechanism whereby self-accusation is transformed into accusation of others, always to the detriment of one's system of social relationships.

The divorcé must not have worked out a personal adjustment which proves personally demoralizing or loses him status in his group. However much a homosexual adjustment, for instance, may appeal to the person who has suffered a setback in his hetero-sexual love life, it is a solution which costs much more than it is worth, and the same might be said of the orientation and way of life generally known as Bohemian.

Throughout, the divorcé must have avoided avoiding his problems by adopting a way of life enabling him to keep his conflicts and make his neurosis perpetual. There are, of course, some complications of emotion which one conceives to be of the very essence of himself. To wish to keep these subtleties and reserves that are one's self is not, however, the same as to wish to experience forever the sweet pangs of sorrow. The distinction is a difficult one, but no man can assimilate a divorce who does not make it.

These are the things which the divorcé must have avoided doing,—so much for the negative answer. A tentative answer of more positive nature can be based upon our four criteria of the assimilation of experience. It will be remembered that these were:

(1) The experience must be accepted by the ego, (2) The affect, or emotion, connected with it must be relatively dissipated, and (3) There must be a more or less stable rearrangement of the fundamental impulses in whatever pattern is necessitated by the new conditions of life created by the experience, and (4) This pattern must be such that the experience is utilized in a positive fashion.

One must accept the experience of divorce, not dodging its reality or its significance in any way whatever. There must be no splitting off either of the idea or of its emotional concomitant. There must be no rationalization by which reality is taken from the experience, no false hope that after all it may not be so. If the break has been, it must be accepted as such. But it must not only be accepted, it must be accepted calmly. It can only be so accepted after it has been at length fully reacted to, i.e., after one has fully expressed all the emotions to which it gave rise. Life must have resumed an accustomed course, and this must be a satisfactory course. The experience of divorce, further, must be utilized in a positive way. One cannot avoid establishing once more a habitual way of life, for we are all Methodists under the skin, but it is more difficult to establish a way of life that is satisfactory, and it requires the utmost sanity and wisdom to make the most of one's experiential resources. And only they win through who sell the past to buy the future.

After so many words of discouragement, it is only fair to add a few of hope. There are many cases of well-adjusted divorced persons which show us that the trauma can be healthily assimilated. And there are not a few to whom divorce has been of positive value, and that not only on the principle, *"Forsan et haec olim meminisse iuvabit."* For divorce, necessarily and to all persons a disrupting experience, may to some few who have, if not wisdom, the gifts by which it may be obtained, be the means of acquiring a better hold on life, a hold based upon a true understanding of one's self in relation to his fellows. Most people come out of a broken marriage with personalities in need of repair, but those who are willing to profit from the experience by making a thoroughgoing reorganization of themselves may ultimately be all the stronger for it. A word to the wise is commonly said to be sufficient, but divorce is a whole course of lectures for those who are willing to listen. Still it is a little group of willful men who hear the closing words of the last lecture; only a small number of hardy ones are ever able to squeeze the experience dry of all that it may hold of benefit.

There may be those who have hoped as they read this book to come upon some bit of advice, some words of understanding, and some soothing imperatives which would be of help to them with present problems. This is a rôle which we are reluctant to assume, for reasons that should be obvious enough. Yet it is a responsibility which we cannot quite avoid.

Perhaps what one wishes to know most is what attitude he should take toward the past. This is not altogether a matter which can be controlled, for an attitude in any case is called out by one's past experience and the situation in which he is involved. This discussion, however, may be introduced as another element in the situation, and may as such assist the divorcé in reorganizing his impulses and deciding what shall be his reasoned attitude toward the things which have happened to him. The divorcé must first realize that the past is there, changeless, indestructible, as such irremediable. The next thing that the divorcé must realize is that the past is not there, not there because he cannot live in it any more. What has been can for that very reason never be again, and this should demonstrate finally the futility of trying to live in the past. "He has lived" is more than a euphemism; it is a law of psychology.

How, then, shall we define our attitude in this paradoxical situation? Here is the past, we cannot escape it, yet we cannot change it. We must not forget it, but we must not continually live it over again. Only one answer is possible. Let us, accepting the past for whatever it may have been, adopt a from-this-point-on orientation. It is true that what one now is is determined by what he has been in the past, but it is also true that understanding of that past can enter as another factor in the determination of our conduct. Admitting the past for what it is, admitting its continued influence over us, let us try to understand it, accept it, and profit from it. Futile, after all, to rebel against a universe. Let us accept ourselves and our past and accepting learn to understand. Only so can we regulate the future more intelligently than we controlled the past. Let us put the past behind by making it useful in the present.

So likewise must we accept the present. Rebellion is ever a wasteful emotion. If it comes, or seems to come, from an inner urge that will not be denied, it must perhaps be humored, but one must sooner or later learn to live without it. It is no good blaming the former mate, for he probably has his own problems, no less severe than one's own. One's parents, relatives, in-laws, friends, the world,—all these are part of the universe and must be accepted as such. The basic conditions of life are just there; only by accepting them can we make the most of them.

A second bit of advice is that we should not shut up our troubles in our own breasts. It is a strange reflection upon the essential gregariousness of man that an experience is only assimilated, as a rule, when one has shared it with another and found that he is accepted by that meaningful other person experience and all. It is in a sense a commendable spirit that prompts one to want to solve his own problems, to bear his own burdens, and to refuse to weight another down with crosses that are not his own. Yet this is quixotic, for it is easy after all to bear the misfortunes of others, and the invitation to give advice is a form of flattery few men can resist, so that we may feel sure that in return for the sympathy and understanding which the other person may give us, and which will be of inestimable value to us, we are giving him ego-gratification which will in most cases far outweigh the depressing effect of our confidences.

Although it is certainly indicated that every divorcé should have a confidant, it is also indicated that one must be very careful in his choice of a person or persons to whom to tell his troubles. For one must be sure that this individual to whom he is revealing all his inner difficulties will keep his secrets. There are very ingratiating persons who wish to receive confidence only to violate it. The social world of many a divorced person has been disrupted by an unworthy friend who scattered the information concerning his intimate difficulties to a world that was all too eager to gossip and all too reluctant to understand. Such experiences are traumatic for persons in the best of mental health; they are likely to be real catastrophes in the lives of those who are already upset. And the person to whom one is to talk about his post-marital tribulations must be one who will accept him nevertheless; the father confessor must disapprove sometimes, but in the end he must absolve the penitent. After all, it is his trade.

Divorced persons who seek someone to whom they may open up their hearts should be warned of the danger of transference, or rather of the fact of transference, for the benefit as well as the danger of talking things over is intimately associated with the fact that the person to whom one talks then sets up as very meaningful in his life. Transference occurs when people tell things which they have not ordinarily told; emotions are supposedly liberated and cluster about the confidant; the process is hastened by a discreet show of sympathy. In the normal course of events the affection of transference is in time largely dissipated, and the individual who has talked away his troubles becomes emancipated from the confidant. But this confidential rapport should be understood and evaluated as such. If the confidant happens to be of the opposite sex, the affection of transference must not be confused with bona fide love; getting a transference is frequently a part of the rebound mechanism. If the confidant happens to be of the same sex, then the attraction that is felt should not cause one to worry about a possible homosexual drive, but should be recognized as transference and evaluated as such.

Unquestionably the best person to whom one may talk is a psychoanalyst, for he will not only avoid giving further trauma by not understanding and not accepting, but will take advantage of his special technique to probe a little deeper than another person would be able to do, and will be able at the end to invest his suggestions with more compelling force than most others are able to summon. But psychoanalysis is expensive, and there are few psychoanalysts and many divorcés, to say nothing of others in need of psychoanalytic treatment. In lieu of analysis, the writer recommends that every divorcé set himself the task of saying everything there is to be said, of expressing every emotion that he can verbalize to someone who will understand and sympathize, who will encourage frankness and keep confidences; those who follow this prescription will find themselves benefited, the conditions as to the choice of the confidant being observed.

But if it is good to tell one's troubles to someone, it is not good to publish them to the world. Not all people understand, not all people approve, and one who puts away his marriage partner must still fortify himself against the disapproval of the public. Certainly one must not exhibit his bleeding heart to the multitude, nor wear his martyrdom as a badge. One must undress sometimes, but he is best clothed if he goes abroad.

Some persons will find it difficult to talk to anyone about the experiences connected with their divorces. These must at least cultivate the utmost frankness with themselves, a task at which they should strive doubly because it is doubly hard to do alone. Above all they must not fall into the error of thinking that their problems are peculiar to themselves. This is a prevalent fallacy in this neurotic world, and one which makes any affliction immeasurably harder to bear. (A brilliant colleague to whom students and others in need of guidance frequently have recourse for advice has a little trick which enables him to demonstrate in most striking fashion the fact that after all their problems are not unlike those of others. When their dreadful tales are half complete, he interrupts, "Wait! Now I'll tell you the rest of it.") The divorced person must remember that there are a few million others in the United States, and that no matter how trying his problems are, there are others who are facing very similar ones, perhaps solving them without difficulty.

In general, one must strive to take a constructive attitude toward his marital experience. Destructive criticism may be very well for neurotic young persons who wish to appear brilliant; as a philosophy of life it never works. Destructiveness in thought is the characteristic of the half-liberated. The real sophisticate is ever credulous.

Downhearted persons are likely to think that no good can ever come from their agonizing experiences. It may be pointed out to them that other persons have gone through the same experiences and received benefit from them. What is one man's food, of course, is another's poison, and if this is true on the physical level it is more profoundly true on the mental. People to whom life itself is a grand experience can derive much benefit from even the unpleasant parts of it.

What can one get from divorce? Those who are used to speak, and to think, of the "things of the spirit," could well say that one can derive from it valuable discipline, on the old courageous principle that "What does not kill me, strengthens me." Certainly there is produced a stiffening of morale from rallying all one's resources to meet an exigent and painful situation,—if one is strong enough to meet it he will be stronger after he has met it. Intellectually, one may gain immensely from the experience of

divorce, he may make long strides toward understanding himself, toward seeing himself and others
as they are, and may arrive at length at that twin
achievement of comprehension and faith which takes
place when one knows what people are and yet accepts them. The effects upon one's personality of
having had one's own troubles are often very mellow-
ing, one who has suffered himself is often made
reluctant to inflict pain upon others and eager to
alleviate it where it exists,—he comes at length to
identify himself with suffering man. Courage, understanding, sympathy,—these are rare qualities, and
perhaps they are cheaply bought at any price.

Contrariwise, one must avoid the destructive attitude. Guilt feelings? Why have them? One's own
human nature is probably about as good as that of
others, and, strangely enough, nearly every person
who has guilt complexes is in fact considerably more
scrupulous than those more robust persons whom
conscience does not trouble. Self-pity? Why? Others
have been through the same experiences, smilingly.
Besides, self-pity has a most insidious way of making people unhappy. But instead of reasoning with
the reader who has these attitudes, let us resume our
rôle and advise that he probe within himself and
find out why he wants to be unhappy. Understanding, he will perhaps no longer wish to be so. There
is comfort, too, in the thought that if consistent unhappiness is a habit of self-dramatization in a
pitiable rôle, then happiness is merely a habit of
playing a more fortunate rôle. If people tire of
bread, let them eat cake!

During the period of divorce one must use great
care in determining his attitude toward his friends
and acquaintances. He cannot, and must not for-

swear the society of happy men, but must have social contacts on as high a level as before. He must not think that the laugh of every passer-by is a jest directed at his own misery or imagine that when his friends are clustered together they are always talking about him. Nevertheless, he must remember that he is in a delicate situation in his social group, and must carefully and tactfully establish his definition of it. He must meet his friends, as friends, must speak of his troubles frankly, perhaps regretfully, utterly without dispraise of the absent mate,—must make his bids for friendship as before without implying anything as to what the attitude of his friends should be toward the person to whom he was married. Even if he does not, perhaps on account of the experience of divorce, any longer approve of the mores of his group, he must never flaunt them, or commit himself to active opposition to them—for the time may come when he will once more give the Ten Commandments his personal endorsement. If, seeking solace for his perhaps unspoken unhappiness, he turns to a Bohemian orientation as the best one, he will do better in most groups to keep this fact to himself. And he will do very well indeed if he rejects the prevalent rôle of the divorcé as a sophisticated, hardened and reckless person whose pleasure is in easy women and hard liquor and whose mornings always find him with a headache.

The friends of the divorcé can help him by accepting him as he was accepted before his marital experience, as one who has had a misfortune but lost no status by it. They should be ready to receive any confidences, and when these come they should hear them calmly and sympathetically, wholly without condemnation of either party involved. The one or two friends who are chosen as special confidants can help by tactful suggestions which may keep the divorcé's social relations from becoming unduly complicated as a result of his driving inner necessities; the others can be of greatest assistance by refraining from suggestions or evidences of curiosity.

If the divorce has revealed no fundamental personality defect which would incapacitate the person for marriage, or has produced no emotional complications which have the same result, the divorcé should in most cases arrange his life with ultimate remarriage in view. It is obvious that this should not follow very closely upon divorce, not alone for reasons of prudence and one's standing in the community, but because of the psychological hazards involved in a relationship assumed too soon after a disrupting experience. The divorced person has an excellent opportunity to rebound: here is the love of a person who has treated him badly, and it may be released by talking to a member of the opposite sex and come to be attached to her; here is the opportunity to strike a vengeful blow at the person who caused his misery, to show her that he can get along without her—those seem to be the essentials of a rebound. If there is no rebound, remarriage should still be postponed until it is clear that no danger may be anticipated from the persisting emotional involvement with the first mate.

It is within the power of society to prevent much of the evil that goes with divorce. Now that divorce has become so prevalent, and access to it is so readily had, so that the use of this kill-or-cure remedy is encouraged rather than frowned upon, society must maintain a more consistent attitude toward it, one which does not encourage a breach and then exact a penalty for it. Durant Drake has well said:

"What we must clearly recognize is that it is not divorce itself which is the evil, it is unhappy and demoralizing marriage. Divorce is simply the operation that aims to remedy the evil. The operation is sometimes a mistake, sometimes causes greater evils than it set out to cure, as is the case with surgical operations. But it would be silly to be prejudiced against surgical operations, unpleasant remedies as they are. It is equally silly to be prejudiced against divorce, for all the heartache that may go with it; it is the drastic remedy for mismating. Much of the heartache and bitterness that go with it are needless, a result of the cruel conception of divorce as a disgrace. In any case, it is the unwise marriage that one should be ashamed of, or the failure to make it a success, rather than the divorce." [2]

People at large can help those who have marital difficulties by trying to understand them, and by not condemning them for isolated acts of which they do not know the background. This writer has found that the more he has learned about any person the less he has been inclined to condemn that person for anything which he did; even those quite heinous breaches of the law which precede a divorce may be more easily pardoned if we see how they shape up in the subjective history of the person who committed them. No one who is not in a situation can really understand the powerful urges that are activating those who are in it; let outsiders stand outside, and keep silent.

Throughout this work the author has stuck fairly close to his subject; which is gigantic enough that goodly peregrinations can be performed within its

[2] Drake, Durant, *The New Morality*, Macmillan, New York, 1929, p. 114. Reprinted by permission.

boundaries. He has presented a first treatment of the problem of readjustment of personality after divorce,—a problem great enough in the number of people affected, and in its seriousness for all who are involved to merit a much larger volume. But there are one or two very closely related problems which the writer would like to solve, and with the indulgence of the reader he will indicate their nature. It may turn out when he has finished that he has after all not gone far afield.

We need to work out new definitions of situations with regard to the relations of the sexes, both in marriage and out of it. In these days women are doing men's jobs, and men are taking over the traditional tasks of women; as a result, we need to give thought to a redivision of labor into that which truly belongs to man and that which rightfully may be assigned to women. We need to recast our rôles in such a way that rivalry between the sexes may not so often arise, or if it does arise, may not disrupt families. This is no plea for the old, and carries with it no suggestion as to what is the proper sphere of either sex, but men must know what is manly and women must know what women should do. The psychiatrists have shown what importance infantile uncertainty as to one's sexual rôle has in the production of neurosis; this same sort of uncertainty has results equally important in marriage.

If we would do away with divorce, and the problem of readjustment connected with it, we must do away with unhappy marriage. Marriage is strongest when people know what is expected of them in it, and happiest when it is strongest. We must take thought and evolve a form of marriage, with duties and privileges of both parties strictly but not rigidly defined, which will work in the modern world. And then every detail of every arrangement, with the responsibilities involved in every privilege, must be written on the walls of every schoolroom. Love cannot conquer all and sex is not enough to keep people together, especially if they do not agree as to the manner of its expression. Let us work out new matrimonial institutions and begin preparation for marriage with birth. For one way of making everybody happy—surely a worthy object—is to let everybody know what to expect. This is a gospel of unfreedom. We may justify it by pointing out that duty is the background without which self-realization is barren. The true epicurean must be a stoic first. A free man is a logical impossibility, and as freedmen we can never quite forget our previous condition of servitude. For that which binds us to our fellow man is more ancient than Adam. The slavery is in us, and if we tear it out we die. As slaves we live or as freedmen die; surely slavery is happiness and freedom melancholy mad.

CHAPTER FOURTEEN

The Methodology of This Study
(See Table of Contents)

A METHODOLOGICAL statement enables the reader to check the data, logic, and conclusions of a scientific study by reference to the laboratory notes. In this sense the methodological note should be obligatory, and the present discussion is included with the object of fulfilling this requirement. Sometimes a methodological note contributes something to the acroamatic doctrines of a science, but it is our purpose here merely to explain how we have collected our facts and generalized from them.

The present volume is a report upon an investigation. The investigation was begun with the purpose of finding out what the major problems of the divorced person are, what processes of adjustment are gone through, and what mechanisms of psychological and sociological nature are involved in these processes. The books on the subject of divorce, or the books in which divorce enters as a topic, have usually dealt with it as a final thing, as the end of a process, the end of a marriage. From a formal and legal point of view this is no doubt true, but from the point of view of personality it is certainly untrue, for divorce in many cases is followed by the most serious personal problems and by intricate and elaborate attempts to reconstruct. This period following divorce represents a gap in our knowledge of persons and in our knowledge of family disorganization, a very important lacuna in our learning which one volume is by no means sufficient to fill. The writer has felt also that the study of things that happen after crises might reveal facts which would furnish a new connotation for the statement, "Personality is formed in crises, is the result of crises." This is no doubt true, but the writer would insist that we should think, not of the great crises after which the life situation is changed, but of the myriad smaller crises which ensue upon such a cataclysm.

There are two kinds of scientists, especially social scientists, those who want what they say to be true and as demonstrable as possible, whether it is significant or not, and those who do not so much care whether what they say is exactly true as whether it is significant if it is true, or if it has some truth in it. It is clear, of course, that the present writer belongs to the latter school. Both sorts of scientists have their little idiosyncrasies. The former may sink to the parroting of facts which are "perfectly true, perfectly obvious, and perfectly meaningless." In the extreme case, his life becomes a feverish search after facts which can be organized neatly and put into courses and books, relations between the facts being unperceived to the end. This person deals, not with life, but with its dregs from which the essence has been thrice distilled. The latter may of course become unscientific and may, developing stereotypy in his age, spend his time in mouthing formulæ which have meaning to him because they are verbalizations of his unreconciled emotions, and may see the world in terms of these formulæ—which is autistic thinking. But really it is much simpler than all this:

the danger of overlooking meaning in the search for solid truth is that what you say will be true but meaningless, and the danger of paying relatively little attention to the canons of truth when searching for significant relations is that you may make a mistake.

The method of study which has been used is that of the case study, but that fact has no necessary connection whatever with the dichotomy mentioned above, for statistics may be used imaginatively, and case studies may be used unimaginatively. What the use of the case study method implies is just that the writer felt that he would arrive at a better understanding of the divorcé by an intensive study of a few cases than by collecting facts about many. If there were enough cases the statistical method could be employed, and if there were enough facts statistical investigations might come to have the completeness of case studies.

The case study method is based upon the notion that what happens in one case will happen in another, and that understanding can be had from a study of the ideal typical, which may represent nothing which ever happened but something which always tends to happen. There is no need to defend this method or to pronounce encomiums upon it. It has its dangers which are epitomized in the statement that one inevitably sees the thing for which he looks. It has its advantage, which is that any reasonably intelligent person who uses it can see something. An unfair and somewhat unintelligent criticism is made of it, that one who generalizes from but few cases is giving out "glittering generalities." Now no generalization can be so clearly buttressed by facts as one which is definitely supported by one or two well understood cases;

generalization from statistics is ever more tenuous and inconclusive than generalization from persons.

Thirty-three cases were included in this investigation. Of these perhaps five were studied with a thoroughness approaching that of the study which a psychoanalyst makes of his patient. On ten more cases fairly complete subjective documents were obtained, and a reasonably good insight into the subjects' minds was apparently obtained. These studies were based on successive interviews, the time spent on the interviews ranging from three to fifteen hours. A series of interviews would imply giving the subject insight and checking up on diagnoses by submitting them to the person diagnosed. In the remaining cases incomplete subjective accounts, or complete narratives, with interpretations interpolated here and there, were obtained. Three of these cases were careful character studies made by other persons than the writer, but fully as competent to analyze personalities, and very well informed concerning the history of the person described. Three life histories written by the subject himself were included in the list. In addition to these cases, there was a good deal of material of a different sort. Some literary cases were used as background, but no such material was used in the body of the work. In addition there were available a number of psychoanalytic cases in which divorce was one of the major problems. Valuable material illustrating mechanisms discovered by the analysis of particular cases was found in the newspapers, periodicals, and conversations with friends, and the writer has not thought that the hearsay evidence rule should apply here. There were thus available a very large number of cases illustrating certain points. Where the writer was unable after making a contact with certain subjects to obtain interviews with them he nevertheless often learned in the course of a general conversation much concerning their life organization and their attitudes. Several subjects permitted the writer to examine their letters, writings, or other documents which would give an insight into their points of view. Others wrote letters to the investigator. Others were willing to check up on a preliminary statement or to read the finished product with a view to proving or disproving its main contentions by reference to their own cases. Some most valuable suggestions were obtained in this fashion. Most of the cases which were singled out for special study were on the higher intellectual and social levels. They possessed sufficient insight that the writer found it very easy to lead them to uncover valuable material; his main task was that of recording impressions, and analysis came after. The cases which were studied were nearly all responsible persons with fairly high intelligence and a reasonable degree of social mindedness. The results will have to be evaluated with that in mind. It has been suggested that a selective factor has operated to exclude from the study persons who having remarried successfully are unwilling to talk about their unfortunate first attempt. This is probably true. It is also true that but little information was available concerning divorced persons who had custody of one or more children.

With regard to other circumstances the cases were rather well distributed. There were cases of old persons; the writer talked at length with a man of sixty-five who had been divorced two years before. The youngest subject was twenty-two, and had been divorced two years before. Some persons were interviewed when the trauma of divorce was very recent, as recent as the week preceding the interview, and others were seen when the divorce was ten years past. One subject had been married twenty-five years, another man had slept with his wife but one night. Some remarried almost immediately after divorce, having apparently transferred their affections before the final break with their mates, and others had not remarried in a decade. Some subjects were powerfully heterosexual, others apparently had strong inclinations toward affairs with their own sex. There were marriages of love, marriages of rebellion, marriages of rebound, marriages for financial reasons, and marriages of many other sorts. There were marriages in which there were children, and these always entered in some way into the reorganization of the parents (but this could not be made out surely, nor was it thought best to study the children, since the matter in hand is the divorcé himself). Alimony entered in some cases. There were a few more women than men among the persons most thoroughly studied, perhaps because a cross sex transference is more easily established. At any rate, women were more willing to be interviewed and much franker than men. (The great resistance of many male subjects led the investigator to suspect that perhaps men were really more hurt by the experience of divorce but this may have been due to any of a number of other factors.) In addition to these cases of divorced persons, there were available a number of cases of broken love affairs, bereavement, and of marriages which apparently were going to be broken up, or which obviously had lost their assets.

Before beginning his controlled study of cases, the

writer prepared a short statement from his general knowledge of the mechanisms which he thought to be involved, as a sort of hypothetical framework for his investigation. This was also submitted to certain divorced persons whose cases could not be studied in full for their comments, and to sociologists and psychologists who were interested in the subject. Unquestionably the preparation of such a statement was not without effect upon the conclusions ultimately reached. But the preliminary statement was not referred to in the course of the investigation, only its main points being kept in mind, and every effort was made to find other mechanisms not included in the preliminary statement and to test the real existence of those mentioned in the paper. About half of the book as it is finally written concerns matters whose treatment was not contemplated at the time of preparing the first statement.

Chief reliance has been placed by the writer upon life histories prepared by himself from interviews with persons who consented to be studied. He has planned to spend with each person as much time as seemed worth while to both parties, never cutting a subject off voluntarily with less than ten or fifteen hours of interviewing. At the beginning of the interview, the writer explained what he was studying, stated the completely confidential character of these interviews, and encouraged the subject to tell his story in his own way. The formula, "Tell me what you think I ought to know about yourself in order that I may understand you, your marriage, and your divorce," was often found useful. If the subject talked with difficulty, questions were sometimes asked. Sometimes it seemed best to let the subject take control of the interview; usually he allowed the conversation to drift around to the subject of his divorce. During these interviews notes were taken where possible, but if this seemed to distract the person they were taken immediately after the interview. Resistance was encountered on certain points. This usually took the form of a sudden reticence or a violent change of subject. If a very good rapport was already established, a point blank question would sometimes carry the interview past this difficult point, but usually it seemed best to let the subject come back to this difficult matter of his own accord. When he did, he usually had sufficient momentum to carry him through. An interviewer should always be able to assume complete control of an interview, but should never attempt any very direct self-assertion until he feels that he is well established; therefore these crucial questions were often postponed. It was usually possible to deal with them in time.

Immediately after each interview the entire story was recorded, in the words of the subject if possible. The writer found it possible to catch the spirit, and to remember most of the words of the conversation, after he had trained himself in this sort of thing. Where notes were taken the write-up could be depended upon as having a high degree of reliability, but even where the notes had to be taken after the interview was finished the product was usually fairly correct. In both cases the results of the interview were checked by showing them to the subject. In addition to the subject's story as told to the investigator, this first document contained a description of the subject, outstanding physical, mental and personality traits, and a preliminary diagnosis. It must be admitted that this preliminary diagnosis was often wrong, but as the work went on, it was right more frequently, and in any case it always pointed out important lines of inquiry. In the second interview the investigator, having established a more favorable rapport, was able to assume more direct control, and to guide the conversation so that it would cover such points as were not touched before. Here might be introduced dream analysis or the analysis of Freudian slips. This would usually point out further lines of inquiry, and the relationship and the process would be from that point on pseudoanalytic.

Although he is fairly familiar with the theory of psychoanalysis, the writer at the beginning of this study had no intention of using this technique. However, he soon found himself almost forced into the rôle of analyst by the attitude which the persons who made themselves the subject of studies took toward him. One must make himself something of an analyst if he is to deal intelligently with the analytic mechanisms. In addition, there were some things about any case which were capable of description in analytic terms and not in any other, or not nearly so conveniently in any other. If a subject has complexes protruding from his ears, a reasonably thorough case study must include them. Also, the writer found the analytic method very useful in establishing a desirable rapport with his subjects, and did not find such rapport apparently possible on any other basis. For instance, even if the analysis of a particular dream was not revealing, it was usually profitable in that it released certain blockings of information which proved to be very valuable for the purposes of this study.

Anyone who attempts a study of this nature must learn to recognize and to deal with resistance and transference. Resistance is a mental set not to reveal certain facts concerning one's self. Its existence tremendously complicates the process of carrying on an investigation of this kind. The writer has perhaps learned more concerning resistance from his failures than from his successes.

One prospective subject was met at a social gathering at which this investigation was discussed. Quite of his own free will he divulged the fact that he was himself a divorcé and offered to submit to an interview. A tentative appointment was made for the following week. This appointment was not kept, and a week later the subject was called once by telephone. Again he professed his complete willingness to talk, but declined to make a further appointment. Some days later he sent word through mutual friends that he did not wish to be called on the telephone. He stated roundly that any intelligent person could solve his own problems and that he saw no reason why he should talk them over with a total stranger. A number of things come out here. Apparently the man conceived himself to be hotly pursued, which would indicate an inner conflict,—perhaps a conflict strong enough to make him think that telephone calls which came from other persons came from the investigator who was after his secrets. The writer apparently blundered in stating by inference that the man would gain some understanding of his own case by talking it over. It would have been far better to suggest that the man call for a little informal chat, to give his reflections on divorce in general, and to wait until a more favorable transference had been established before going ahead. But notice also the parapathiac combination lock by which this man's secrets are guarded. He will not talk his secrets over with a stranger. It happens also that he will not talk them over with his friends, and that he values most highly those friends who seem least aware of the fact that he may have some problems of personal adjustment.

Resistance through breaking appointments is frequently enough encountered in the general course of psychiatric treatment. Some types of resistance which would only display themselves when one is making use of the technique of psychoanalysis for purely investigatory purposes were also found. After the first reaction, "Certainly I'll talk it over with you," there would come this, "Why study that? You can't find out anything. People won't tell you the truth. And you can't possibly help anybody else, because everybody has to work those things out for himself." Or, "Why study that? It's all very easy. The whole problem of readjustment depends upon the cause of the divorce. That's what governs what one does afterwards." The first reaction is equivalent to, "I don't want to tell you anything about it,"—of course the franker form was encountered also. The second is a more refined attempt to avoid probing, and this sort of reaction was responsible for many valuable hints which have been incorporated into the study. The attitude, "My case really is not worth study. Nothing at all happened," was found to be usually indicative of a very interesting and valuable story when once it was obtained. More refined forms of resistance were met with in those who said, "All right, let's talk now. How long will it take, fifteen minutes?" or in those who really could not tell their story but would gladly answer any questions. Sometimes the resistance took on a frankly humorous character, as in the case of the man who said, "Certainly I'll answer your questions, but I want to sit down with a sheet of paper, too, and for every question that you ask me I'm going to ask you one." Sometimes the humor was unconscious, as in the case of the estimable girl who declined to tell her own story but secured two substitutes from her circle of acquaintances. (All of which may lead the discerning reader to suspect that the technique of the writer in securing contacts left something to be desired. It is not intended to deny this charge, but it should be remembered that one who is making case studies for purely scientific purposes has considerably less leverage than the professional psychiatrist who can hold out the hope of material benefit, and ensure coöperation by high fees, and who sees his people after they have declared themselves bankrupt and gone into the hands of the receiver. And none of these remarks concerning resistance should be construed to mean that the writer did not find people in general very willing to talk about their divorces.)

The problem of resistance calls up the technical matter of how to deal with it. In general, the point is not to go ahead until a favorable transference has been established, not to frighten the person with questions or a display of acuity until he is anxious to talk. One is always aided in overcoming resistance by the fact that the urge to tell and the urge not to tell occur together.

Since he is not a psychiatrist the writer had to hedge himself about with certain safeguards in the use of the psychoanalytic technique. In the first place, he never dared to be as clever as he could, and endeavored to remain always on the stupid side of safety in his diagnoses of persons. He attempted to make out only the major outlines of a personality, using the psychoanalytic technique to peel off the outer layer of resistances in order that he might see them a little better. But he never proceeded much beyond the most obvious interpretations, preferring to be correct and safe rather than to be brilliant and unsafe, departing from the general policy to which he committed · himself a few pages back. In the second place, this technique was used, except in the case of two or three persons who were obviously in trouble and wanted any help that the writer could give them, only for diagnosis. This implies that the writer did not tell his people everything that he thought he knew about them, but preferred to avoid giving them any insight which might prove to be dangerous. The writer would suggest that this is a very good rule, and that with the exception of the most obvious matters which must be gone into before a reasonably good understanding of the subject can be had, amateurs should confine themselves to suggestive therapy, and very little of that.

The indebtedness of the writer to the psychoanalysts is, as we have indicated, not slight. Their technique has been used without any further reservations than that imposed by an imperfect mastery of it and by non-professional status. The writer has appropriated a number of psychoanalytic concepts, and has explained some of his own findings by reference to certain psychoanalytic presuppositions. This course, it is thought, can be justified. The psychoanalytic technique works. Psychoanalytic concepts, furthermore, are convenient terms, labels which a large number of people understand, and the only names we have for certain mental mechanisms. If some of them have no more explanatory value than other names, they are useful as names. As to the psychoanalytic presuppositions, the writer is aware of their logical weakness. For him, psychoanalysis is primarily a means of getting certain results and not a theory of human nature. It is a technique, however, which has made important contributions to knowledge, and a technique whose usefulness is by no means exhausted.

The writer prefers to think of this study as a contribution to the field of social psychology. He has used psychoanalytic concepts in no finalistic way but as a means to understanding the complete human being in his system of social relationships, and he has had as his object the understanding rather than the manipulation of human beings. These two considerations would seem to differentiate this study from technical psychiatry. Nor is it difficult to mark it off from the more conventional sort of academic psychology. A cynical colleague has remarked that it is social psychology rather than psychology because it is an attempt to understand human beings living in a certain situation rather than an enumeration of the reasons why such understanding is impossible. Although the psychologists would probably grant that there is some truth in this statement, we shall not insist upon it. It seems fairer to say that this study is social psychology rather than psychology proper because it is a discussion of human beings, group-conditioned content of consciousness and all, rather than a mere discussion of or search for mental mechanisms.

This brings us to another point. It has been stated that people will not talk freely, that they will not tell the whole truth, and that they may even tell untruths. Without impertinence one may ask, What of it? We cannot know that what a person says is true,

but we can know that this is what he says. And one
is not utterly without canons which will enable him
to differentiate truth from falsehood; he is not altogether powerless in these relationships. Certainly information which one gets in a series of case studies
is much more reliable than that which one gets by
sending out a questionnaire. This is also the argument for the life history based upon interviews as
contrasted with the life history prepared by the
subject himself. In an interview one learns more, and
more important things, and things which are more
likely to be true. In an interview one has the opportunity to evaluate statements, to check up, to give a
person an opportunity and an invitation to qualify
them, to ask brazen questions, to demand to be told
the truth. Here again psychoanalytic concepts are of
great utility. In the first interview what was usually
obtained was the rationalized account, the statement
prepared for publication, the carefully edited story.
In later interviews this was often qualified, sometimes contradicted, and not infrequently things were
revealed of which the subject himself had been
unaware at the start. The writer is of the opinion
that in general people were about as frank with him
as they were with themselves. The most damaging
things, sexual episodes, masturbation, prostitution,
abortions, etc., were readily told. This is of course
the easiest material to get, it is harder to get at those
things which are more intimately subjective, but even
here the close observer and the alert questioner can
learn much more than people are at first willing
to tell.

The fact that many of these persons were studied
some years after their divorces took place constituted both an advantage and a disadvantage. It was

an undoubted advantage in that one could see what rôle the divorce had really played in the person's life, for it could then be seen as an integral part of his whole history, underlying which there was a certain onward movement. One could not have perceived that onward movement if he had seen the person at the time of the divorce, for the meaning which the divorce had would not then have been made clear. (This also takes us into the question of the causation of divorce, which the writer has hitherto studiously avoided, although much of the case material concerns the history of his subjects before the divorce. The writer feels that this method of studying divorced persons some years after they receive their divorces could with profit be applied by those who wish to study the process of family disorganization. To cite but one example, the writer is aware of certain cases in which at the time of the divorce the discord of the pair seemed a simple matter of sex incompatibility, whereas it later came out that the difficulty represented as well a deep-lying rivalry between the marriage partners.) But if the advantage of getting these people some years after their divorces is that the experience has then assumed its proper place in their lives, it must be admitted that the disadvantage lies herein too, for the people have then had a number of years in which to prepare their highly rationalized account, and a good deal of practice in telling it, so that they are much less likely to be caught off their guard. The only remedy for this is increased alertness on the part of the interviewer, and a prolongation of the interviews.

Scientifically, it would have been much more valuable if these cases could have been published entire, with analyses and interpretations as they went along, even those which were later found to be wrong. This would have furnished a very helpful manual for those who wanted to do case studies later, illustrating how they should not be done as well as how they should be done, though perhaps not illustrating how well they should be done. This idea of publishing some cases as they were brought out, with current notes, is one which the writer has surrendered with reluctance. In the first place, much of the material collected was not to the point although it was necessary to collect it in order that a correct interpretation of that which was in point could be made. (Some of this was also collected as a means of establishing rapport.) In the next place, the time is simply not ripe for a field manual of case studies.

Instead, a highly schematic, relatively compressed treatment was adopted. The writer has confined himself to explanation and illustration of mechanisms, and has used his case material with that in view. He does not intend that his study shall have any quantitative implications. The words, rarely, infrequently, occasionally, sometimes, frequently, generally, often, usually, nearly always, always, etc., are to be found in the book. The writer does not care to change them, but he is quite willing that his readers should do so; they are uninvited guests who have come in by the back door when they were chased out the front, and the host feels no responsibility for their treatment. The writer has limited himself to the study of the ideal typical, and has attempted to help the reader to understand what may happen in certain cases. These are the generalizations which he has drawn from the cases which he has studied. No doubt some of them will be disproved. It is hoped, however, that some of these generalizations will be found to be both true and important, and that even those which are untrue may point out significant lines of inquiry for the future.